# Praise for *Lead Together*

"Just the table of contents is a treat! Every chapter is well structured, directly applicable and peppered with interesting examples. If I were out there trying to build a different kind of organization, I would take this book on my journey and go back to it all the time."

**FREDERIC LALOUX** author of *Reinventing Organizations*

"There's a calling in the world for new-century leadership. So many hear it, long for it and need it. Many leaders live the values underlying this boldly collaborative way of being. Yet we still enact 'old' ways of operating our businesses for lack of new, values-aligned patterns. *Lead Together* provides those patterns, along with the inner practices, that allow them to work."

**LYSSA ADKINS** author of *Coaching Agile Teams*

"*The authors bring* such an ethical framework to commerce that *business* no longer has to be considered a dirty word. This is twenty-first-century thinking, in which *scale* no longer means growing your business as big as possible, but—like any living thing—as vibrant and vital as it can manifest."

**DOUGLAS RUSHKOFF** named one of the "world's ten most influential intellectuals" by MIT and host of NPR's *Team Human*

"The time has passed for investing in businesses applying extractive philosophies and methodologies to scaling. *Lead Together* shows leaders how—beyond the critical pairing of money and talent—to innovate the ways we work to be more human, purposeful and values-aligned. If you are a leader who, like me, dreams of scaling companies that are fun, inspiring and contributing meaningfully to people, planet and healthy profits, this is the book for you. *Lead Together* is practical, refreshing and what's needed for this time. The authors have done a superb job."

**MIKE WINTERFIELD** founder and managing partner, Active Impact Investments

"Who knew that joy could be a serious pursuit of business leadership? Or that hierarchy isn't the best way to build a strong, adaptable team? You did. You always knew there was a better way. Now you have a great book to show you how others have done it. More importantly, *Lead Together* authors Brent Lowe, Susan Basterfield and Travis Marsh share their collective wisdom and give you ample reflection moments so you can unleash the change agent burning inside of you. Get reading, start changing!"

**RICHARD SHERIDAN** CEO and chief storyteller, Menlo Innovations, and author of *Joy, Inc.*

"There is a growing community of leaders who desire to fulfill bold purposes beyond the goals of traditional business. These leaders see the need to shift business norms, assumptions and patterns. *Lead Together* offers concrete, practical, hands-on approaches for enacting this shift, and is an essential resource for every leader who believes the world is ready for and in need of businesses that are a force for good."

**RYAN HONEYMAN** partner/worker-owner, LIFT Economy, and coauthor of *The B Corp Handbook*

"Ahhh, the authors pull back the curtain on a dream coming true. No-holds-barred, *Lead Together* urges us to include all voices in organizing and managing our work *now*. Without glossing over any of the transformational challenges, we are guided along a path to distribute more freedom and more accountability to every person. Festooned with practical advice, short chapters illuminate how to scale this work up and out. The focus on leaders learning how to be in charge but not in control is particularly useful. This is a perfect moment for *Lead Together* to inspire deeper change."

**KEITH MCCANDLESS** coauthor of *The Surprising Power of Liberating Structures*

"*Lead Together: The Bold, Brave, Intentional Path to Scaling Your Business*, from Brent Lowe, Susan Basterfield and Travis Marsh arrives just in time for the northern fall grape crush. Like a fine wine, it fills the intellectual palate with a sense of possibility for scaling human-centric organizations. Despite the occasional rocky terroir of business uncertainty, the flavors of self-managed purpose, power, responsibility and leadership are bold and exciting, with a smooth, approachable finish. The creators lead a generous tour of the back room, allowing the reader to barrel taste challenging topics like compensation, decision-making, conflict and diversity. *Lead Together* should be paired with every scale-up."

**DOUG KIRKPATRICK** author of *The No-Limits Enterprise*

# Lead Together

# Lead Together

## The Bold, Brave, Intentional Path to Scaling Your Business

**Brent Lowe,
Susan Basterfield,
Travis Marsh**

 **PAGE
TWO**
BOOKS

Cataloguing in publication information is available from Library and Archives Canada.
ISBN 978-1-77458-016-5 (paperback)
ISBN 978-1-77458-017-2 (ebook)

Page Two
www.pagetwo.com

Edited by Kendra Ward
Copyedited by Crissy Calhoun
Proofread by Alison Strobel
Cover design by Fiona Lee
Interior design by Setareh Ashrafologhalai

leadtogether.co

*For those who believe something better is possible when we lead shoulder to shoulder and create the conditions for the development of all.*

# Contents

# Preface

"… the level of consciousness of an organization cannot exceed the level of consciousness of its leader."

**FREDERIC LALOUX**[1]

A S COAUTHORS our work together began as an experiment in cocreating a blueprint for leaders interested in reinventing their organizations' work patterns and governance. That initial experiment has resulted in three books. In all of our work, we've held a common value of transparency. In our previous two books, *Reinventing Scale-Ups 1.0* and *Reinventing Scale-Ups 2.0*, we wrote about the challenges and sometimes frustrations of cocreation. We are a decentralized team of diverse thinkers, brought together through our collective intention to share what we have learned from experiments within our work and with the organizations we support. Our aims for this latest book are to share more stories and pull back the curtain on the processes and practices of our own lived experiences.

In November 2018, as we finalized our plan to write *Lead Together*, we created guiding principles for the project. We want this book to be meaningful for any leader or emerging leader bumping up against the limitations of their current leadership practices and looking for new actionable ideas. We imagined these leaders might be experiencing:

**Ineffectiveness and poor business results** "I am doing all I know how to, running this business to the best of my ability using well-established ways of working... and it's not going as well as it needs to. I'm ready to explore new ideas."

**Intellectual curiosity and desire for personal growth** "I am a game changer and a rebel. What can I learn to help me be a better leader and help our team be more effective and happier?"

**The need to deal with complexity** "There are big problems to be solved and we won't solve them using the same ways of thinking and doing that created them. We need new ways to thrive within the volatile, uncertain, complex and ambiguous world we now find ourselves in."

**Leader frustration and burnout** "Being the single point of accountability and decision-making in this business [or team] is exhausting and stressful. I need others to step up and share this responsibility with me."

**A lack of joy** "The way we've been working feels rotten. It is not fun, inspiring or meaningful. There must be a better way. I want to enjoy my work and feel fulfilled."

We invite you to experiment, and we offer specific actionable ideas anchored in the emerging paradigm of self-organizing and self-managing. In this book you will find us using these terms interchangeably, although there is a slight difference in their meanings. In both cases, there is a primary shift away from having a manager responsible for determining the who, how and what of the work. **Self-organizing** teams are responsible for deciding and enacting their own work processes and have a mandate to make many decisions, including *how* the work gets done and *who* does the work. **Self-managing** teams have the added responsibility of deciding *what* work is done and taking on activities such as prioritizing work, overseeing budgets and setting strategy. They also take on aspects traditionally handled by human resources, such as hiring and onboarding.

We aim to help you sufficiently understand the importance of your own development by focusing on the *self* in *self-management* and *self-organizing*, and we've shared the inner experiences of leaders in self-organizing systems to support you through the challenging journey of personal change, offering *Lead Together* as an easy reference guide for the trip. We use the words *team* and *organization* in our writing to connect with CEOs and founders as well as leaders of all types in various contexts. Throughout the following pages, we will frequently invite you to self-reflect, which is an essential practice for developing new and different leadership abilities.

We hope to inspire you to experiment by sharing success stories from a variety of companies and learnings from leaders in more than sixty diverse organizations. A full list of the companies profiled can be found at the end of the book. Each one began as a start-up. Some are still in the early stages of finding their way, while others have grown significantly. Most are now in a phase of scaling up; they've made it through their first couple of years, are sustainable in their current configuration and are actively considering "What's next for our organization?"

Our aim is to speak to the challenges faced by leaders within growing businesses. We interviewed many founders, CEOs and natural leaders within organizations of 200 people or fewer. If you are in that group, the ideas in this book will apply directly. That said, *Lead Together* offers ample learning and practical actions for leading in *any* context. Leaders of scale-ups face a unique set of challenges and a steep learning curve. The personal and professional growth that spans decades in other contexts are concentrated into a few short years.

We have spent the last four years traveling the world, both physically and virtually, to learn from the best thinkers and doers about the future of work. We have come to embrace five principles that are woven into the chapters that follow. We believe these are essential to building an influential and thriving organization. These principles are anchored in the belief that investing in creating the right environment increases the probability of scaling up a sustainable, prosperous company.

**Principle #1: Individuals thrive when they are engaged in meaningful work.** When we unearth a clear, shared and inspiring purpose beyond the profit motive, work becomes more personally meaningful and fulfilling for everyone. Accountability and responsibility increase too.

**Principle #2: Organizations evolve and require freedom to emerge over time.** The dogmatic approaches used in most organizations lead to taxing bureaucracy and limited potential, while a blank slate induces chaos. With a minimal amount of helpful scaffolding, the character and capabilities of an organization surface as patterns and a workable system takes shape.

**Principle #3: Psychological safety is essential.** When we invite our colleagues to bring more of themselves to work—free from fear of personal judgment—creativity and learning follow. Doing so requires conscious effort.

**Principle #4: Business challenges provide the best learning and development curriculum.** Deliberately leveraging the needs of the business as a platform for personal development allows for ongoing business growth. Business growth in turn creates new opportunities for personal development.

**Principle #5: Transparency, trust and agency are core to a culture of accountability.** When everyone in an organization has access to the same information, is invited to share opinions and is entrusted to make decisions, the result is shared context, ownership and a sense of accountability.

Warning: by pursuing the ideas that follow, you will be seen as an outlier and a rebel. Now is a good time to ask yourself, "Do I want to lead a business that follows a well-worn path or do I believe my company should be brave, bold and intentional?"

We like to question long-held beliefs about what makes a truly successful business. Although many of the ideas in *Lead Together* are not yet widely embraced, they have been honed by a variety of progressive, successful companies introduced throughout the book. These early adopters are illuminating an alternative and healthier leadership path. The world needs progressive leaders to be successful and lead the way.

Between us, we have more than fifty collective years of working with start-ups and scale-ups across five continents, and we are passionate about supporting leaders like you. Your work will lead us all into the future. We do not profess to have all the answers for your unique circumstances. Instead, we believe you are best positioned to be your own case study—learning, iterating and growing. Our goal is to provoke thought and invite experimentation. As you experiment, we invite you to share your stories and connect with us at leadtogether.co.

# Introduction to an Emerging Paradigm

"If you want small changes in your life, work on your attitude. But if you want big and primary changes, work on your paradigm."

**STEPHEN COVEY**[1]

"SOMETHING BETTER is possible. I've seen flashes of it. I've experienced the flow of coming together in a project—with no one questioning purpose or trust or intention. It's just there, in the room with us.

"But then everything goes back to normal. I get grumpy about the lack of collective ownership of the sales numbers, about managing Tom who never really liked Nadia, about playing referee between product management and the developers. In the blink of an eye I'm back to my old mindset. This doesn't feel good.

"How can I leave this place better than I found it? I want our company to provide meaningful work for those who choose to be here. I can't do it on my own, and moreover, I don't want to. This is a team sport, and together we can create something we are all proud of. We get to decide what sport this is, what the rules are and who plays. No one said we couldn't write our own playbook! Do we dare?

"I know in my bones that there isn't a magic recipe, and that suits me because I don't want to be a clone. This can be a place where we all get better, do better, *be* better together.

"But I ... we ... don't know how to do it ... yet."

So thinks the leader who wants to lead together.

Whatever generation or geography we each belong to, one thing is certain: the systems in which we work and live weren't created by us. They were shaped millennia ago and have evolved along with us humans ... and we're still evolving.

Any new endeavor requires that someone takes a risk, becomes a first mover. The great minds of the last century implored each of us to examine the systems shaping and steering our progress. As Albert Einstein reportedly said, "No problem can be solved from the same level of consciousness that created it." And Buckminster Fuller: "You never change things by fighting the existing reality. To change something, build a new model that makes the existing model obsolete."

Often it feels comfortable simply doing our best within a system that has brought so much bounty to society. When the machine is humming and the cogs all spin in unison, we feel a sense of fulfillment and pride. Optimizing for efficiency, reliability and reproducibility becomes our ultimate prize. But what happens when our current systems begin to fail us? When what we're taking from our planet far outstrips Earth's ability to regenerate? When individuals revolt against oppression or a lack of opportunity? When pandemics mushroom because of a lack of clarity, unity or cooperation? When our ways of working serve neither businesses nor employees?

We all carry with us a backpack filled with limiting beliefs— about ourselves, our organizations, the people within them, our customers and more. These beliefs are based on our experiences and biases. They help make our organizations feel safe and predictable, controlled and measured. Our limiting beliefs also keep us and our organizations stuck. They restrict our evolution. What is the unseen potential waiting to be unleashed if we move beyond the organizational structures of the past? Does answering that question make you feel scared *and* enlivened? If so, it's time to learn about a new emerging paradigm.

WHY DO we need a new paradigm for organizing work? In *Brave New Work*, Aaron Dignan proposes: "If I showed you a house, a car, a dress or a phone from 1910 and asked you whether it was modern or antique, you'd have a pretty good idea. Because almost everything has changed. But not management."[2] The traditional hierarchical model of work, with a concentration of power at the top, has persisted since the Industrial Revolution, when assembly-line labor was in its infancy and Taylorism—which treats people as cogs in a machine to improve productivity—was the scientific management practice of the day. As we enter the next societal evolution, we are operating in a far more complex global economy. "Somehow, amid a period of relentless innovation, including the internet, mobile computing, autonomous vehicles, artificial intelligence and rockets to space that can land themselves," Aaron notes, "the way we come together as human beings to solve problems and invent our future has stayed remarkably constant."[3] The observations and ideas highlighted by Aaron are not new. Writings and lectures by Mary Parker Follett from as early as 1927 contained references to transformational leadership, the interrelationship of leadership and followership and the power of collective goals of leaders and followers.

Maintaining our current leadership style and ways of organizing is all too easy. We might choose to believe "there is no compelling reason to do things differently" or "the system is too big to transform." It may or may not be helpful to recognize that we are all complicit in propping up the socio-political-work paradigm we were born into. This complicity creates in us a tremendous resistance to change.

## Teal and Adjacent Concepts

Our hypothesis is that you are reading this book because, at some level, you are interested in a leadership or organizational alternative. One clear option is emerging—referred to by some as Teal—in which, rather than a pyramidal hierarchy, an organization is seen as an ecosystem or interconnected network.

Frederic Laloux, author of *Reinventing Organizations*, the book that popularized the Teal movement, suggests that there have been four definable paradigms of human organizing over the last 10,000 years. First were the Red chiefdoms, followed by the Amber age of agriculture, state bureaucracies and organized religion, which appeared around 4000 BCE. The next leap—Orange—fully emerged in the Industrial Revolution: the metaphoric organizing principle of the machine to be optimized. Finally, in the last century, the emergence of Green represented the organizing principle of family, with benevolence and egalitarianism as defining features. Starting in 2012, Frederic began to find examples of, and propose, the next organizing paradigm, Teal.

**Self-management** Teal organizations operate effectively, even into the thousands of people, with a system based on peer relationships. They set up structures and practices in which people have high autonomy in their domain and are accountable for coordinating with others. Power and control are deeply embedded throughout the organizations, no longer tied to the specific positions of a few top leaders.

**Wholeness** Whereas Orange organizations encourage people to show only their narrow "professional" selves, and Green organizations introduce the concept of engagement, Teal organizations invite people to reclaim their inner wholeness and exercise this wholeness at work. They create an environment wherein people feel free to fully express themselves, bringing unprecedented levels of energy, passion and creativity to work.

**Evolutionary purpose** Teal organizations base strategies on what they sense as their unique contribution to the world. Nimble practices that respond to new information and recognize emerging patterns replace the machinery of plans, budgets, targets and incentives. Paradoxically, by focusing less on the bottom line and shareholder value, Teal organizations generate financial results that outpace competitors.

We often hear leaders and organizations strive to be Teal as if it's a fully understood and defined paradigm, but Teal is not a destination in itself. People familiar with Teal often think that it transcends practices from the other paradigms, such as the establishment of hierarchy, and that these practices simply cease to be if you are "doing Teal right." But approaching this work as *including and transcending* previous paradigms is key. The emerging Teal paradigm still incorporates, for example, hierarchy but in a more dynamic form than at other levels. If and when Teal fully emerges, it will take decades to become a predictable and widely adopted pattern of human organizing. However, we don't need to wait for Teal to fully emerge before we begin leveraging the philosophies and practices already tested and proven to be helpful.

Various organizing principles and patterns are emerging as concepts adjacent or related to Teal, some discretely different and others only slightly nuanced. These include conscious capitalism, sociocracy, Holacracy, agile, self-organization, self-management, Management 3.0, beyond budgeting, complexity theory and many more. Some models, such as Holacracy and conscious capitalism, have an organization stewarding the model. Others, like the agile movement and self-organizing, are broader terms defined in different ways by different people.

## The Messiness of Emergence

As a new paradigm of work emerges, one that encompasses Teal and adjacent concepts, its path can get messy, with elements being debated and challenged. One specific critique of Frederic's Teal work comes from Tom Nixon, who shared his thoughts in the article "Resolving the Awkward Paradox in Frederic Laloux's *Reinventing Organizations*":

Laloux describes a paradox in these [Teal] organizations. As they become more decentralized, the CEO or "top" leader exerts less and less formal authority in developing strategy, and managing its people and operations. However, simultaneously they have to play a vital, centralized role in "holding the space" to ensure its progressive, decentralized practices do not regress back to a more traditional organizational model. Further, there appears to be clear evidence that the CEO in all the progressive organizations are highly visionary leaders and play a key role in setting the vision at the highest level.

On the one hand, Laloux describes these organizations as being like ecosystems such as rainforests, where "there is no single tree in charge of the whole forest." But clearly, the role of the founder or CEO is quite unlike any other, and the task of holding the space is vital for the health of the entire system. So in fact they aren't truly decentralized. It's an awkward paradox that doesn't fit Laloux's model of the next generation of organizations.[4]

Source is a conceptual model by Peter Koenig, who proposes that creative endeavors of any kind—artistic or business—manifest from one human. Every human initiative—from projects to parties to entire businesses—start with one founder, the source. This person takes the first risk to realize an idea and the role can be passed along in a line of succession.

We have all experienced leaders who tap into a vision that mobilizes others. US president Kennedy's declaration to the American people that "We choose to go to the moon in this decade and do the other things, not because they are easy, but because they are hard" offers a famous example of someone tapping their source power and evoking an evolutionary purpose.[5] That evolutionary purpose continued on with others leading the mission that landed on the moon, six years after Kennedy's death. Human ecosystems will change, grow, morph and evolve, and along with them so can their purposes. As Tom points out, Frederic notes a clear connection between specific individuals and an organization's purpose when he says the heroic leader does not have a great vision, but rather a wonderful force chooses a leader to help in the manifestation process.[6]

As often as not in recent years, stories have surfaced of high-profile organizations adopting and then dropping self-management, as if it were a comprehensive operating model that could be completely adopted or dropped. Self-management is more a journey and way of being than a comprehensive operating model in and of itself. Rather than being disheartened or seeing stories of companies walking away from the self-management journey as proof of its futility, we can better understand the next paradigm as one still in development. Because of the messiness and complexity of the development phase, an approach used by another team applied directly to your situation will at best offer a place to start.

## The Journey from Here

We are on a modern journey of discovering a new relationship to work and leadership. In the following pages we unpack the elements of this emerging paradigm through stories and by introducing experiments. We'll use a variety of terms including Teal, self-management and self-organization. These words are used only to help frame our conversation. Dogma is unhelpful. The following chapters invite you to carve your own unique path for your company. Don't force it. Notice and document. Reflect and iterate. As long as you work consciously and with intention, the right path for your team will emerge.

# 1

# Leadership Redefined

First, Bravely
Look Inward

"The important thing is not to stop questioning. Curiosity has its own reason for existing."

**ALBERT EINSTEIN**[1]

L*EADERSHIP* AND *POWER* are possibly the two most loaded words in business. This is especially true for leaders interested in new ways of working and being. Traditional businesses operate using command-and-control, top-down management. Emerging business philosophies prioritize peer-based responsibility and freedom. The reason to build a culture of individual responsibility rather than a do-what-I-say approach is obvious. But the practice of bringing it to life is much harder.

People often say that a well-performing business reflects the collective strengths and contributions of the team while dysfunction traces back to poor leadership. The reality is more complex, yet it's hard to downplay the impact leaders, especially founders, have on teams. For this reason, leaders need to start by looking inward.

SideFX is a thirty-year-old, 100-person visual effects software company and a global leader in its space. Despite its age, the company still has the feel of an early stage, scaling business. Kim Davidson is a cofounder and has held the title of CEO since the organization's inception. Immensely passionate about his industry, he is beloved by his team and customers. Kim has stewarded the business through year-over-year growth, and he readily admits that even after three decades, he continues to learn daily what it means to be a leader.

At a lunch before SideFX embarked on a refresh of its vision, purpose and values, Brent, one of the coauthors and a coach to the team, asked Kim what he thought these elements should be going forward. Kim's answer was immediate and resolute: "I don't know, ask the team. They are in the best position to decide." When pushed for a sense of direction, Kim's answer didn't change: "Really this isn't up to me alone. The team knows what's working and what isn't."

Kim stayed true to his word, allowing the team both the freedom and responsibility of charting the next phase of the company's journey. He remained an active contributor throughout the project but provided little direction, making only minor tweaks. In the end, the team was heavily invested in the changes, and Kim was fully aligned with the result. This is how he has led his team since day one.

In an ideal world, all of your colleagues would show up fully capable, knowing exactly what to do and how to do it. The team would be perfectly coordinated, workloads would be perfectly balanced and business growth would be perfectly smooth. You would know exactly what to say and do to steward optimal progress.

Every leader can attest that this is never the case.

How do you want to show up within your company, especially in the chaotic moments? Embracing radically new ways of working requires leadership. Not the kind indicated by job titles but the kind that comes from deep within. It's a role open to anyone and everyone within an organization.

The SideFX story demonstrates three qualities we see as inherent to successful leaders on this journey: curiosity, creativity and drive for results. These leaders also share common beliefs about how organizations should be structured, have a similar leadership mindset—one of courage, authenticity, transparency, love and empathy—and understand their role as a leader.

## Leadership and Hierarchy

Let's tackle a common myth about self-managing organizations. These organizations are often referred to as flat, suggesting there is no hierarchy and therefore no leadership. As a result, they can be mistakenly seen as disorganized or chaotic with no one leading anything. In reality, every organization has hierarchy, including those operating in the self-management paradigm. As Lotta Croiset van Uchelen from Schuberg Philis, a self-managing IT organization based in Amsterdam, explains, "In a group of people, there is always hierarchy. The difference is that people say, 'I trust you for this leadership role' or 'I trust that you're going to solve this issue for me.' Traditionally we think of being called a leader, the big boss, and now I have to make all these decisions. Alternatively we can come in, show what we're good at, that we're an expert in something but not everything. It could be that I'm good at knowing when we should go in a certain direction or having a vision."[2]

Embracing emerging leadership philosophies doesn't mean hierarchy needs to disappear, but it does need to become dynamic. Leadership isn't held consistently by a small group of individuals. It shifts based on who has the most knowledge and experience in a specific context. Those wanting to move away from top-down management often become fearful that hierarchies suggest self-management isn't taking hold. A more useful perspective is that individuals will leverage their areas of expertise to guide the team at specific times in helpful ways. Our invitation is for you, as a leader, to reduce your attachment to hierarchical authority while embracing your unique genius in the areas where you can help your team achieve more together.

## Being Leaderful

Do you believe people are fundamentally good and inherently aim to do great work? Or do you believe people generally put themselves first, prioritizing personal gain over what's best for the business? How you show up as a leader depends on which of these two beliefs resonates most. Leaders who connect more with the first statement believe their colleagues are motivated by internal factors such as the opportunity to contribute, learn and grow.

The alternative philosophy states that people are motivated by external factors such as rewards for good work and punishment for poor performance. Achievement-oriented bonuses and strict policy enforcement fall into this category. The external-motivator approach to leadership tends to generate compliance. When consistency and speed in mechanical tasks are the priorities, external motivators can be effective.

Nowadays, however, more and more companies rely on knowledge-based work and creativity. In these areas, *engagement is more important than compliance.* Leaders need to invest heavily in strengthening their own abilities to connect with colleagues' internal motivators. Many examples of tapping internal motivators lie in the pages that follow, including supporting autonomy through decision-making processes, creating a culture rooted in learning and growth and communicating shared purposes that everyone on the team finds meaningful.

## Leadership Roles

If your role *isn't* to use positional power to control the team or leverage external motivation to incentivize behavior, then what *is* your job? Leaders in the new paradigm focus on ensuring six necessary roles are filled in their organizations, with founders and CEOs often taking them on. But these roles could be filled by anyone with the passion and skill to do them. Who stewards them and how they go about doing so will be unique to each team. The more purposefully your team goes about naming and assigning these roles based on individuals' personal gifts, the stronger your team will be.

### Space holder
Holding space (physical, mental and emotional) is perhaps the single most important leadership capacity needed in self-managing organizations. In environments where speed and complexity are

becoming the norm, leaders are called upon to see and integrate all that is evolving around them. This requires the capacity to be— and to help others be—comfortable in ambiguity, welcoming the unknown while remaining grounded in a bigger purpose. By holding space, leaders can engage with the unfolding future and guide the organization based on what is happening in the moment rather than attempting to control what can't be controlled.

Holding space requires leaders to listen, think and engage differently. Those who excel at this cultivate curiosity and engage with (rather than resist) whatever comes up in the moment. They respond from an inner knowing that moves beyond what the data, analysis or plan might otherwise suggest. The process of holding space can appear passive to an observer but is an active, deliberate and often demanding leadership practice.

## Purpose-sensor, strategist and inspirer

Someone needs to steward and champion the team's purpose and associated strategy. The individuals filling this role tend to be visionary, passionate and driven. Teams benefit when these gifts are shared in the form of inspiration. It's difficult for everyone on the team to stay focused on the big picture while executing day-to-day operations. Keeping the team's North Star clear and at the forefront, as well as sharing progress updates, helps everyone remain aligned and focused. We dig into this role further in chapter 6, "Purpose."

## Communication orchestrator

We started this chapter by comparing a top-down bureaucratic approach to one that is more entrepreneurial and freer flowing. For a team to operate with a greater sense of freedom and responsibility, it needs access to the same information available to its leaders. The more transparently information flows through an organization, the more empowered a team will be. Leaders help set team-wide expectations through their actions. The amount of information that gets shared by leaders and how that sharing happens will go a long way in determining how communication flows throughout. Chapter 17 explores transparency in more detail.

## Culture steward

Company culture is formed the day two people start working together. It evolves over time, including each time someone new joins. Culture is a living thing, and like all living things it requires a strong immune system to stay healthy. Cultures are compromised by the worst behaviors demonstrated or permitted by the team. The best cultures are cocreated and subsequently kept healthy when the team proactively decides how it will work together. This process inoculates against unhealthy behavior. Culture also requires regular reviews—booster shots—to keep it well and strong. Although culture is a collective creation, leaders play a vital role in intentionally stewarding its foundation and ongoing health.

Many of the following chapters provide insight into how leaders participate in the cocreation of unique company cultures. Chapter 8 on creating safe space is of particular importance.

## Resource balancer and role-design coach

When a team is properly resourced, it does its best work. Unfortunately, people and money are usually in short supply. Helping your team balance available resources, find new resources and clarify roles is invaluable. When eager and skilled people are free to go about their work, magic happens. Finding the spot where passion and skill align for each team member, while supporting their continual development, is a never-ending puzzle we explore in chapter 11. Chapter 12 will help you shape decisions about limited resources. Chapters 20 and 21 focus on recruiting and onboarding new team members.

## Organization protector and boundary holder

Of the six leadership roles shared here, this one is the most vulnerable to misuse. In the words of Simon Wakeman, managing director at UK-based digital agency Deeson, "If you try to be a very directive leader, you can break the [self-managing] system very quickly. But there are times when you have to be directive because you need to stop something from going off the cliff."[3] As leaders, we can fall into the trap of protecting our team from every pothole. When a team hits a pothole, it learns. When it drives off a cliff, it dies. At Deeson, day-to-day pothole avoidance and the associated learnings are left to individuals and coaches. Leaders intervene at limited times and in limited ways to protect the organization's well-being.

Lee Manning of Carpenter Oak, a UK designer and builder of timber-framed buildings, shares a similar perspective:

> After moving from managing director into the chairman role, my work became purposely about not having control... but at the same time sensing when something is about to fall over or take a direction we won't come back from. It's being able to sense when those moments are, and there have been three moments in the last three years when I've had to try to get people to see what I see. It has meant asserting some power and that's been really tough. I've had to ask myself... "Should I actually do this or not?" Fortunately the three times I've interceded seem to have been beneficial to the organization. Things have since evolved to the point where I no longer need to exert power. Transparency now runs through the organization enough not to allow personal agendas to have too much influence. My role has changed from chairman to that of a non-executive director, while continuing to hold a finance role.[4]

The role of organization protector is critically important and frequently misunderstood. Too often leaders overstep the bounds of their role. We're all familiar with the term *micromanagement*. Karin Tenelius from Tuff Leadership Training warns about going too far the other way: "The common misunderstanding is that you abdicate and you have to stand by and watch people making stupid mistakes. And that's not the case because you're still there. But instead of directing people, you give the team feedback. So if you see risks for big mistakes, you can always say, 'When you talk about this opportunity or this decision, I get really scared because I foresee this or that.' You still participate, but not from a position of command-and-control."[5]

## The Role of Source

One more role often associated with leadership deserves special attention—the role of source. The company founder is the most prevalent example of a source, as the founder is often the person who had not only the creative spark of the initiative but took the first risk to bring it into being. The founder manifests the seed and plants, waters and fertilizes it, until a business is born. Recognizing the time, energy and effort required to be a source, and the special connection these individuals have with the purpose of the business, is important.

Tom Nixon is the founder of Maptio, an online software tool for pioneering organizations that prioritize creativity and agility over traditional management hierarchy and processes. Tom helped popularize the concept of source as defined by Peter Koenig. In Tom's words:

> It's okay to accept that somebody is the author of a particular vision or a part of a vision, and wants and needs to take responsibility for their vision. And to invite other people to connect to it in a loving and empathic way and understand what it is that the author is trying to create and what's the need they have that's driving them. The role of CEO or founder in self-managing companies is certainly about facilitating a process of coming up with the vision. But it is more than that. It's accepting responsibility for the whole and that involves a lot of listening and it also involves authority. That's not a thing to be afraid of.[6]

In Koenig's model, as an organization grows older and bigger, sub-sources will emerge, each holding the role as sources of initiatives within the company. Self-managing innovation design firm The Moment was founded in 2011 by Mark Kuznicki, Greg Judelman and Daniel Rose. They are seen as the original sources and continue to fill that role, even as the organization evolves and others take on leadership roles. In Mark's experience, "Being the source is about a feeling, and a sense of meaning, not just work to be done. Storytelling is important to the identity of the initiative, so that it may continue to evolve with a solid connection to source and purpose."[7]

## What's Your Leadership Role?

None of the leaders we've met have been exceptional at all these roles, nor do they aim to be. Instead, they show up as imperfect role models on a journey of learning. They understand their colleagues will sometimes make poor decisions, just as they will. Their focus is on creating an environment where passionate people work toward a common purpose, learning and growing along the way. When things go awry, these leaders look inward first.

In what leadership roles do you excel? Where do you want to apply these personal gifts so others welcome your leadership? How might you amplify the leadership roles discussed in this chapter to help you or your organization overcome a current limitation?

Critical to all leadership in this new paradigm is introspection—a willingness, when challenges arise, to look first at the ways your own emotions, assumptions and habits may contribute to the problem, and how you may need to adjust as a result. If you would like an additional resource to help create a look-inward-first mindset, check out *Leadership and Self-Deception* by the Arbinger Institute. It follows the story of a CEO transitioning from an outward-looking to an inward-looking leadership approach.

# 2

# **Power**

Acknowledge It
and Transform It

"In any system with humans in it, power relations exist, whether you formalize them or not ... If you refuse to define power structures, informal ones will emerge almost instantly. Not expressing these can be extremely harmful to your organization."

**FRANCESCA PICK**[1]

WHEN WE ARE children, the role of our caregivers is important. In our earliest years, those older than us know more than we do. Our caregivers protect us from harm and guide our growth. The same is true in business: those with deep knowledge and experience in a given area guide colleagues who have not yet gained that experience. They leverage their broader perspective in service of the team and steward that area of the organization.

## The Side Effects of Power

Dacher Keltner has been a behavioral researcher for more than twenty years. Along the way he completed an experiment he calls "the cookie monster study," bringing groups of three into a lab and randomly assigning one of the three to a position of leadership. They were then given a group writing task. Thirty minutes into their work, Dacher placed a plate of freshly baked cookies—one for each team member, plus an extra—in front of everyone. In all groups each person took one cookie and, out of politeness, left the extra. The question Dacher wanted to answer was "Who will take the last cookie?" In almost every case, the person who'd been named the leader did. "Studies show that people in positions of corporate power are three times as likely as those at the lower rungs of the ladder to interrupt coworkers, multitask during meetings, raise their voices and say insulting things at the office. And people who've just moved into senior roles are particularly vulnerable to losing their virtues, my research and other studies indicate," Dacher writes.[2]

Power leads to a sense of status or privilege. A study out of the Rotterdam School of Management demonstrates how that status negatively impacts organizations. When led by higher-status (powerful) team members, projects that would otherwise die on the vine continued to receive support because those with less status (the powerless) feared voicing negative opinions and providing critical feedback.[3] We'd all prefer to view these studies as pointing to the flaws in other leaders, but we're all prone to being the cookie monster. Status and privilege are addictive.

Stewardship, however, is different. Stewardship protects, guides and nurtures. Power leverages title and position to exert personal will and preference. When power is used to exercise personal will, it's a form of control. Being a steward does not make us more powerful than others. On the contrary, it puts us in a position of care. In the case of SideFX from chapter 1, Kim stewarded the process of redefining the company's vision. All participants understood that the final say on the new vision, purpose and values fell to Kim. He did not, however, use his position as CEO and shareholder to control the process or predetermine the outcome.

Exercising power over a colleague without their permission creates an asymmetrical relationship, which often causes the other person to feel powerless. It's easy to have good intentions and still build an organization full of powerless people. Sharing power broadly with colleagues brings everyone onto the same plane; even when specific individuals steward specific roles, everyone can be powerful. This collective sense of working in concert is core to agile and self-managed organizations. It brings people together, builds shared understanding and fuels group commitment.

## Four Types of Power

Power is woven through all our relationships, shaping our interactions and permeating our organizations. Rarely, however, do we acknowledge it. Jane Watson, a participant in the five-week Practical Self-Management Intensive, a course designed and run by Susan (a coauthor of this book) and her colleagues at Greaterthan, describes her new learning about power this way: "Saying power is invisible doesn't quite get at its intangible quality. I think it's more accurate to say that it's unseen, because so frequently we're not even looking for it. [The Practical Self-Management Intensive] brought me face-to-face with how limited my personal vocabulary for talking about power was. Subsequently, I began to notice power in my surroundings and my relationships. And once I'd seen it, I couldn't un-see it."[4]

Power shows up in our own behaviors and those of others in four different ways: power over, power for, power with and power among.

So far in this chapter, our use of the word *power* has referred to **power over**.[5] As implied by its name, power over is the directive and controlling approach one person (such as a boss) takes over another. In this dynamic, one person dictates while the other is coerced to follow regardless of their feelings. The power-over dynamic is rampant throughout traditional organizations and is especially problematic when anyone, and especially a leader, tries to use the organization to fulfill unhealthy or unaligned personal needs.

**Power for** comes into play when one person advocates on behalf of another. A caregiver might make decisions or manage resources on behalf of their elderly family member. In a work context, a more seasoned team member may make decisions on behalf of a colleague who is still learning their role.

When we work collaboratively to make decisions and negotiate resources, we are exhibiting **power with**. Power over, power for and power with exist within a transactional paradigm. One person acts over another, one person acts for another or one person acts with another. In all three, a finite amount of power is divided between two or more people.

**Power among** is much more expansive. Fully self-organizing systems operate with power flowing among and through system participants. One person can use their power to advance the interests of the organization without anyone else feeling powerless. For example, as we'll explore in chapter 12 on decision-making, anyone in an organization can steward big decisions using approaches that ensure others with opinions meaningfully contribute.

You might ask, "Is it ever appropriate to exert authority in a way that may feel like power over?" In a coaching conversation about authority and power that Brent had with a founder, the founder said, "Our ultimate goal is to get stuff done. We don't start companies because we want power. If any founder exercises power, it's because they feel it's the best way of getting to the next step." So how do you get things moving to the next step without the use of power over?

As a leader stewarding important roles within your team, you might, at times, be best positioned to make mission-critical decisions in the interest of the team. Doing so can be appropriate and necessary. The feeling of power over experienced by a team comes more from *how* a leader exerts the authority inherent in their role. Grabbing control and issuing directives out of frustration, impatience or personal preference leaves teams feeling powerless. ("I've waited long enough for you to introduce the new test equipment requested by our customer. I'm done waiting. I've made the decision.") Making critical decisions transparently with a mindset of collective learning helps teams feel valued and included. ("I've looked at the work you've done so far in selecting the new test equipment. You committed to communicating a decision two weeks ago. I was in a meeting yesterday with our biggest customer and they were pushing for an answer. In my role as CEO I had to make a final decision or risk losing the customer. Let's spend ten minutes understanding what we can both learn from this experience.")

Although Kim at SideFX naturally limits his power-based decision-making, Kurtis McBride, founder and CEO of Miovision, a Canada-based traffic data and solutions company, is more intentional in his approach. Miovision has recently embarked on an effort to clearly define all roles within the company, including the decision-making scope of each role. That includes leaders. This creates transparency—everyone has clarity on what decisions are within their scope versus those that will require consultation with others. This also encourages leaders to act as coaches and mentors, cultivating effective decision-makers and keeping decisions where they optimally belong: with their teams.

## Reflect and Act on Your Preferred Power Card

Susan served a team in Western Australia as its 1,200-person organization transitioned to self-organizing teams. During the transition the existing executive team members decided what they, themselves, collectively needed: a stronger commitment to disperse their power. Or, as one member put it, "We need to come together to break up." The team paid attention to which facets of power they favored or, put more bluntly, which power card they tended to play. They asked the following questions of themselves, and we encourage you to ask yourself the same as you move toward a new way of working:

- Am I attempting to influence the outcome?
- Am I advocating for my preferred solution?
- Am I wielding the fact that I hold the most context?
- Am I leveraging my authority?
- Am I trying to reinforce my status?
- Am I making decisions on my own?

Most of us are attracted to forms of power and favor certain expressions of it. When you can acknowledge and recognize your habits, you're more likely to be able to transparently and account- ably disperse some of these decisions to others. In doing so, you are supporting the shift from power over to power among.

## From Power Over to Power Among

Sometimes intentionally, sometimes unintentionally, power over thrives in organizations through the excessive use of positional authority. As a leader desiring to lessen your positional authority or give it up altogether, your power needs to go somewhere. At some point on the journey to self-management, all leaders learn that simply releasing positional authority does not work. The team continues looking to you for decisions and solutions. If you con- tinue to fulfill that role, you are back to positional authority. If you remain silent, the team will likely grind to a halt.

Shortly after beginning the shift to self-management, Peter Aprile, founder of Counter Tax Lawyers in Toronto, gathered over lunch with a few of his colleagues to discuss the company's bene- fits program. During the conversation Peter noticed he was doing most of the talking. No one else seemed to want to propose solu- tions or make decisions. He left lunch ruminating on the thought, "Why do I need to do everything?" At home, he realized, "I've trained them. This is 100 percent on me. I need to start doing things differently."

When you move away from positional authority, power needs a new home among the team. This shift will only occur by dispers- ing the power to organizational practices, cocreating agreements and defining roles and purposeful structures. The team, leader included, needs a map and some guardrails.

Perhaps the best-known set of self-governing practices and agreements exist within the Holacracy framework. Honed over twelve years and through 1,000 organizations, Holacracy is based on a set of rules outlined in a constitution. Once a team signs and adopts the constitution, power shifts from one or more individuals into the system itself. Everyone lives by the same set of rules and practices. We explore Holacracy and alternatives in chapter 25. For now, know that whether you follow Holacracy or a different approach, agreements and practices provide clear lanes for everyone to follow.

## Supporting the Shift

Shifting power requires intentional grit and a preparedness to stand firm in your beliefs, even when doing so is super challenging. Never has role-modeling been more important. If you are not ready and willing to stand in the fire throughout the transition, it's best to wait until you are.

Soon after Peter from Counter realized he needed to start doing things differently, his will was tested as the firm suffered significant revenue losses. In the past, Peter would have gone into overdrive to fix the problem himself and save the team. In Peter's words, "I just stayed in that space. Team members weren't holding each other accountable. Everyone wants to be held accountable, but they don't want to hold others accountable in return for fear of having the finger pointed back. We're learning to hold each other accountable in the right way without one person always having to fill that role."[6] As painful as this lesson was, it became a turning point at Counter. Others started noticing and naming the lack of accountability, and team members started addressing accountability with each other.

As you explore the shift away from positional authority, first ensure you and your colleagues are ready to give self-management a try by exploring the topic and seeking consent to start experimenting. Scaffolding for the shift is provided in the next chapter. Second, develop a minimum experiment for your first iteration. What are the practices, agreements, roles and structures you will prototype? As your prototype unfolds, focus as a team on defining and assigning mission-critical roles first and quickly.

At the outset of the journey, identify coaches within or, more likely, outside your team to proactively guide learning. We three authors are coaches, and there are many other talented coaches available around the world. Identify facilitators within the team who can give permission and raise the profile of grassroots initiatives. Honoring and supporting initiatives started by team members who were not previously in positions of authority provide valuable early wins. Finally, watch for shadow hierarchies that emerge to fill the positional authority void and act fast by having the necessary conversations.

In preparing to shift, start practicing. Next time a decision comes your way, ask yourself these questions:

- Is someone else on the team capable of making this decision?

- Does the learning offered to my colleagues in making this decision outweigh the risk to the company?

- Is the decision reversible if things go awry?

If you can answer yes to these questions, step back and let others decide, even if it's uncomfortable. If you find yourself unable to answer yes to one or more, why is that? What can you learn about your relationship to power?

# 3

# Transition Stages

Journey to New
Ways of Working

"Operating in self-organization requires heightened awareness. We're always practicing... it's never done."

**TIM JONES**[1]

MAGINE STANDING at the starting line of a marathon. The banner overhead reads "The New Ways of Working Endurance Run." Are you excited to be here? Is this your first marathon? How long will it take you? What's the terrain? Are you prepared? Have you completed training runs? Worked with a running coach? Stretched? Have you thought about fuel stops along the way? Do you have a support crew?

Running a marathon is an adequate analogy for the journey to the next paradigm, and there are a few differences worth calling out. In this marathon, the terrain changes every mile of the race in unknown and unexpected ways. Parts of the course are unlike anything you've experienced before and no training will prepare you. The length of the course is unknown but it's long. Lastly, some of your running mates aren't ready to run this race with you.

Our goal in this chapter is to help you set reasonable expectations. Transitioning to new ways of working is challenging. How challenging? Peter Aprile, founder of Counter, describes it like this: "We've done a lot of hard things. I didn't realize how hard this would be. Not even close. This is the hardest thing ever. Without question. On so many levels." But is it worth tackling? "Counter has become an environment in which people are exploring the potential in themselves—what they believed to be the limits of their potential and then going beyond. We've reached levels personally and as a group that I don't know how we could have got to otherwise... It's helping me become a better human, lawyer, colleague, husband and father."[2]

Many who are well into the journey describe the shift to self-management as going from unconsciously incompetent ("I don't know what I don't know") to consciously incompetent ("Wow, I'm not very good at this") to consciously competent ("With effort and focus, I can do this") and finally to unconsciously competent ("I work in these new ways naturally, without thinking about it").

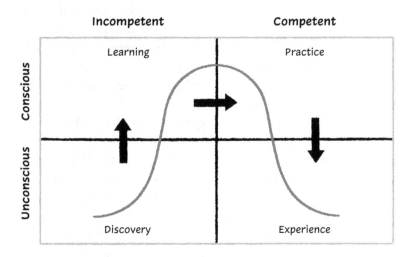

Bryan Peters is a member of the team at Sobol.io, a software platform for distributed and self-organizing teams. In the early stages of his journey, despite being well versed in the theory of self-management, he needed to work through an ego hit. "I thought I was good at this self-management stuff," he recalls. "As our team moved deeper and deeper into new ways of working, I realized I had a lot of personal work still to do. I was incompetent in areas where I really needed to be better, and [I had to] break some old habits no longer serving me or my team."[3]

## Three Stages of the Journey

Edwin Jansen of the Ian Martin Group, a fully self-managed recruiting firm, has written about how the journey to embracing and embodying this new paradigm can be seen as having three distinct stages.[4] Although presented here as linear steps, the experience is much more cyclical. As you begin your own journey, think of these as loops to be completed over and over again. Instead of getting stuck at stage one, push on, iterate, then iterate again.

### Stage 1: The head (or the intellectual stage)

First you need to understand the core concepts of self-management. At this stage, you begin to see your organization as an ecosystem built on trust rather than as a management pyramid. This is a fundamentally different way of working, requiring different practices and different skill sets. A successful transition requires both personal development and organizational shifts. Reading and revisiting this book and the variety of resources listed in the resource section will help with this part of the journey. You're ready to move beyond the head stage when you can begin answering these questions affirmatively:

- Am I starting to understand this new way of working?

- Can I define it for myself and others with some clarity?

- Is my definition aligned with the definitions of others in our organization?

- Do I think this way of working can be beneficial for us?

### Stage 2: The heart (or the emotional stage)

A new paradigm, such as self-management, requires all involved to take an ongoing, honest and emotionally difficult look at themselves. The move from unconsciously incompetent to consciously competent (and eventually to unconsciously competent) will have you in a constant battle with your ego. It requires that you surface and examine deeply held beliefs. This stage is often accompanied by major emotional realizations and sometimes tears. For previously high-ranking team members, moving through this stage can be accompanied by a feeling of becoming unprivileged. For others, the need to make more decisions and express more opinions can tap inner uncertainties.

Moving through this phase provides the emotional strength necessary to operate in a self-organizing system. It reorients you from being primarily focused on your own needs to serving the needs of your team, of which you and your needs are a critical part. You are ready to move beyond this stage when you can begin articulating answers to these questions:

- How is the move to self-management personal to me?

- What emotional turmoil is showing up for me (anger, frustration, fear, and so on)?

- What long-held beliefs and personal views am I reexamining?

- Which emotional attachments to the past do I need to release?

### Stage 3: The habits (or the behavioral stage)

We move through our days relying on well-established patterns. Our ingrained habits are often reflexes operating without conscious thought. They show up in our use of language, emotionally charged responses and repetitive actions. Many were established long ago by our egos to protect us from our fears. Leaders in traditional contexts may come to expect deference to their ideas, see their opinions as holding more sway and reflexively delegate, but their new team agreements might ask that they listen more than they speak and allow others to take ownership of roles and responsibilities in a project.

When shifting, you need to establish new healthier habits through deliberate practice. Doing so is easier said than done. As we all know, old habits die hard. This stage is best maneuvered with vulnerability, conscious behavior change and public account-ability. You know you are making progress here when you can begin answering these questions:

- What previously unconscious patterns have been getting in my way?

- What habits am I ready to work on changing?

- What healthier habits would I like to create?

- Where can I start being more open and vulnerable with others about the source of my unconscious patterns?

- How can I incorporate public accountability to support my desired behavior changes?

## Tactical Elements of the Transition

Every individual and team transitions differently to a new way of working. As you shape your own transition, here are some helpful tips.

### Avoid being a fast-paced purist

When learning about successful self-managing organizations, you might find yourself wanting to implement everything at once. Per-fection is an understandable desire, but as a goal, it's bound to fail. The journey from unconscious incompetence to conscious competence takes time and energy—both of which are in short supply as the team focuses on delivering the business's products and services.

In retrospect, Simon Wakeman from Deeson would have been less of a purist about things: "We did a lot of reading, watched lots of talks and got quite evangelical about some of the principles. We went quite big on it and we went a little too big too soon. The organizational shock of the first iteration was quite disruptive. We then pared it back and built it up gradually. That made more sense.

The real underlying reason for why it wasn't that effective the first time was that people weren't ready for it. Real self-organization demands a load of competencies from team members that they've never had to think about before."[5]

### Be directive at times

For many, traditional ways of working are comfortable and predictable. Moving to a new paradigm can feel like moving from your favorite à la carte restaurant to a gluttonous buffet. Too much choice, at least in the beginning, can be overwhelming for some. For this reason, quickly aligning on a few critical elements, including roles, decision-making, meetings and governance, will be helpful.

### Take action

Change requires action. Kathryn Maloney from The Ready, a self-managing consulting firm, summarizes change this way: "We can teach people new meeting structures, decision tools, communication technology, teaming structures, et cetera, all day long, but if you aren't prepared to give up what you know to make room for what you don't yet know—and feel slightly off balance in the process—much less new and different will occur."[6]

Taking action by stepping into the unknown is scary for many. This fear keeps us stuck dreaming and planning. The move to self-management requires everyone to act and then to act again. It's through this repetitive and iterative process that a level of stickiness and virality emerges. Without it, the transition will never occur.

### Don't force change, invite it

When transitioning in an already established organization, clarify boundaries around those who are choosing to work in new ways. This allows a defined group of team members to experiment in real time. Those who choose to step into the new space commit to trying new things.

A 2,500-person Dutch ecommerce company, Bol.com, chose to begin its transition with a team of forty people, who started experimenting with the principles of Holacracy. Over time they created their own Holacracy-influenced way of working called Spark. The members of that team became promoters of Spark. This excited other teams and they joined the movement. Five years later, more than 1,500 employees are working with Spark. Harm Jans of Bol.com describes Spark as "Bol.com's way of working for self-organizing teams. It allows for high autonomy, high engagement, clear roles and responsibilities, agile decision-making and very effective meetings." From his experience, "This way of working is not easy, but if you and your colleagues commit, your team will develop faster than ever before."[7]

## Graduate to self-management

Some teams feel it's illogical and unfair to expect anyone to transition overnight from one way of working to another. An alternative is to offer a period of learning and experimentation so that each team member can fully adopt self-management at their own pace.

Everyone who works at the law firm Counter becomes a Counterpart. The team recently introduced the term New Counterpart for those who are still learning the core self-management skills; all new members of the team begin as New Counterparts. The team is now figuring out what markers indicate if and when somebody is ready to be invited and to accept the Counterpart Friend role and eventually the Counterpart-ner role. Unlike the traditional three- to six-month probation period, this graduation is based on demonstrated skills, not time. Peter has also come to realize that some people will not graduate and will need to leave the organization. In his words, "We expect that some people will leave Counter and take a different path. And I'm confident that will put all parties on the ideal path."[8]

## Practice

We often use the term *practices* in self-management. It's a deliberate word choice to remind us that we are always learning. When we're practicing something, we do that thing over and over again. By doing so, we get better. We develop an awareness of how we are currently performing and how we are progressing.

Samantha Slade, author of *Going Horizontal* and founder of Percolab, an international cocreation and codesign firm based in Montreal, uses playing the piano as an example: "When we play piano, we don't just get better by playing randomly. We give ourselves a little framework. I'm going to play piano on Tuesdays for thirty minutes. On Wednesdays I'll play for fifty minutes. And on Saturdays I'm going to give it an hour. I'll play the same piece during the weekdays. On Saturdays I'll challenge myself with a new, more complicated piece. Naturally we give ourselves frameworks to challenge us to be developing forward as learners and practitioners. And so it's bringing that again into the workplace."[9]

## The Management in Self-Management

Many leaders on the self-management journey share the same message based on their learning. It's best described as going from one extreme to another. The next-generation organization needs a rebalancing of management with more individuals managing themselves and less directive leadership coming from others. In attempting to create that new balance, many leaders admit to going too far.

Leo Widrich, cofounder of social media software platform Buffer, writes, "Prior to implementing self-management we [cofounders] were in a more traditional management role, making decisions and guiding teams and areas toward goals and setting milestones. In our first iteration toward self-management, we completely let go. We stopped having 1:1s with people to help them grow, we stopped making decisions, we intentionally avoided creating a vision. We generally took on similar roles to everyone else on the team: Joel [Gascoigne] would do day to day product work, I would do marketing on a daily basis again. We quickly learned that that wasn't the best way for the two of us to spend our time."

Stepping back too far too fast can slow down learning and leave the company directionless. Leo continues, "In our current iteration of self-management, Joel and I have again taken on a higher-level role. We brought back mentoring and coaching. We also brought back higher-level decision-making about vision, product direction, etc. What we left off is the management part, meaning people don't report to us and we don't tell people what to work on."[10]

Helen Sanderson, founder of community support provider Wellbeing Teams, had a similar experience. "Honestly, I think I stepped back too much," she admits. "I was confused by what not being a traditional CEO anymore meant. I think being in a self-managed team calls us all to step into leadership roles and I stepped back a bit too far. I'm better at that now and have learned to behave differently, stepping into my leadership role alongside my colleagues."[11]

THE NEW Ways of Working Endurance Run only begins when you take the first step and then the second, and then you jog from head to heart to habit and around again. As you practice, your self-managing muscles and those of your colleagues will grow. Missteps are not only part of the journey but a requirement. Without them, your progress will stall. Invite experimentation and celebrate the learning.

# 4

# Conscious Language

Know That
Words Matter

"We cannot problem-solve our way into fundamental change … This is not an argument against problem solving; it is an assertion that the primary work is to shift the context and language and thinking about possibility within which problem solving takes place."

**PETER BLOCK**[1]

WHEN YOU BECOME aware of behavior patterns in your workplace, notice too the way you use language to reinforce those patterns. Our word choices influence behavior and reinforce triggers and reactions. Taking the time to achieve alignment on definitions is incredibly important and potent—your team will develop a consistent shorthand language that helps support and create your cultural identity. Bear this in mind when bringing in new team members—and take the time to initiate them to your unique language.

Some words are so common that most of us don't think twice about them. Words like *feedback* and *performance*, *collaboration* and *management* and *leadership*. The issue is that these words, like our other assumptions about the workplace, are so commonplace. We don't bother to check the definitions with ourselves (let alone our colleagues), or try to reach a level of coherence and agreement on their meanings.

Spend the time to scratch past the surface of words and clarify their meanings within the context of your organization and team. Getting caught in the loop of semantics is easy, but defining what you mean is important work, especially when it comes to the words attached to your needs or identity—what we call "baggage." For example, one of the most troublesome and often used words is *trust*. What does it mean? Does it mean I believe you will tell me the truth? Does it mean you will do what you say you are going to do? Does it mean I am ceding my authority to you because I believe you will act on my behalf? Does it mean I know you have my back? How might trust play out in a team? Is it a blanket statement? Is everyone to take everyone else at their word? Can we check back with one another once trust is given? Should we? To us, the authors, trust has two components: I trust your intentions, and I trust your capacity. You might mishear someone who says "I don't trust you" and assume it's about your intentions when it's about your capacity.

Things get even more complicated when, in an effort to explain a new way of working, you bring in words that a person's never heard before, at least in the work context—like *Teal, Holacracy* or *self-management*. You need to take the time to align on a common understanding of new terminology. Even introducing words that people know and understand in other contexts, such as *democracy* or *hierarchy*, can cause confusion if you assume they have objective meanings. We all have our personal interpretations of these words, and when we use them to inform change, collective understanding is essential.

Jason Cottrell, founder and CEO of Myplanet, a Toronto-based software studio, gives a lot of thought to words. For example, what should the leadership team of the company be called? "I know that some look at me as silly when I debate these items since there are 'established norms' in our industry. However, most are established around a hierarchical approach to management. I do believe our language choices signal our intent."[2]

## Teal-y Buzzwords

When groups of people work, live or grow together, they create language. It happens organically. Jargon is something that helps people belong; adopting the lexicon is part and parcel of adopting a community identity. It enables "the in" to feel together, but for those who are "not in," it can be a barrier to understanding—suggesting an exclusive, insular culture—or simply be annoying. Here are some commonly used words within Enspiral, a participatory community that supports people in launching and building all sorts of initiatives, projects and world-changing ventures. These words are not unique to Enspiral and can be heard in many self-managing organizations.[3]

**Buzzword:** Check-in

**How you might hear it:** "Let's do a quick check-in before we get started. What's on top for everyone just now?"

**What it means:** Inviting everyone in the room to speak at the beginning of any meeting or gathering. Brings all the voices in right from the get-go and makes it okay to talk about anything going on that might affect how we are *showing up* (see below).

**Buzzword:** Check-out

**How you might hear it:** "Let's do a quick check-out. How is everyone leaving the session today?"

**What it means:** As with *check-in* (see above), check-out is a process that invites everyone to say whatever they need to say before a meeting or gathering comes to an end. Often quick and lighthearted.

**Buzzword:** Ecosystem

**How you might hear it:** "They aren't really in the community but are definitely part of the ecosystem."

**What it means:** Borrowing from nature, *ecosystem* is used to describe the whole landscape of interconnected people, projects and companies relating to a specific community, idea or conversation.

**Buzzword:** Followership

**How you might hear it:** "We don't celebrate followership enough!"

**What it means:** Less talked about than leadership but no less important, *followership* is best described as offering active, visible support to someone who is taking a lead on something, such as agreeing to show up to a first-time event and making it known to others.

**Buzzword:** Harvest

**How you might hear it:** "Who's up for harvesting everything we've discussed today?"

**What it means:** It's not picking apples from a tree. *Harvesting* generally means to collect and write up all the big ideas or actions from a discussion, workshop or gathering. A harvest might look like mind maps on big pieces of paper, photos of the Post-it Notes on windows or notes in a shared online document.

**Buzzword:** Hold space

**How you might hear it:** "Thanks for holding space for us so beautifully on this retreat."

**What it means:** The act of creating and maintaining the optimum physical and social conditions for other people to do what they need to—to meet, converse, decide, debate, explore—without seeking any specific outcome.

**Buzzword:** Sense

**How you might hear it:** "My sense is we're really close to something here."

**What it means:** Something unnamed, a thought or process that hasn't quite landed yet. Something being sensed is still a bit fuzzy; sometimes it is an idea or insight that's not quite fully formed.

**Buzzword:** Show up

**How you might hear it:** "We need to keep asking ourselves how we want to show up."

**What it means:** Showing up doesn't just refer to going along to meetings or parties. It also refers to being conscious of the mindset we bring to a project or activity, being open-minded, reflective, gentle or considered, for example.

Choosing to introduce such words into your own vocabulary as a leader offers several benefits. Changing your words leads to changing actions and modeling new behaviors. Language offers others an insight into our thinking. If we aspire to lead differently, language is an easy first step to prototype and practice.

Alignment is everything when teams decide to work in new ways. It's not done once; it's done continually and it's the role of everyone to practice. Beyond building a level of awareness about the vital importance of language and words, you need to bring a level of intentionality and consciousness to what you say and mean. It's also about checking each other when you fall back into old language patterns by regularly asking for clarification.

Once a level of alignment is reached, you can start practicing how you might use words to clarify, reinforce or enliven team values. One of Buffer's values is listening. To help bring this value to life, they prioritize using less declarative and more uncertainty words, such as *might, maybe, sense, probably* and *hunch*. They do this by approaching everything as a hypothesis, Buffer's Courtney Seiter explained in a blog post:

> At Buffer, it's rare to hear definitive words like *definitely* or *certainly*. You're far more likely to hear:
>
> It's my intuition that . . .
> I sense that we could possibly . . .
> Might it work to . . .
> I sense that it could work to . . .[4]

You can also experiment with language as you begin to move away from traditional titles and consider roles as increments of accountability. Many teams have a lot of fun by creatively naming roles. For example, the role of board liaison can be renamed "board whisperer" or expense approver can become "steward of the coin." Of course, it's not compulsory to have fun with language!

As with each invitation in this book, working with language comes down to awareness first (naming things for what they are), then consciousness (doing something with intention while understanding the implication). Become aware of the words you use and the effect those words can have. Decide together how to elevate the language your team uses to propel you into your new way.

# 5

# **Resistance**

## Work Through
## Inner Opposition

"Everyone has a little voice inside of their head that's angry and afraid. That voice is the resistance—your lizard brain—and it wants you to be average (and safe)."

**SETH GODIN**[1]

THROUGH SHEER WILL or bloody-mindedness, we fight against our lizard brain every day. Our instinct to stay safe, conserve energy, do just enough is an inbuilt mechanism that, if we allow it, overrides the better angels of our nature. Each day we need to re-recognize our resistance and decide to challenge it—to work with it, and learn to dance with it. Even those of us who see ourselves as fearless in almost every way—as eternal optimists—will resonate with the words of Steven Pressfield, author of *The War of Art*, from his blog post "Resistance Wakes Up with Me":

People ask me sometimes, "When in your day do you first feel Resistance?"

My answer: *"The instant I open my eyes."*
In fact maybe sooner.
Maybe before I even know I'm awake.
I feel it.
It's like Resistance is this huge, rapacious bear that sleeps in bed at my shoulder. By the time my feet hit the floor, it's already lacing up its shoelaces.
Resistance is waiting for me.
He's wide awake.
He's ready to rumble.

He does not give me .0001 second of slack.
What's the answer?
What's *my* answer?
The only way I've found to beat this bear is to tackle him head-on
from Microsecond One.
I get up.
I stagger to the bathroom.
I'm grumbling, I'm muttering to myself, I'm waiting (miserably)
for the first positive thought.
But in my mind I have set myself to face that bear and beat him.[2]

If we're honest with ourselves, this metaphorical bear is an "every day in every way" occurrence in our lives. Fear, resistance, whatever we choose to call it, is as much a part of life as breathing. From the day we lose our innocence (in one way or another) until our last breath, the struggle is real. Asking "What are you afraid of?" surfaces a few core possibilities. The fear we might hurt ourselves or others is a biggie. Dig a level deeper into "hurt ourselves" and things get a bit more interesting and somehow simpler.

Take the idea of physical harm or the deprivation of physical needs (food, shelter) out of the equation, and we're left with the possibility of being emotionally, psychologically or spiritually hurt. Hurt might arise as guilt or shame. A colleague of ours often tells the story of his "loss of innocence" and hence his core source of resistance: "I remember being seven or so, year two at school. I had something really clever to share with the class, and I excitedly raised my hand. When the teacher called on me, I spoke, and to my utter horror, the entire class, including the teacher, started laughing at me." That emotional pain of feeling ridiculed, rejected or stupid is real. For many of us, our resistance to change of any magnitude can be traced back to the fear of being made the butt of a joke, or cast out. Leading a team on the journey to self-management will trigger these same fears.

Traditional ways of working are so deeply ingrained in our psyche that the mere suggestion of doing things differently can feel like we've hung a "make fun of me" sign around our neck. Is it any wonder that most leaders, even the most progressive ones, have convinced themselves it's easier to stick with the long-held management paradigm?

## The Journey Hurts

Resistance is natural. We all face it to varying degrees and at different times, and we all have ways of dealing with it. It often leads us to avoidance, such as an implicit fear of introducing new ways of working together, so we put off experiments. Sometimes the fear presents as anger or frustration with ourselves or others. When you initiate change within your organization, it's absolutely essential that you interrogate your personal beliefs and work on yourself.

Edwin Jansen from the Ian Martin Group reflects, "I've experienced tremendous growth when I uncover and explore the things I'm most deeply afraid of. I look for feedback, and then notice when I'm emotionally triggered or defensive at hearing how I could be better. Then I ask myself, 'What am I afraid of?' And try to find the courage for vulnerable action."[3]

Susan worked with the CEO of an organization with more than 1,000 employees whose personal (limiting) belief was not uncommon, and it boiled down to "I assume that because I am the boss, everyone thinks I have the best ideas and/or that I'm the only one who can execute on them, and that if I imagine that's not true, I am either letting them down or I am a fraud."

So there it is: *exploring resistance will hurt.*

The hurt will continue years into the process of exploration—and so will the learning and growth. Not every day, and not always in the same way, you will find yourself asking, "What's the point? Am I the only one who cares about this?" And guess what? Others on the team will be asking themselves the same questions too. We all know change is not a linear process. Even when you embark on a quest as noble as creating a more human organization, you as a leader of the change may consistently be the biggest obstacle to it. And that's okay.

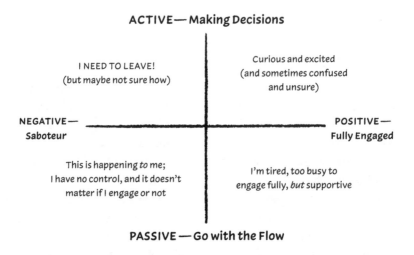

ACTIVE— Making Decisions

I NEED TO LEAVE!
(but maybe not sure how)

Curious and excited
(and sometimes confused
and unsure)

NEGATIVE—
Saboteur

POSITIVE—
Fully Engaged

This is happening *to* me;
I have no control, and it doesn't
matter if I engage or not

I'm tired, too busy to
engage fully, *but* supportive

PASSIVE — Go with the Flow

Acknowledging and naming our resistance helps. This simple quadrant map provides a useful tool for identifying where each member of a team is on the journey to self-management. It can be used, for example, at the beginning of team meetings as a check-in, to see how people are feeling in that moment. Draw it on a physical or virtual whiteboard, or use handouts, and ask people to plot themselves. Teams that use this tool frequently learn it by heart and can draw it themselves.

You can use this tool in many ways, and people who use it report feeling like they move between quadrants every day on their self-management journey. There is no right or wrong quadrant, only truth in the moment. This map is useful in helping teams understand that it's not only okay but expected to not feel great about the process all the time. Often we'll find ourselves actively engaged in the freedom and responsibility of self-management.

Sometimes we become passively disengaged, feeling helpless as we're swept along in the current. At times we are engaged but only passively, feeling a surge of momentum only to be overcome with the busyness of our workload. And sometimes we need to proactively step away for a while—and that's okay too. It's unrealistic to think we can be all-in all of the time.

Dr. Robert Kegan's Immunity to Change process is a great resource for deeper exploration of your own internal resistance. Greater-than Academy's Practical Self-Management Intensive program uses Immunity to Change maps to help participants interrogate their mindsets and behaviors, identifying assumptions about what they think will happen if they change their behaviors. By asking ourselves questions, we can come face-to-face with our own resistance. The process also asks participants to test their assumptions by creating low-risk experiments. Through experimentation, we get to see a more nuanced view of how our fears are both useful and hindering to our bigger purpose.

## Where Emotions Live

The move to self-management and managing the accompanying resistance—our own and others—are rooted in emotion. Frederic Laloux puts a finer point on the shift to Teal: "If it comes from the head only, it never works. There is always a counter-argument from someone resisting change."[4] The intention for change needs to come from our personal stories and life experiences that spur us to explore something new, different and better. Again and again, you will encounter the argument that emotional work doesn't belong in the workplace. But this perspective is blind to a simple fact: emotion is already in the workplace, playing out every single day. We have become amazingly adept at ignoring, stepping around and squashing anything that triggers fear.

Think about a time at work when you thought your team was perfectly aligned on a project and then you were blindsided by a conflict. It may have been with a team you'd worked with a lot and people you knew really well. Then suddenly you felt your shoulders tighten and fought hard to refrain from reacting angrily. "How can this happen," you may have wondered, "with people I've worked with for ages and who feel like a mature and communicative team?"

Although we can be aware of triggers like not being heard or feeling we've been excluded from an important decision, frustration and rejection can still surface in our minds, our bodies and our hearts. In traditional workplaces, openly processing these reactions would be seen as bad form or a sign of weakness, certainly not something to "waste time on" in the workplace. Is it any wonder people suffer at work? When the default is to ignore or ridicule feelings, we are forced to bury or dismiss what is true for us. We humans know how to avoid hurt. By the time we enter the workforce, we have spent decades perfecting sophisticated practices of dodging pain.

## Resistance and Fear

If you decide to dance with your resistance instead of ignoring it, begin with awareness, discernment and naming feelings. Here are some steps to help you slow down and explore what might be going on for you. Ask yourself the following questions, perhaps answering them in a journal:

- Can I accept that I have internal resistance here? (If you cannot accept your own resistance, explore your resistance to resistance, asking, "What am I resisting?" Be specific and be honest in your responses.)

- Is this resistance bringing up any fears, and if so, which fears? (Fear often underlies resistance.)

- Can I find any wisdom in my fear or resistance? (Often, though not always, resistance points to something that is meaningful but hidden, or at least not obvious.)

Explore and unpack the emotions that arise for you during this process.

Creating a safe environment where others can explore their emotions in this way is a great gift. This is one of the offerings of the emerging Teal paradigm. Rather than suppressing our feelings, and especially our fears, on the journey to a better workplace, we bring them forward.

Leading a team on a transformational journey will trigger resistance and fear for many. Jurriaan Kamer from the self-managing consulting firm The Ready speaks of the challenge of changing an organization this way:

> It feels really like simple work, but it's actually one of the hardest kinds of work; the hardest kind of change is to change a system. It's important to realize that any change, or any creating of something within a system which is different, automatically provokes a response of the immune system of the organization, [which will] probably try to get rid of this abnormal state. If you're aware of that and have the courage to continue even if that happens... continue to speak up with the idea that you're actually trying to pursue something that's better, that is very important. Try to be courageous and not get disappointed, or you will get disappointed and it will cause a lot of pain.[5]

When you encounter organizational resistance, you can take steps to work through it. Try not to think of resistance in teams as something to be overcome but, as with personal resistance, something to be curious about and work with. Resistance offers valuable insight into what is going on. By concentrating first on the people energized by new ideas, you'll create the capacity in them to help those who may be struggling.

When listening and exploring resistance, notice what's being said and the needs behind the words, and moreover practice explicitly asking each person what they need. You can then name whatever you agree with in the resistance, such as valid concerns that need to be addressed. The goal is to clear up misconceptions and ensure your colleagues feel heard and understood.

APOLOGIES FOR the lack of pat answers in this chapter. All we can promise is that if you choose to be in, you will have a moment, like when Dorothy steps outside her house after landing in Oz, of seeing color and light that was not there before.

# 6

# Purpose

Know the Guiding
Reasons for Your
Work Together

"Purpose is a central, self-organizing life aim that stimulates goals, manages behaviors and provides a sense of meaning … [It guides] the use of finite personal resources … offers direction just as a compass offers direction to a navigator."

**PATRICK MCKNIGHT AND TODD KASHDAN**[1]

NGAGING IN purpose-driven and meaningful work is the highest ideal we can hope for in our professional lives. For most people, securing a livelihood is the core motivation for work. The ability to align our personal values and tap into our own intrinsic motivators is a privilege. A North Star, or guiding reason, for an organization's existence is powerful, and also difficult to articulate. A thriving consulting industry exists to help unearth the missions, visions and values of organizations—but once arrived at, these statements can easily fall flat and fail to drive the intended behavior. Discovering and articulating a purpose for your organization is a critical piece of the self-management puzzle. We can't effectively self-manage within a system without a sense of shared purpose to guide us.

As with so many of the words, terms and phrases explored in this book, *purpose* is fraught with varying interpretations. When considering the usefulness of purpose, cultural architect Caterina Bulgarella challenges us to distinguish between purpose as a means to an end (financial growth) and as the catalyst for transformation. She writes in *Forbes*, "Many companies today probably recognize the importance of purpose, but only a minority use purpose as a goalpost in decision-making, and many employees, especially millennials, feel a lack of affinity with their employers' purpose. These two issues are symptoms of the same affliction—using purpose for linear growth (i.e., evocative forward pull), instead of tapping its transformative qualities (i.e., evolutionary or upward growth)."[2]

Frederic Laloux expresses a similar sentiment in *Reinventing Organizations* when he writes, "Executives, at least in my experience, don't pause in a heated debate to turn to the company's mission statement for guidance, asking, 'What does our purpose require us to do?'"[3]

Meaningful purpose emerges from an organization's "big why," often over years of reflection and exploration, stewarded by people with strong personal values and a shared vision of what could be. Whether it's building software to create a great user experience or, as in the case of the WD-40 Company, "to create positive lasting memories in everything we do."[4] North Stars can be brilliant arbiters for decisions and strategies as well as aspirations for transformative work.

In an attempt to capture and communicate purpose, we rely on the inadequacy of statements. As hard as we try, words remain inanimate. They are important and helpful but insufficient. Beyond its founding, your organization brings to life its own purpose, and the job of everyone in the organization is to listen to what "it" needs to do next. The idea of an organization having its own say may sound bizarre, but consider the following example as an analogy.

A river in New Zealand has recently become the first in the world to be recognized as a living entity with its own rights and values and given the legal status of a person.[5] The Whanganui River, located in the north island of the nation, has a special and spiritual importance for the Māori people. The New Zealand Parliament passed a bill that gives the river the ability to represent itself through human delegates, one appointed by a Māori community, known as Iwi, and one by the Crown government. The legal status of the Whanganui River, or Te Awa Tupua, is believed to be unique in the world. The Māori people recognize the river as part of the living mountains and the sea. Chris Finlayson, who negotiated the treaty, said the Whanganui Iwi—a Māori tribe—had fought for recognition of the people's relationship with the river since the 1870s. Te Awa Tupua has its own legal identity with all the corresponding rights, duties and liabilities of a legal person. As Chris notes, "I know the initial inclination of some people will [be to] say it's pretty strange to give a natural resource a legal personality. But it's no stranger than family trusts or companies, or incorporated societies."[6]

Introducing the idea that an organization is a living entity with its own evolving purpose (known in Teal as *evolutionary purpose*) helps individuals separate their own wants and needs from those of the organization. In the above example, the river has two appointed spokespeople. In your company, you can invite everyone to be a representative of the organization. Principles, ideas and values can be distilled into writing, but activating the organization as the holder of its own purpose requires *sensing* on the part of the team. This practice moves beyond the merely intellectual to include imagination and intentional reflection. The need for ongoing sensing comes from the simple distinction that *evolution describes a gradual directional change in needs* that could be easily missed. When adequately sensed, evolution leads to opportunities for growth and development.

In many organizations, teams try to concoct a purpose rather than sensing into changing needs. In *Reinventing Organizations*, Frederic Laloux describes the process of discovering evolutionary purpose simply: "Instead of trying to predict and control the future, members of the organization are invited to listen and understand what the organization is drawn to become, where it naturally wants to go."[7] At the end of this chapter, you will find a series of exercises to help you tune in to your organization's unique and evolutionary purpose.

## Reflect and Act on Personal Purpose

For founders and stewards, achieving a level of certainty about your unique vocation comes before realizing the organization's purpose, and is the first step in leading with purpose. Do the following statements resonate as true for you?

- I have a good sense of what makes my work meaningful.
- I know how my work makes a positive difference in the world.
- My work helps me better understand myself.
- I appreciate how my work contributes to my life and my personal growth.

If not, take some time to reflect on your current journey and how you could shift to bring more meaning, and thereby more purpose, to your work. Personal purpose is found at the intersection of individual passion (areas that fire you up), skill (honed through education and experience) and service of an external need.

## Intent, Being and Doing

Purpose is a declaration of the significant ways a team chooses to use its time; the place where intent, being and doing come together. For example, the team at Ian Martin Group has declared that their purpose is connecting people in meaningful work. This is their intent. They've chosen to operate with a triple bottom line of people, planet and profit. A certified B Corporation, the organization "believes in using business to benefit all stakeholders in our society and [is] committed to doing good for people, our communities and the environment." When team members are honestly embodying those ideals, they are being, or living, the best version of their purpose. Some on the team use the mantra of "getting people done through work" rather than "getting work done through people." By acting on that mantra and investing in their own personal growth, they are "doing" in alignment with their intention to truly live their purpose.

Purpose is *not* a description of a company's value proposition or a snazzy marketing slogan. Articulating a clear, actionable purpose that creates alignment is incredibly challenging. In her paper "The Power of Purpose: How Organizations Are Making Work More Meaningful," Alison Alexander suggests the connection between purpose and work resides in the place "where a company aims to activate and develop more fully its employees (and the organization in general) to produce greater value for business and society."[8] The invitation here is to look to where personal development pulls you and your colleagues.

For some, the concept of purpose is too soft and nebulous. If that's the case for you, think about your company's *promise* instead. Social-innovation design pioneer Cheryl Heller defines a company's promise as "the commitment a business makes to each of the people who interact with it. It's a promise that defines what is unique about the company and what people will get for their money and their time, whether they are a customer, partner, investor or employee."[9] In every purpose statement, there is an implicit promise. The invitation is to make that promise more explicit.

## Organizational Purpose in Action

Articulating authentic purpose brings energy and focus to a team. It acts as a gravitational force for people sharing a similar vision of what's possible. Let's look at some examples of purpose statements. If on first read they seem somewhat superficial, digging into the essence of the companies reveals the power these purpose statements hold for those teams.

### TOMS

TOMS's purpose—"We believe we can improve people's lives through business"—originated from founder Blake Mycoskie's personal experiences while traveling and volunteering in Argentina.[10] The company is most known for its commitment to give a new pair of shoes to an impoverished child each time it sells a pair of shoes.

## Decurion Corporation

Decurion Corporation operates subsidiaries ranging from entertainment centers to seniors' living facilities and commercial real estate. Its purpose statement is "to provide places for people to flourish." The organization is committed to the belief that profitability and human development are not mutually exclusive, and it works to enact this belief at every level of its businesses. As a result, Decurion is defined more by why it exists and how it operates than by its commercial portfolio. Believing business is a place for people to thrive, it espouses many self-management principles. One example is a ten-week course offered to employees called the Process of Self-Management, which explores personal purpose, skillful speech and servant leadership.

## Crisp

Crisp, whose purpose is "to enable consultants to be happy," was founded in 1999 by consultants, for consultants.[11] In their own words, "We are not a regular consulting company. We have no CEO and no managers. All consultants are self-employed." The Crisp team released their unique operating model as an open source reference.

Does your organization have a documented purpose? Does it still hold true today? Does it reflect and integrate your values and individual life purposes and those of your colleagues? Is it something you talk about and reflect on regularly? How would it feel to realize the purpose has changed, evolved and as documented is no longer reflective of the organization?

## Exploring Purpose

The process of unearthing your purpose begins by asking and answering questions until a coherent message begins to emerge. This may take months or even years. Personal and organizational purpose blends throughout the process. The following exercises are offered as potential starting points.

### Start uncovering your personal purpose in five minutes

In his TEDx Talk, Adam Leipzig walks his audience through five simple questions.[12] The same questions can be applied to you personally or to your organization as a whole. The answers need not be any more complex than the questions, and you need take only five minutes to respond.

- Who are you?
- What do you love to do?
- Who do you do it for?
- What do those people want or need?
- How will they change or transform as a result of what you give them?

### Who, why and how does your organization serve?

The folks at the research and consulting firm Imperative have a brilliant worksheet that guides organizations through three critical decisions. By forcing a decision on each of these questions, your purpose will begin to take shape:

**Who does our work have the greatest impact on? (Choose one)**
On society
On organizations
On individuals

**Why is our work necessary? (Choose one)**
To ensure a fair and level playing field for everyone
To remove barriers that keep people from reaching their full potential

**What is our core competency? (Choose one)**
Creating communities and connections
Addressing issues that people face
Uncovering knowledge and information to share with others
Building systems that are able to continually create remarkable results

## Questions to test your company's purpose

Below are five questions you can use to test your organization's purpose:

**Is your purpose evolutionary?** Has your team taken sufficient time to listen and understand where the organization naturally wants to go? Or have you fallen into the trap of attempting to create a future that a limited number of stakeholders prefer and that diverges from the messages being sent by the broader ecosystem?

**Is your purpose clear enough?** A fluffy or generic purpose statement, or one that reads more like a marketing slogan or value proposition, will not provide you and your colleagues with a helpful North Star. When articulated well, your purpose statement will be a meaningful guide to how you spend your time and limited resources, and to how you serve those around you.

**Are you prepared to shift?** In sensing and responding to an evolutionary purpose, change is a necessity. The timing of those changes will depend on the needs of your organization and the world around it. Your purpose could remain unchanged for years at a time or adapt more frequently. What elements of your purpose seem fixed for now, and where are you sensing an emerging need to evolve?

**How will you resist short-term temptations?** Your purpose will be tested. Short-term pressures will surface. What are your team's non-negotiables—the things you feel so strongly about that you won't waver on?

**Does your organization's purpose speak to you?** As a leader, you are a channel for your organization's purpose. If it doesn't speak to you, you will not be an effective channel. What, if anything, would need to be different for the organization's purpose to connect with your own?

THE ABILITY to clearly articulate your purpose is different from knowing your purpose. Knowing is an internal sense that can be hard to express, even to ourselves. Articulating purpose is the often challenging process of finding the right words to explain that internal sense. Both parts may take time and play off each other. The best you can do is describe what you believe to be true today. In the process, you may find yourself refining your internal knowing. It may not be sufficient for the long term, but it's a foundation from which you will build. The purpose journey is a balance between reflection and action. You are likely to find yourself toggling back and forth between certainty and doubt. Refinements will emerge with new information and changing circumstances.

# 7

# Values, Principles and Aspirations

Articulate the
Deeper Connections
of Your Work

"Values are like fingerprints. Nobody's are the same, but you leave them all over everything you do."

**ELVIS PRESLEY**[1]

I F VALUES ARE the representation of how we move through the world, or our uniquely individual and deeply rooted guide-posts, principles are the guardrails, or hard boundaries, we set for ourselves to describe what we stand for. In addition to values and principles—our own or those of our teams—we aspire to (sometimes) utopian ideals of a future state of greatness: a team so well oiled and aligned that literally anything we put our minds to is possible. Leading in this new intentional paradigm requires understanding the function of values, principles and aspirations, and creating the conditions for your teammates and the organization to express them.

## Values

Values are alive within each of us and our teams, whether we identify and verbalize them or not. Values reflect our beliefs and motivations, and they are relative to each person, not universally held. They provide the frame for how we interpret and interact with the world: what's important, what's possible, what's dangerous.

According to Jackie Le Fevre of values consultancy Magma Effect, values lie deep within the unconscious: "Values are energy-laden ideas that sit in the limbic area of the brain where there is no language. The limbic functions in terms of what it feels rather than what it 'thinks' or 'knows.' Together our beliefs and values function as a kind of background operating system. This gives us an internal autopilot sense of how the world works and where we fit in, enabling us to develop our own shorthand ways of navigating everyday events."[2]

Landing on a set of shared values for a team may or may not be possible, and it's not always necessary. Ask whether the collective alignment of your personal beliefs (values) is more or less important than how they get expressed (principles). If you know that in order for your team to express its unique purpose, everyone's core values need to unambiguously align, then invest in that hard work of defining your shared values. Otherwise, focusing on principles can make room for diverse values and leverage that diversity for broader impact.

One of the first realizations when moving to a less hierarchical way of leading is that in traditional organizations, the articulation of what's important comes from those at "the top"—whether that is the founder or CEO, their team or another group with the necessary context and mandate. By questioning the usefulness of this approach, everyone in the organization can challenge their own previous powerlessness of trying to enact what they imagine their managers think is important. Instead everyone can start intuiting and articulating what they sense is appropriate for the organization.

When values are less visible and hard to interpret, we sometimes find our values colliding with others'. Just as we can all relate to the idea that like attracts like—that we are naturally more attracted to those who value the same things we do—we also all have the experience of being "caught up" in that assumption, whether in friendship or romance or at work. Caught in the flush of a new relationship, we see what we want to see, and that's often mistaken as a reflection of shared values. We become dismayed when, over time, the other person shows their "true colors."

Natalia Lombardo from consulting company The Hum offers her perspective:

When I say "values," I think about a list of characteristics and ideals that are important to me. Ways of being that I try to embody or grow into. So when I think about being "values aligned" with you, I assume that your list of values is similar to mine. But it's not just the items on the list that matter, it's also the order in which we prioritize them.

For example, let's say that my values—in order of importance—are:

- Respect
- Integrity
- Care
- Honesty
- Autonomy

And yours are:

- Autonomy
- Freedom
- Enjoyment
- Care
- Integrity

According to that list, we share many of the same values. But the fact that we each place them with different importance in our list will make us act in different ways.[3]

If you do go down the values path, it's incredibly important not only to land on your value words but also to demand precise definitions, as Helen Sanderson and Jackie Le Fevre point out:

Compare these two descriptions of *compassion*. The first from a large hospital trust and the second from Wellbeing Teams.

1. Compassion means "we use a person-centered approach in all our interactions with colleagues, patients, clients and their families."

2. Compassion means "actively hearing and sensing another's thoughts and feelings, being kind and finding empathetic ways to support individuals and each other to achieve positive outcomes."

Nothing wrong with either and some description is far better than no description, particularly if arriving at the description has been a participatory process.[4]

## Values in action

The best test of meaningful values in an organization is if and how they are used in guiding decisions. The team at Ecosia, a social business and internet search engine provider, uses their values as guideposts. Even with a strong social purpose, they routinely rely on their values—impact, integrity, sustainability, leadership, user focus and happiness—when making difficult decisions. "Should we scale right now? Should we invest our limited resources in improving the product? Are we pushing ourselves too hard and risking burnout? Are we giving each other good feedback and enough of it?" Each of Ecosia's values is further defined using a short statement and brief paragraph. They hashtag their values in internal communications when team members propose projects or changes that are values aligned.

## When values conflict

An organization may have two values that conflict. ET Group, a self-managing technology integration company looking to bring harmony to work and workplace with technology, has four guiding values: accountability, growth, customer collaboration and teamwork. The value of growth encourages "building capacity through financial stability, profitability and efficiency," while customer collaboration means "proactively partnering with our clients." In the short term, partnering with clients can cut into profits and take extra time. Conflicting values challenge the team to consider trade-offs, speak candidly about the issues and find solutions that best further the organization's purpose. These are the hard yet necessary decisions required to keep ET Group on track.

Because our values most often lay hidden, they remain implicit, not clearly visible to others and often not even to ourselves. Principles, on the other hand, can be negotiated and openly declared by a team. Our principles can help us form explicit agreements on how a team works together and how individuals conduct themselves.

## Reflect and Act on Personal and Organization Values

What personal values do you hold and how do they shape your decisions?

Clarifying your values and making them transparent are crucial steps within a self-managing organization. A great place to start is by completing the free Personal Values Assessment from the Barrett Values Centre (valuescentre.com/tools-assessments/pva). It takes less than ten minutes and provides more information than you would expect for a quick test. You can also reflect on and review your values one at a time by asking:

- Why is this value important to me?
- In moments when I deeply live this value, what behaviors do I exhibit?
- How might I react if this value was not being honored by others?
- How do I want this value to show up in my career and my life?

Good values in an organization are best unearthed rather than invented. The company 1-DEGREE/Shift partners with organizations to define and align on their values. It names five parts of a good value definition: a single word to name the value, a short definition of the value (five to seven words max) to add clarity, five behaviors that show this value in practice, two or three behaviors that signal the value might be slipping and a story that illustrates the value in action. Using these five elements, LifeLearn, an organization that educates and communicates solutions to improve animal health and wellness, articulates its value of passion this way:

**Value:** Passion

**Short definition:** Improving animal health with gusto!

**This looks like:** Bringing energy and a positive attitude to difficult challenges, creating space for fun and humor, being open to new and better ideas, celebrating wins both externally and internally.

**What's unacceptable:** Spreading negative energy, saying, "It's not my job," just showing up.

**Story:** It's like a dog happily engaged in active sport.

## Principles

Principles are the terms of engagement. They articulate our hard boundaries, and unlike with values, all team members must agree to act within the intent of team principles. If they can't or won't, they need to be somewhere else. What are your team's uncrossable lines, your principles?

Based on his experience working with Morning Star, a California-based tomato processor built on a foundational philosophy of self-management, author and TEDx speaker Doug Kirkpatrick is unambiguous: "First, human beings should not use force or coercion against other human beings. Second, people should honor the commitments they make to others."[5] He notes that the company ran solely on the basis of these principles for years before they were further fleshed out. And to this day, if you do not agree to abide by these principles, you can't work at Morning Star.

One of our principles as coauthors is open and honest communication. If you wanted to join the team, you would have to agree to this principle. The principle then informs two team agreements: we say what we mean, and we ask for what we need.

Each time a new team comes together, the members need to determine a set of principles or adopt a set already established elsewhere. Enspiral's guidance for support pods (teams within the Enspiral ecosystem) offers prompts for establishing principles that new groups may choose to apply:

- We acknowledge and articulate our personal boundaries.

- Once agreed, we respect our timing and other logistical requirements.

- We acknowledge the source of our ideas and/or the lineage we are following.

Compared with some of the other ideas in this book, this section may feel jarringly staunch. It is intended to be: we posit that we can't and won't walk through life as our whole selves if we are constantly asked to renegotiate and acquiesce our core principles— our uncrossable lines. So much of this book is about calling "what is" into our awareness in a way that is unflinching. Sometimes we need to be unflinching.

## Aspirations

Aspirations—intentions of how a group would like to work together that are not yet fully true—are yet another set of ideals often confused with current values. It's not uncommon for teams to believe that "because we name a principle, it must be true and present."

When new teams come together, they clearly aren't yet aware of their capabilities or capacities. As with everything, we learn what's possible by and through doing the work together. For some teams, just kicking into the work may be appropriate. Others find benefit in taking the time to articulate higher-level intentions of potential. A recently formed team that Susan is working with articulated their aspirations in their second meeting together:

### We are creative
We channel our collective creative energy to achieve our goals. We optimize our ways of working for flow and moments of delight.

### We are excellent
We hold ourselves and each other to high standards. We're highly capable in our roles: we play the music, not the instrument.

### We are idealistic
We strive to be the best version of ourselves, and we support each other in those aspirations. We assume good intent from others, and we give feedback in the same way—candidly, honestly and kindly.

### We are pragmatic
We recognize constraints and we adapt to the times. We're time-and-space agnostic: we default to asynchronous communication and create artifacts for others to augment and share—but we understand that there are also times to come together and optimize for connection.

### We are resilient
We handle setbacks by finding alternatives. We avoid single points of failure and step in to support each other in our roles.

When challenges arise, we recognize them clearly, articulate them and find ways to solve them.

This team has no idea yet if the above is true, but for them it was important to set the intention—their aspirations. It has given them something to circle around as they spin up. They intend to check in on these aspirations frequently, in order to collectively surface patterns and practices that may help to realize them. Eventually, these aspirations may become lived values or they may evolve into something else.

EVERYONE NEEDS points of orientation. Purpose is one. Values, principles and aspirations provide additional bearings. To be effective within a team setting, you need to work with your colleagues to bring awareness to the precise definitions, collective understanding and shared intentions of each of these orienting features. Think of starting a long journey by car with your teammates as fellow travelers. First, you need a sense of where you are heading and why. As you drive, it's helpful to have clear boundaries, guardrails along the most treacherous portions and Do Not Enter signs ensuring you don't make a wrong turn. You don't need these tools at every moment of the journey, but having them at key points can be the difference between thriving and barely surviving.

# Psychological Safety

Create and Foster Space
for Creativity & Impact

"[Psychological safety is] a belief and expectation that no one will be punished or humiliated for speaking up with ideas, questions, concerns or mistakes."

**AMY EDMONDSON**[1]

LET'S SAY AARON has been hired to work in a small and growing ecommerce company. He needs to navigate between three owners who don't always agree on the business's priorities. This challenge is exacerbated by his tendency to focus on fixing problems and keeping everyone content without highlighting the misalignment. He picked up this habit of not rocking the boat when he was climbing the ranks of a traditionally structured Fortune 500 company.

Part of him knows he has a lot to learn. He also knows he was hired because he has relevant experience, and he wants that to show. In his role, he needs to expand the warehouse team—and he does—but turnover is higher than he expected. He asks the owners for ideas and gets nothing back but silence. So, he muscles through, doing what he can to support and grow the team.

After six months, he receives surprising feedback in the form of a rumor. One of the owners isn't happy with his performance. He asks the owner about it and receives a cryptic response about failing to ship out product with 100 percent accuracy every day. The feedback feels vague, but he's learning that asking questions can be dangerous and opens him up to more judgment. What can he do?

This story is fictitious, but it is a plausible scenario that shows some of the challenges when there isn't psychological safety. Similar experiences play out in teams everywhere.

## Popularizing Psychological Safety

Although psychological safety has long been a driver of team performance, it has only become a more common leadership topic in the last ten years. This is in large part because of a study completed by Google. Leaders at Google became curious about why some teams within their organization excelled while others floundered. Committed to understanding the "secret sauce" of a flourishing team, Google began a comprehensive study. After examining the performance of 180 teams, the researchers were stumped. "We had lots of data," a manager in Google's people analytics division was quoted as saying in *New York Times Magazine*, "but there was nothing showing that a mix of specific personality types or skills or backgrounds made any difference. The 'who' part of the equation didn't seem to matter."[2]

The researchers persevered until they eventually found a strong correlation. They discovered that the level of psychological safety within a team is the number one determinant of its success and productivity. When there is a shared belief that the team is safe for interpersonal risk-taking, team performance improves. In contrast, as seen in the scenario at the opening of the chapter, when people feel unsafe because of team dynamics, team performance declines. In the simplest terms, how we treat our colleagues is directly related to how effective our team is.

The term *psychological safety* was coined by Amy Edmondson, Novartis professor of leadership and management at the Harvard Business School. When she measures psychological safety, she does it by assessing individuals' levels of agreement with these seven statements:

1. If you make a mistake on this team, it is often held against you.

2. Members of this team are able to bring up problems and tough issues.

**3.** People on this team sometimes reject others for being different.

**4.** It is safe to take a risk on this team.

**5.** It is difficult to ask other members of this team for help.

**6.** No one on this team would deliberately act in a way that undermines my efforts.

**7.** Working with members of this team, my unique skills and talents are valued and utilized.[3]

Using these statements to diagnose the example that opened this chapter, we can see that the new team member interpreted his mistakes as being held against him (number 1), he couldn't bring up tough issues (number 2) and it was difficult to ask for help (number 5). Other factors may have been at play as well. In her TEDx Talk, Amy offers three simple things individuals can do to foster team psychological safety:

**1.** Frame work as a learning problem, not an execution problem.

**2.** Acknowledge your own fallibility.

**3.** Model curiosity and ask lots of questions.[4]

As the researchers at Google dug deeper, they found two specific behaviors present only in teams with high psychological safety. In high-performing teams, all team members speak in roughly the same proportion—known by some as equal talk time. Some voices may be more dominant for any given topic, but in the end, everyone is heard. Second, stronger teams can sense how others are feeling by tuning into tone of voice, body language and other social cues. This enables the team to monitor its own emotional health. Being part of a remote team makes this second behavior much harder. Marin Petrov from self-managing organization Hack and Paint shares his experience:

Many of us have come from hierarchical structures and big companies. Changing those habits is difficult because they're quite ingrained. It's something that takes a lot of time and effort. For me personally, I've struggled working remotely knowing that when you're in an office with people, there's a lot of feedback coming from everywhere, including from people's body language and from the environment itself. For us, we work in more of a distributed nature. When you don't have that feedback, it can be a bit harder to break down those fears that might be present. Building up confidence might take a little bit longer as well.[5]

Psychological safety is a necessary element for every high-performing team, and it's critical as companies scale up. In this phase, team membership is changing frequently and everyone needs to learn fast while working in a complex environment. When people cannot talk about their challenges openly and instead feel they have to protect their image as competent contributors, there is little room to learn and grow individually or as a team.

## Trust

Trust is at the core of psychological safety. It isn't just a team skill but also an environmental condition. And psychological safety is required not only within the walls of our organizations. Teams can expand to encompass partner organizations, suppliers and customers. Simon Wakeman shares how Deeson builds psychological safety with its clients when launching a new project:

> We talk a lot about one team, which means we have to get to know each other a bit. We do a warm-up exercise. We also do a fair amount of social stuff outside the workshops at the start, which is really about us getting to know the client and the team members getting to trust each other. Mutual trust, the ability

to give each other clear feedback, and the context of that feedback is really, really important. Once we get into the nuts and bolts of doing this work, we need to be able to talk to each other and communicate effectively. One of our learnings is that people have their own approach to communicating. Some people are very confident and some are more introverted. If we get the team balance wrong and haven't established that mutual trust, that's when problems come up and we have to do more coaching than we would expect.[6]

We need to trust that being vulnerable and taking social risks will not result in judgment or negative repercussions. We all share a deep desire to be valued and respected as individuals and colleagues.

## Getting in Our Own Way

Most people spend a disproportionate amount of time in the workplace navigating the delta between how they want to be seen and how they think they are seen. This starts the first day on the job, wanting to appear competent, reassuring the boss that they made the right choice.

From a young age, we are trained to manage impressions. No one wants to appear ignorant, seem incompetent, come across as intrusive or be labeled as negative. We develop protective habits. To ensure we don't appear ignorant, we choose not to ask questions. To avoid appearing incompetent, we keep weaknesses and mistakes hidden. To ensure we're not perceived as intrusive, we stay quiet and don't offer ideas. We don't critique the status quo so as not to be seen as negative.

Likewise, we can encourage these protective behaviors in others. Interrupting to criticize a colleague's ideas in a brainstorming session demonstrates how easy it is to shut down free-flowing ideation—the literal opposite outcome of what was intended. Before our colleague can finish explaining their idea, we instinctively run it through our internal filters, compiling a mental list of why it won't work. We place too much value on past experiences and become wrapped up in our own thoughts. As a result, we fail to give sufficient airtime to alternatives, instead nudging our colleague back into managing impressions.

We all manage impressions to some extent. Where do you find it easiest to slip into judgment or criticism? Are there certain situations, for instance when talking to individuals in perceived positions of power, where you are more likely to avoid looking ignorant or incompetent? What patterns can you notice about your tendencies to want to influence another's opinion of you or preserve your sense of safety?

Despite the temptation to protect themselves, some people wake up every morning willing to break free of these unhelpful habits for the betterment of their team. The more psychologically safe we feel in our environment, the easier it is for us and our colleagues to get out of our own way.

## Psychological Safety and Accountability

Increased psychological safety can be confused with decreased accountability. Each is its own independent factor. High safety and high accountability can and should coexist within the team. This combination drives learning and positively affects motivation. An environment can be safe for sharing mistakes while still setting a high expectation for performance. For example, you can expect your colleagues to perform well, share their learning for everyone's benefit and take ownership for ensuring their mistakes get fixed. This can be done without placing blame. Amy Edmondson uses a model to visualize the relationship between psychological safety and accountability:

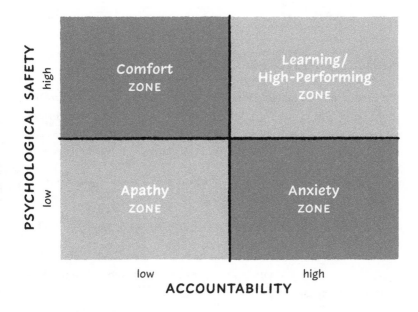

There is a risk of creating an environment that is too safe. When you shift from safe to too safe by keeping accountability low, you slide into the comfort zone. Work gets done, but you stifle meaningful progress. Teams living in the top right quadrant work hard to stimulate idea generation as a way of learning. When one person's idea is replaced by a better one, the previous idea is valued as a discussion starter.

When you and your peers have multiple priorities in common, you might find it all too easy to slip into the comfort zone, letting commitments to each other slide with the justification that everyone is very busy. This results in a drop in organizational accountability, and teams slide out of the performance zone. Check out chapter 10 for tips on boosting accountability.

## Reflect and Act on Psychological Safety

The next time you sense yourself or others falling into the comfort, apathy or anxiety zones—perhaps by shutting down new ideas or narrowing in on one idea too quickly—experiment with your own version of the following language:

- "Let's challenge ourselves to build on that idea and see what we can learn."

- "Can I propose an alternative to play with for a few minutes?"

- "Admittedly, I'm pretty excited about my idea. That said, I'd like you to challenge me on it to see what I can learn in the process. Perhaps something better will come up."

## Tips for Supporting Psychological Safety

There is no secret sauce to building psychological safety within your team. Continue experimenting with practices that encourage and support interpersonal risk-taking. Here are ten practices to try.

### Reframe problems

Framing problems through a lens of learning rather than one of execution shifts the conversation. Make explicit the uncertainty that lies ahead, along with the interdependence required to solve the problem by setting an intention of learning together. The future does not equal the past. "Let's see what this challenge has to teach us."

## Acknowledge your own fallibility

Creating a psychologically safe space where everyone speaks up freely, sharing ideas, asking questions, expressing concerns and calling out personal mistakes, requires that someone goes first. Your team will be more confident in taking social risks if they see you doing so. Be vulnerable. Share your mistakes—the bigger, the better. Have fun with it. "I'll bake cookies for anyone who helps me see what's in my blind spot."

## Get personal

Share something personal with your team that wouldn't otherwise come up in day-to-day business conversation. Traditional workplaces prioritize the rational part of the human experience and discount the emotional, intuitive and spiritual parts. By getting personal, you show your team that all components of being human are seen as valuable elements of business. Start meetings with a round of not-yet-revealed fun facts.

## Model curiosity

Our brains can only be in one of two places at a time—judgment or curiosity—but not both. Most of us default quickly to judgment as a way of making ourselves feel safe. Give curiosity a try as a tool for zapping assumptions. Every time we assume something about a colleague's intention and we're wrong—which is often—we risk damaging psychological safety. Become a friend with the question, "May I check something with you?"

## Create shared experiences

At the core of psychological safety is respectful and supportive human-to-human communication. This level of communication becomes easier the more we know each other on a deeper level. A team barbeque, hike or evening out creates the opportunity for relationship-building that lives on long after the event is over.

### Unpack it together

Relaying difficult messages is hard. If you find yourself delivering some tough love to a colleague, ask to unpack what just happened. "It was challenging for me to deliver this message to you. I tried to be clear and kind. Is there something I could have said or done differently that would have been more helpful to you?" Being curious shows that this is a developmental journey for both of you and opens a space for mutual learning.

### Build a vulnerability muscle

The willingness to be vulnerable takes time to develop. The team at Barcelona-based Cyberclick, an online marketing and digital advertising firm, worked at building their muscles over a few years. In 2012, they introduced the idea of measuring happiness and started sending an email every day to each person on the team with three questions: In what mood did you come to the office this morning: green, yellow or red? How have you left today: green, yellow or red? From one to four, how much have you enjoyed your day and your tasks? Responses were anonymous at first, but after a year, the team had built enough trust to add names. In their weekly meeting, checking the traffic lights became the top agenda item. They made decisions based on what they'd learned, with a commitment to leave the meeting with an idea of what to do based on that learning. They've since dropped the email and instead complete the exercise together in their meeting.

### Check in during meetings

Important emotional cues can get missed when meetings move too quickly or are virtual. Consciously tuning in to emotional cues allows us to determine if the nod of a head really means the other person is on board with what's just been said. Before moving to a new agenda item or wrapping up the meeting, try asking, "Does anyone have any lingering tensions?"

## Develop the skill of listening

Active listening builds trust and rapport and is a skill like any other. Reaching a higher skill level requires a concerted effort. Practice paraphrasing back what your colleagues say to enhance understanding. Watch for reactionary phrases that indicate you've shifted from listening to giving advice, interrogating or explaining. Lastly, use eye contact and verbal acknowledgments to signal you are listening.

## Celebrate successes and failures

Failures are a sign of progress as long as we learn and act on that learning. The Johnsonville Foods factory team has a Mistake of the Month Club to stimulate discussion about errors and to learn from them, and a Shot in the Foot Award for the person who makes the biggest mistake from which they learned the most.[7] Awards like this make experimenting fun and exciting rather than boring and scary.

HERE IS an honest reflection from a member of an organization in New Zealand who craves more behaviors that support psychological safety in her team:

> I often struggled to operate within the bounds of this working group which I've distilled down to two learnings: 1. Lack of whanaungatanga (Māori for relationship, kinship, sense of family connection) amongst the group. There needs to be a level of trust created, which takes time and generosity and is more than "the work." 2. Lack of kawa (or "how our small group chooses to be with one another"). I often felt muted in our meetings, with concepts and language inaccessible for me and no clear way into the group dialogue.
>
> Both kawa and whanaungatanga assist me in understanding the edges of things which results in me feeling safe, confident and able to work well with others. Without these, the cracks are less forgiving, intentions are forgotten and people can feel backed into a corner, which I think, in part, is what is going on here.

Psychological safety is an area where many teams are uncon-sciously incompetent. The move to competence takes time and focused effort. Is everyone on your team free from punishment and humiliation when speaking up with wild ideas, dumb questions, personal concerns or tragic mistakes? We invite you to build safety by experimenting with one or two practices from this chapter and then expanding when you and your colleagues feel ready.

# 9

# Radical Responsibility

Learn and Help
Others to
Take Action

"This is a story of four people named Everybody, Somebody, Anybody and Nobody. There was an important job to be done and Everybody was asked to do it. Everybody was sure Somebody would do it. Anybody could have done it, but Nobody did it."

**UNKNOWN**

"WHEN EVERYONE IS responsible, no one is responsible" is a well-worn phrase. It's also a well-worn misinterpretation of self-management—the idea that not having bosses leads to a free-for-all. Nothing can be further from the truth in successful self-managed teams. Fleet Maull, author of *Radical Responsibility*, defines the term this way: "Radical Responsibility is the voluntary choice to assume or embrace 100 percent ownership for each and every circumstance we face in life. It is the choice to take our power back and focus on finding solutions rather than someone or something to blame. In the workplace, Radical Responsibility requires each team member to be 100 percent responsible for their personal behavior and contributions to a project, and therefore more invested in creating positive outcomes."[1]

Tom Nixon of Maptio references Charles Davies who said responsibility can only be taken, not given. The act of radical responsibility looks like this in practice: "I'm Trish and in my chosen role as product design lead, I am responsible for crafting the next version of our product. I will complete my initial draft by November 30, will be held accountable by Stephan and Victoria and ask them to do so by checking on my progress at our biweekly meetings. Either of them has the obligation and right to challenge me if I am not meeting my commitments." Let's break down five important elements in this example to show how Trish is taking, rather than being given, responsibility:

- Trish self-selects a role for which she has the energy, capacity and capability.

- She states her criteria for completion.

- She states who her accountability partners will be.

- She states how she wants those accountability partners to hold her responsible.

- She states their rights and obligations.

In this example, the loop doesn't close until Stephan and Victoria agree to fulfill the responsibilities Trish has laid out for them. But in those last two points, many well-intended role processes go wrong when people try to give or cede accountabilities to others without confirming that they have agreed to take up the responsibilities.

For many new to self-management, stepping into radical responsibility feels foreign. Björn Lundén is the founder of the 115-person Swedish knowledge and software company, Björn Lundén AB. He says it takes about a year for new team members, especially those coming from academia, to become comfortable with radical responsibility and the freedom that comes with it:

> New team members will say, "You mean I can go and buy a new computer if I want one?"
>
> Our response is, "Of course you can because you are the one who can decide if you really need one. Nobody else can do that."
>
> "Then I can buy a luxury computer, spending 40,000 crowns instead of 15,000 for a cheaper one?"
>
> "Yes, you could, but everybody will see you as a poor decision maker, so that will stop you from doing it."[2]

Some of us are wired to take radical responsibility and embrace the freedom that comes with it. Others of us may struggle because our past experiences have taught us that stepping into radical responsibility takes us into unsafe territory. Björn's example shows how, when we act with the intention of fulfilling an organization's purpose, use team values to guide our decision-making and respect the social system we're in, being responsible is the most sensible way to work.

## A Team Sport

This transformation is about more than cooperation and collaboration. It's the act of taking radical responsibility for ourselves *and* our teams.

Learned helplessness, which comes from a real or perceived lack of control, can trap us in a self-perpetuating pattern of deflecting responsibility. For the large majority of workers, a lack of control is real. We've all had the experience of crafting a well-articulated, pragmatic solution only to have it ruled out of hand by a person with power and control over us (read: a boss). Or we've been told outright that our opinions and ideas aren't relevant. If you've had these experiences, you may be able to see how team members could perceive themselves as powerless even once invited to take radical responsibility.

The great adventurer and humanitarian Sir Edmund Hillary said, "There is something about building up a comradeship—that I still believe is the greatest of all feats—and sharing in the dangers with your company of peers."[3] Moving from learned helplessness to radical responsibility takes courage and fortitude, and you can't do it alone. The transformation only takes place within a group of peers.

A company well on its way to being fully self-governed democratically agreed to delegate hiring and firing to one leader, consciously ceding sovereignty over those decisions. After one of their colleagues was terminated by the individual holding the official responsibility, the team was furious. They didn't agree with the decision. What would the experience have been like if this team instead agreed that any and all performance issues be fully transparent? What if the responsibility for improvement rested on the entire team? In other words, could an agreement be struck to move the delegation of these decisions from one person to a development opportunity and responsibility held by the entire team? That's radical responsibility in action.

But let's face it, the *most* difficult thing to take responsibility for in a self-managing environment is calling out your colleagues when they have not met their responsibilities. Doing so is at the heart of radical responsibility.

When in a team that is building trust (and love), we are much more reluctant to be perceived as tough by demanding our peers keep commitments. In a team without a boss, encourage everyone to invite another team member to be an accountability partner. This simple role-swap involves one colleague standing alongside and supporting another by asking accountability questions, such as "Have you met your metrics this week?" If the answer is no, the next step is committing to a solution. The relationship doesn't need to be one-to-one. Teams may decide to have a single accountability partner supporting all team members. This act of radical responsibility makes any deficiencies within the team the purview of the entire team.

## Reflect and Act on Radical Responsibility

Taking radical responsibility for your work requires you to hone a variety of personal and interpersonal skills. In *Radical Responsibility*, Fleet identifies the following steps for taking radical responsibility when working through conflict with others:

- Recognize when you are in a drama triangle, filling the role of villain, victim or hero.

- Pause, so you don't act when triggered.

- Own your feelings, whatever they are, as a helpful signal.

- Make space and shift your state to something more helpful.

- Identify your needs and communicate them clearly.

- Create a boundary when necessary.

Each of these steps requires its own set of skills: self-awareness, self-reflection, self-care and self-accountability, to name a few. These elements are vital for just about any self-development, un-learning or reframing we take on.

## Radical Responsibility and Individual Needs

What gives each of us energy and what causes unnecessary anxiety or frustration influences how likely we are to take radical responsibility. Tom Nixon suggests the following exercise to help get clear:

> Ask the team to make a list of everything they are working on and put it into two columns: stuff that is energizing and stuff that doesn't energize. In other words, work that feels like paddling upstream and activities that feel like paddling downstream. When we look at the stuff that's not energizing to people, [it's] where you can expect them to be underperforming, behind schedule, not delivering or where there's more of a need for a

kind of formal accountability practice to get them to just deliver on that thing.

In the energizing column will be things that will happen of their own accord because they are energized by it. The mistake so many companies make is thinking we need more systems and processes to make people more accountable for things that they don't really want to do. Why don't we just remove those things that don't energize us from the list and absolve ourselves of the guilt that we feel every day by not doing the thing or not doing it well? We'll free our headspace for something else. And that's a much more productive way to work.[4]

Of course, you probably can't remove everything that doesn't energize you from your responsibilities. You can't stop paying the rent just because no one likes doing it. By clarifying and being transparent about what does and does not energize each member of the team, you create an opportunity to shift accountabilities so more ends up in each individual's energizing column. Finding ways to take radical responsibility for your own needs and experiences is the best thing you can do for your team.

# 10

# **Agreements**

Make Accountabilities
and Commitments
That Work

"[Anyone] holding themselves accountable to nobody ought not to be trusted by anybody."

**THOMAS PAINE**[1]

T HE TEAM AT Sylius, a Poland-based open source ecommerce platform, noticed they were using phrases like, "I don't want to manage you … but could you possibly find time to do this for me?" New to self-organizing, the team was learning to navigate a reality where everyone was free to negotiate, accept and reject projects. How does work get done when no one has power over another?

Traditional companies operate with the assumption that managers know best, or at least know more, and therefore should determine who does what. As we shared in chapter 2, authority can quickly turn into power over. Power-over-based environments mirror many characteristics of adult-child relationships, where permissions must be granted and consequences doled out. What if your organization was instead built on a strong foundation of healthy adult-to-adult relationships? Successful self-managing teams rely on such relationships and on the agreements, commitments and accountabilities they support.

Over time, the team at Sylius has learned how to shift to healthier adult-to-adult relationships. Paweł Jędrzejewski, founder and lead link at Sylius, explains, "We decided there would be absolutely no power of one person over another. We can negotiate; we need to accept and reject projects. Once we accept a commitment, it's perfectly fine to say to each other, 'When will this be done?; it is needed sooner; you said you would do it and didn't.' We're not more strict but rather more reliable and more assertive with healthy expectations."[2]

## Making and Keeping Commitments

Commitment making and keeping are essential skills for self-organizing. Make too few commitments and nothing gets done. Make too many and you fail to deliver. Quite simply, self-organizing doesn't work unless a team develops the kind of trust that comes as a result of making and keeping promises to each other.

If you are a guest at one of Percolab's team meetings, you could be asked the question, "What, if anything, will you be committing to coming out of this meeting?" As a guest, a likely reaction is "What am I supposed to be committing to?" In response to your question, the Percolab team will smile and quietly wait. As an experienced self-managing team, those at Percolab know that you commit to what you *want* to commit to—to what makes the most sense given your passions, professional knowledge and experience. In such moments, those new to self-organizing begin to realize that they can own what they commit to. They don't have to defer to someone who assigns their commitments.

## Personal Commitments

Each time we promise something to a colleague in our day-to-day interactions—to send a file, finish a project by a certain time or make an introduction—we create a new commitment. When we deliver as expected, we meet the terms of our commitment. The more we deliver on our promises, the more trust we build. The opposite is also true: trust degrades with each missed commitment. These misses chip away at the trust bank accounts we have with colleagues and with ourselves.

We can be sloppy in how we make and fulfill our personal commitments. In his TEDx Talk, Bruce Peters of Beyond Teal shares his forty years of experience using a personal commitment scorecard.[3] In a follow-up conversation, Bruce shares, "I make a commitment, I keep track. It sounds compulsive, but what changes in your life when you actually start tracking your commitments? It changes what commitments you make, what you say yes to, what you say no to. It changes how you extract commitments from others. It changes the game."[4] Bruce's commitment scorecard is simple. It contains the date of the commitment, the commitment itself with as much detail as needed and the date it was completed. Bruce goes one step further by tracking his commitment-keeping percentage. Every Friday morning, he does a weekly review of his promises, commitments and action items and leaves time later in the day to deliver on those commitments still outstanding. Absent an emergency, this Friday routine is sacrosanct for Bruce. You may choose to be more or less structured than Bruce in your own commitment making. No matter the process, the skill of delivering on commitments is critical to thriving in a self-managing team.

The chance of misunderstandings in the commitment-making process is high. To reduce miscommunication in casual day-to-day agreements, experiment with your own version of these three R habits:

**Reflect back** "Before wrapping up, let's reflect back to each other the deliverables we committed to so we're both on the same page."

**Recap by email** "I'm going to send you a quick email recapping my takeaways from our meeting to ensure we are aligned. Could you reply to let me know if you agree or if I missed anything?"

**Record live** "Let's pop open a document and capture our conversation and commitments in real time."

Your personal commitments can also be more formally arranged. In some organizations, cocreated contracts between colleagues form the basis of how work gets done. An often referenced example is Morning Star's colleague letter of understanding (CLOU). The CLOU is a document created by each team member in collaboration with their teams. Each CLOU includes a personal commercial mission (PCM) where the author defines their fundamental purpose within the organization; key activities the author agrees to do in pursuit of their PCM; stepping stones, or key measures, by which the author will assess their own performance; time commitments (a self-set date) and a list of CLOU colleagues affected by the commitments, who sign off on the document.

In the next chapter, we explore different ways of defining roles and responsibilities. Similar to CLOUs, roles are a more formal way of documenting personal commitments.

## Team Agreements

Collective commitments, sometimes in the form of written agreements, are a critical step in turning a group of people into a great team. These verbal commitments and written agreements provide a common understanding, allowing the entire team to have a sense of clarity and ownership. Your team already has many of these agreements in place. They might be documented; they're more often the unspoken ways things get done. Are people expected to be on time for meetings or is it normal to be late? Can individuals openly disagree with senior team members or is doing so taboo? Are working hours fixed or flexible?

Team agreements, formal or otherwise, create mutual understanding—for better or worse. When created consciously, they provide a solid foundation upon which a team's ability to trust and be open with one another is built. Team agreements in this spirit foster learning and inclusivity, leading team members to feel, "I belong here. I understand what it means to be part of this group. I can maintain my uniqueness while contributing to this team."

Team agreements fall into one of three categories:

**Governance agreements** The overarching practices and processes that govern how the team makes changes to the team—how decisions are made or how the team's structure changes.

**Social agreements** How the team works and behaves together, ranging from vacation scheduling to feedback practices.

**Operating agreements** The practices and processes used in the day-to-day work of the team, how new projects get kicked off, for example.

In chapter 27, you'll find a sample list of the most common governance and social agreements from the handbooks of self-managing businesses. Operating agreements are context specific and usually arise in response to a need for process clarity.

## Cocreating

Every time you create a team agreement, you are testing a hypothesis. You believe the commitments you're making to each other will be beneficial, provide clarity and work well. It's only over time that you learn whether or not the agreement works. When you treat each new agreement as a prototype, you give yourself and others permission to suggest changes as you learn.

The fast-growing team at Mantle314, a climate change consulting firm based in Toronto, has more than doubled in size over the last year. Laura Zizzo and her brother Ryan Zizzo, the company's founders, started introducing the concepts of self-organizing early, and they quickly realized that to function effectively, the team needed to create shared agreements. Over a six-month period, they created ten agreements, covering compensation to quality control. With Brent's help, they took six steps to arrive at their agreements:

1. In a meeting, the team identified areas that needed more clarity and alignment, surfacing ten different categories. For each area, one team member committed to drafting an agreement.

2. The team reviewed samples from other companies and prepared draft agreements. (Tips for shaping agreements are provided in chapter 27.)

3. The author of the draft then invited two or three colleagues to review the draft and provide feedback.

4. The author created a final version and published it to the full team.

5. All team members confirmed their commitment to the cocreated agreement as being "good enough for now, safe enough to try."

6. If a team member wasn't prepared to sign the agreement as captured, they proposed changes to the author and returned to step 4.

Before joining Mantle314, every new person is introduced to the most important agreements so they know what they are committing to. After joining, they may propose changes to agreements for team consideration and acceptance.

Some organizations have roles or groups responsible for creating team-wide agreements. In all cases, the agreements need to be made available to the entire organization for discussion, reflection and amendment *before* they're adopted. As your team grows to a size where seeking everyone's input becomes challenging or impractical, you may choose to elect a representative decision-making group that leverages the advice process outlined in chapter 12.

Capturing and recording agreements make them real. Try choosing an unwritten, implicit agreement that's working well in one part of your organization to cocreate an organization-wide agreement. For example, if one team has adopted an effective meeting practice or decision-making approach, consider documenting and sharing it as the foundation for a new organization-wide agreement. Consider including the following:

- What are you proposing?

- How can everyone's voice be included in the cocreation process?

- Who is responsible for the actions outlined in the agreement?

- How and when will the agreement and related progress be tracked?

- Is there a specific time frame associated with the prototype, and when will the team stop to reflect on its learning?

- How and when will new people to the organization be introduced to this agreement?

- How can the agreement be changed?

Often the cocreation process is simple and straightforward, but not always. The team at Enspiral cocreate agreements for everything from how money is spent to how diversity is fostered—all documented in their open source handbook. As is the case for many organizations, Enspiral's handbook took shape based on the need to capture the loose arrangements and assumptions already in place. Through rigorous discourse and consent, the team processes, decides on and documents the resulting agreements. Susan shares her experience of cocreating agreements with the Enspiral community:

> Some of the decisions we make at Enspiral are easy; some are incredibly challenging and emotionally demanding. We are a community that values dissenting voices, and the conditions required to hold that in a generative rather than reductive manner requires a lot of care and consideration. I had the experience of proposing a change in governance which would have delegated some aspects of decision-making to a small group of members. I was prepared for dissenting voices, but I wasn't prepared for my proposal to be blocked, which it was. In hindsight, blocking the proposal was the right decision, but at the time I really struggled.

I felt that I had failed to adequately convey the intention of my proposal. In reality, there was a fundamental flaw in my thinking and only because of our culture of encouraging and honoring dissenting voices was I able to accept the outcome without feeling personally aggrieved.

## Changing Agreements

One of the first agreements we suggest creating outlines how changes to agreements will be made going forward. Rodrigo Bastos is a member of Target Teal, a self-organization design firm based in Brazil. In Rodrigo's words, "You need a way of changing and adapting agreements very fast because reality doesn't wait for you. When a big client contract lands or when the team isn't working very well, we may need to change our agreements. How can you change fast and painlessly with little effort and then iterate on that new agreement?"[5]

There are two parts to the change process. The first is noticing when an agreement is no longer sufficient or working well and calling it out. Space needs to be created and regular prompts made so tensions can be surfaced. Aim to create a culture where, if somebody brings up a tension, the team can start to discuss and decide if resolving the tension requires changes to team agreements.

Once it's decided that a change is required, it's time to make the change. In chapter 12, we outline various tools for making decisions. A consent process usually forms the backbone of any change process.

Collective team agreements may go through periodic, structured updating, sometimes referred to as *refactoring*. Alanna Irving at Enspiral explains:

Refactor is a metaphor from software development. It's something programmers do after they've been working on a piece of software for a while and they've developed a better understanding of how it should be working. They clean up how it functions internally to make it simpler, more readable, better performing and easier to change and improve later—usually without radically changing its functionality or reason for being. In software, refactoring is a way to fix technical debt, which comes from old code that works, but makes new changes time-consuming or difficult.[6]

Refactoring applies to the hygiene of a company's culture too. Continually refactoring the core pieces of a team's culture and operating agreements helps bring closure to elements that hinder making new changes. It's not always about adding new things to improve specific culture problems. Sometimes simplifying is more valuable.

## Accountability

If you aspire to lead and work in agile self-managing organizations, individual and collective accountability is a necessary ingredient. Adult-to-adult relationships require a sense of shared accountability between all team members. When a commitment is missed, the responsibility of renegotiation falls to those who failed to deliver. Alternatively, the people affected become responsible for speaking directly and respectfully with the appropriate individuals. These conversations require courage and skill. In chapter 14, we provide practices to help you manage tensions and disagreements.

When those conversations don't happen, leaders often fall into the role of judging missed commitments and doling out consequences. In self-managing teams, leaders across the organization need instead to coach and facilitate. By coaching colleagues to solve their own problems and offering to facilitate (but not judge) when needed, team members learn how to operate with shared accountability and build their own skills and confidence.

## Visibility

We are communal creatures. When commitments are made visible, a sense of peer pressure kicks in. The team is now watching. Miovision uses group accountability rather than leader-driven, top-down tactics. The team relies on the sense of responsibility inherent in daily stand-up meetings (short accountability meetings), open team presentations and weekly and monthly company meetings. In CEO Kurtis McBride's words, "These meetings create public discussion and commitments, break down silos and distribute accountability through the team."[7]

To keep accountability alive, ritualize it. At ET Group, team members weren't tracking their project time, a requirement for recognizing project revenue. The team decided it would be helpful to have utilization rates for all team members shared monthly. Within two months, utilization-rate tracking rose significantly. At the end of supply chain software company Nulogy's annual retreat, a team member volunteered to be an accountability partner by incorporating a review of the team's committed actions into its weekly meetings going forward, until all commitments were completed. Jack.org, with its team of forty-six, is a Canadian charity that trains and empowers young leaders to dismantle barriers to positive mental health. The team incorporated a massive whiteboard metrics wall into their space where they track their progress. Team stand-ups take place in front of the metrics wall and it's a stop on all office tours (including with donors). Rituals such as these incorporate shared accountability into your team's daily routines. (See more about stand-up meetings and rituals in chapter 24.) Implicit expectations become explicit once visibility and a sprinkle of social pressure are added to the mix.

## Handling the Misses

Commitments will get missed. If those misses don't get called out, a culture of regular commitment breaking emerges. Responding to misses is tough. Our automatic reactions tend to be silence (passive-aggressively ignoring the issue), punishment (attacking and blaming) or making excuses. None of these approaches solves the problem. Instead, they diminish trust and rob your colleagues of a valuable development opportunity. Relationships and accountability can be strengthened through honest, respectful and timely conversations about misses. In chapter 13, we delve into the topic of feedback to help with these difficult discussions.

In your role as a leader, your team relies on your demonstrations of accountability. Along the way, you will occasionally make mistakes and fail to deliver on your own commitments. In a fast-paced environment, you are stretched thin and need to reprioritize commitments frequently. To build a culture of accountability, acknowledge your misses and share what you will do differently in the future. Encourage your colleagues to hold you accountable, and respect them when they do.

Making commitments and maintaining healthy levels of accountability are collective undertakings. They require an environment of transparency and rely on adult-to-adult discussion. Team function—and dysfunction—is contagious. Habits spread quickly and are sticky. Next time commitments start to slip, experiment with a quick, collective accountability debrief, asking, "What is the impact of this miss? What's to be learned? What caused the miss?" not to blame or shame but to identify the issues.

A conscious effort is required to avoid two pitfalls: filling the role of an accountability enforcer and missing commitments because of overextending yourself. The first scenario locks an individual—usually the most senior leader—into an unhealthy relationship dynamic within the team. Bypass this situation by experimenting with rituals such as those used at ET Group, Jack.org and Nulogy, described above, and by rotating roles. At its core, the second pitfall reflects an inability to say no—to oneself and to others. In her work, Dr. Brené Brown has ritualized the mantra "choose discomfort over resentment."[8] Learn to limit your promises.

## Integrate Agreements and Accountability

Here are some ideas to help embed agreements and accountability into your organization's DNA. Pick one or two and try them out:

- Add an accountability check-in on previously set commitments as a standing agenda item for an existing meeting.

- Within the next week, talk with someone who failed to keep a commitment. Be curious and ask explicitly what that person needs and, if relevant, how you or the team can help.

- Have the team experiment with creating a version of Morning Star's colleague letters of understanding.

- Create a physical or virtual whiteboard listing the most important and urgent team agreements and objectives.

- Introduce a daily ten-minute standing meeting to review accountabilities from yesterday and reset for today.

If you have doubts about your team's ability to make and keep commitments, get curious. Why is that? Engage the team in conversation around the topic. Do others feel the same? Experiment with your own approaches to making commitments and holding others accountable. As your team's skills mature with respect to agreements, commitments and accountabilities, so will the healthy adult-to-adult relationships that define your team's culture.

# Clear Roles

Align Skills and
Growth with the Work

"Finding good players is easy.
Getting them to play as a team
is another story."

**CASEY STENGEL**[1]

**W**ORK NEEDS TO be done. A team member agrees to do that work. On the surface, it's simply matchmaking skills to needs. The reality of organizational productivity is far more complex: Work goes undone. People fail to meet expectations. Task boredom sets in. Career aspirations require tending and don't always align with business needs. Leading can feel as if you're trying to assemble a puzzle in which both the picture and the shape of the pieces keep changing.

Leaders traditionally play the role of puzzle assemblers. In most businesses, the CEO acts as the chief puzzle assembler. When a new role is needed, a leader defines it. When a team member struggles, a leader deals with it. When it comes time to discuss career growth, a leader determines what is available or possible. Edwin Jansen from the Ian Martin Group believes there is a panacea for overcoming these challenges: remove yourself (or any one person) from the role of matching people to jobs.

Leaders are not mind readers—they don't intrinsically possess the ability to look deep into everyone's soul and extract the relevant information. What do they love to do? What do they do best? How are they motivated and demotivated? In their book *Primed to Perform*, Neel Doshi and Lindsay McGregor investigate how companies build the highest-performing cultures. They look at nine factors that influence employee motivation: performance reviews, governance processes, compensation, leadership, workforce and resource planning, community, career ladders, organizational identity and role design. In their words:

> The most powerful and the most overlooked source of total motivation is the design of a person's role within an organization. Often, jobs are designed entirely around tactical performance. We have a strategy. We turn that strategy into a process. We then write a job description to execute that process. Rarely, however, do we craft a role that inspires total motivation and adaptive performance. Poorly designed roles can make it almost impossible to create a high-performing culture.[2]

Still, leaders invest significant time working with incomplete information. They aim to match people and tactical work, ignoring individual uniqueness. Creating the conditions for each person to take responsibility for their own work, and how they fit into the needs of the organization, is infinitely more scalable and satisfying.

The Ian Martin Group has adopted a self-administered process they call the role advice process, or RAP. In essence, RAP is a way of crowdsourcing the design of a role. Because the Ian Martin Group is self-managed and chooses to work without traditional management structures, no single person is responsible for designing roles or managing team performance. They must work through role-based issues within a self-management scaffolding. A broader set of opinions helps align the needs of the business and the strengths of the individual. It has become a core element of how they operate as a company and has had a dramatically positive effect on the team. For example:

- A person who wasn't performing well put themselves on a three-month probation with the intention of either improving or leaving the organization. Along the way, they discovered an entirely different role, in which they are now thriving.

- A person decided to split their time and salary with another part of the organization that needed help on a project.

- Team members chose to leave the company after realizing their ideal roles didn't exist.

- Everyone else who completed the RAP meaningfully changed their roles, experiencing increased impact and personal engagement.

In Edwin's words, "The role advice process was voted our most effective practice by the team. It really is the closest thing to a panacea that I've ever seen in business. Got a people problem? Try a role advice process."[3]

## A Sample RAP

Think about your role for a moment. Could you increase your influence and engagement if you redesigned your role? Through a RAP, you can define the set of tasks best aligned with your strengths and things you enjoy. Does this mean you get to drop everything you don't enjoy? It does not. At least not until someone else pulls those tasks into their role. Referring back to the puzzle analogy, the puzzle is complete when there are no holes. Holes can be filled in three ways. The first is to reshape the pieces of the puzzle to fit. The second is to hire a new puzzle piece. The third is to reshape the design of the puzzle. Some things left undone could strengthen the business.

Let's look at the Ian Martin Group RAP in more detail. As we do, consider how you might guide yourself or a team member through a similar process.

### Step 1: Embark on a RAP

The process begins with an individual's desire for input into the design of their role. Sometimes it's prompted by the individual themselves. Other times, a colleague may suggest the individual initiate a RAP because they have noticed a significant problem or opportunity.

## Step 2: Announce the start of a RAP

The individual declares to the team that they are starting a RAP with a simple email to the team or a post on an internal message board. The message includes who will be consulted, an open invitation for any team members to contribute advice and the date the individual plans to present the results. (The team places a one-month timeline on RAPs.)

## Step 3: Invest time in self-reflection

The individual answers a series of questions: Why am I doing this advice process? What led to this? What are my strengths, talents and interests? Where are they best put to use? What is my current contribution to the team? What's working well? What could be better? Could I increase my impact by shifting or changing my role? In what ways specifically? What could be gained? What could be lost? Who would assume current duties I'd like to hand off? How do I feel about this potential change? What am I worried about? Excited about? What are the pros and cons?

## Step 4: Seek advice from others

The individual presents their self-reflection and seeks advice from at least three team members. Advice comes from those who receive a personal request as well as anyone who self-selects into the process following the initial announcement. This allows for contributions from any team member who believes they may have valuable input or may be affected. The questions in step 3 can serve as good discussion starters.

## Step 5: Decide

Decision time. Taking all information into consideration, the individual decides what they think should happen next. This could include changing roles, altering the current role or even leaving the organization.

## Step 6: Present results

The individual shares the results with their team by creating a summary document, or the entire process can be documented in a decision-making tool like Loomio (which is what the Ian Martin Group uses). The communication includes their personal reflections, reasoning and thought process; advice they received; the decision and a transition plan.

## Step 7: Take action

In a fully self-managed organization, the final step is to execute the transition plan. If no one objects to the plan, no further approvals are required. The individual driving the change is responsible for ensuring a smooth transition with their colleagues. Any significant changes in responsibility, compensation or employment status need to be fully documented before the change can take place. Compensation changes may require additional steps. We dig deeper into this topic in chapter 18.

IF THE Ian Martin Group process feels like it's too radical a shift from how your organization operates, you can customize the approach. Start slow and test-drive variations. The key is to shift the responsibility for constructing an optimal role from a central figure to each team member. It's critical that the RAP is done in good faith. If an individual is not ready to step in with positive intent, it's best not to use this process.

## Crafting Multiple Roles in Parallel

Similar to the Ian Martin Group, Percolab operates as a self-managed team and has its own process for managing roles. Percolab is an innovative fourteen-person consulting firm with deep expertise in codesigning the future of work, participatory management practices and collaboration. Its role process involves thinking about all the responsibilities necessary to allow the organization to meet its purpose. Those responsibilities are grouped together into roles.

Unlike in traditional organizations where one person is mapped to one job, individuals at Percolab may hold multiple roles or groups of responsibilities at the same time. Percolab transitioned to this role-based structure from a more traditional model. After completing the initial transition, Percolab's founder, Samantha Slade, shared the following process.

### Identifying company roles

Every organization already consists of a set of roles. By observing what is needed for the organization to meet its purpose, these roles can be made explicit. At Percolab, Samantha put on her role-identifying hat for a few months. She homed in on daily life at the company by asking herself, "What is the team working on? What are people talking about? Where do confusions, roadblocks and tensions repeatedly occur?"

In all, thirty-two roles were revealed as necessary sets of responsibilities (eventually merged and narrowed to a smaller number). Many were already owned by team members while others were unassigned. Samantha gave each one a placeholder title: banker, legal protector, video producer and so on. This was done in an open and transparent process. During this time, Samantha resisted the temptation to look outside the company for guidance, focusing instead on what was needed for the Percolab team based on their own unique way of functioning.

### Writing roles into being

Each of the thirty-two roles needed to be articulated in writing. The team completed this process, allowing their collective intelligence to emerge. The created roles included a title that was clear and aligned to the culture, a purpose expressed in a short why statement, accountabilities that defined tasks and decision-making authority and specific measures that articulated if the role was being well stewarded. So, for example, the role of banker looked like this:

*Title:* Banker

*Purpose:* Reduce financial stress of all members of the collective, collaborators and organizations with whom we have transactions.

*Accountabilities:*

Based on laws and obligations, foresee financial provisions and make and document all necessary payments to the government.

Act as contact for Percolab with the government, documenting key information, exchanges and situations.

Remit checks, once documentation is duly completed and, if appropriate, approved.

Inform members if a difficult financial situation arises and work through it openly and collectively.

*Measures of a role well stewarded:*

Financial stress of members is low—collective average rating of no more than two out of ten each month.

Payments are made within thirty days.

No penalties or interest paid to the government.

The team agreed that each member would be responsible for writing four to five roles. They set up a wiki in which people inserted first drafts. For each role, two additional team members iterated the document forward using their wisdom and experience. Everyone on the team committed to reading all the roles at this point in the process.

## Adopting and attributing roles

The team held a two-and-a-half-hour workshop to adopt and attribute the roles to individuals. They began with a short refresher on the purpose of roles. A check-in round followed to see how everyone was feeling heading into the exercise and to give space to any apprehensions. Then small groups discussed and reviewed the roles relevant to them with the intention of proposing three improvements to the role drafts. Each proposal was evaluated using an integrated decision-making process (which we will explore in the next chapter). Together, they agreed upon an implementation date for the new role system, and the roles were then attributed to individuals through a multistep process:

- The name of each role was written on an index card and laid out before the team.

- Team members then wrote on the cards the name of who they thought was best situated for stewarding that role. Including their own name was not allowed.

- The group reviewed the collective perspective that had been revealed. Then each person proposed two roles they had energy to steward. The group let the person know of any objections. If none, the roles were considered attributed.

- In the next round, anyone could propose anyone else for the remaining roles. Again there was a quick check for any opposition until all roles were attributed.

- A closing round was completed to allow everyone to share their thoughts and feelings before leaving the workshop.

Both the Ian Martin Group's and Percolab's approaches remove the leader's responsibility to play matchmaker between people and roles. In both cases, the team benefits from the insights of individual members and everyone can opt in to work that feels meaningful. Would this kind of inclusive process help address current limitations you're facing with role assignments in your organization?

## Playing to Strengths

It's unrealistic to expect someone to excel at everything, yet most companies set this expectation of leaders. Adopting a more dynamic definition of leadership allows your team to better leverage its strengths.

Miovision plays to everyone's strengths in a clever way. The company has managers and leaders but not in the traditional sense. Through prototyping, Kurtis McBride came to realize there are three distinct components found in leadership roles: strategy, execution and empathy (empathy is here defined as knowing how to work with people to get the best performance). Strategy, execution and empathy are distinct in the skills, aptitudes and experiences required for success. Miovision doesn't expect anyone to excel in all three. Instead, Miovision selects leaders based in part on their strength in at least one of those areas. Additional training, mentorship and coaching helps leaders grow their strengths across all three dimensions.

Miovision believes the ideal role for every team member exists at the intersection of passion, skill and need. Passion is uniquely personal. The skill match is negotiated between leaders and team members. Need is articulated through defined business goals. The company is relentless in finding ways to enable each team member to align their skills with business needs while working on things they are passionate about.

Miovision's culture is a constant work-in-progress, but at its core are two philosophies. The business leaders leverage one key strength. Individual contributors merge the genius of passion, skill and need. Kurtis refers to these as "first principles."

## Differentiate Roles and Souls

We are all familiar with the idea of people filling jobs to the point that the person and job seem to be one and the same. Evan *is* the VP of sales. Abby *is* the graphic designer. In self-managing organizations, it can be helpful to differentiate between roles (a collection of related responsibilities) and souls (the human beings). Although it may seem like a foreign concept in many work environments, you do have experience with this differentiation. You might hold the roles of spouse, parent, sibling, team member, community volunteer and more. Some roles you'll hold for a lifetime. Others will come and go. Through it all, you will be a human with your own hopes, dreams, fears, wants and needs. Percolab differentiated the various roles required to operate its business, identifying thirty-two roles, but it had only fourteen souls—team members—to steward multiple roles simultaneously.

Differentiation does not mean separation. In the real world, roles and souls work together, which means it's easy to mix them up. Understanding how each role is distinct while appreciating how they work together provides increased clarity. It allows you to be explicit about why you are taking the lead on certain work or raising specific concerns. You can ask, "Does one of my roles care about this?" Or "How is my relationship with this other human being I work with?"

Undoubtedly these various approaches are not perfect and may not be right for your circumstances. The invitation we offer is to experiment beyond the tradition of defining comprehensive and static job descriptions. Instead, try differentiating between roles and souls and releasing yourself from the responsibility of chief puzzle assembler. Invite your team to participate in a collaborative process of experimenting with one or more of the above approaches.

# 12

# Decision-Making

Unleash New Paradigms for Deciding Together

"If organizations are serious about creating an adult-to-adult partnership culture … participation in decision making is how it happens."

**SAMANTHA SLADE**[1]

D AMIEN DOUTÉ tells a wonderful story that goes something like this.[2] Three friends, Alex, Billy and Camille, want ice cream. They pool their money and discover they have enough for one bucket. So off they go to the corner store and find that only two flavors are available: vanilla and strawberry. Alex and Billy prefer vanilla, but Camille prefers strawberry. How will they decide which one to buy?

There are six types of decision-making processes they might choose from. They might go with the **status quo:** unable to decide, the friends don't buy any ice cream. Or they might be **random:** flip a coin and let fate decide. If the decision were **autocratic**, Alex is holding the money and would get to decide, without considering the wishes of Billy or Camille. However, if it were a **majority** vote, ballots would be cast and Camille would lose. **Consensus,** on the other hand, would see the friends buying the flavor that everyone agrees on. Since Camille's preference differs from Billy's and Alex's, they would endlessly discuss possible solutions until, after an undetermined amount of time, either Camille or Billy and Alex "give in." If they chose **consent**, however, after exchanging preferences, Alex might propose picking vanilla and ask the group if they have a reason not to choose that flavor. Camille might then tell them of a personal intolerance and inability to eat vanilla ice cream. Hearing this, Alex might change the proposal to strawberry. Although not their first choice, Alex and Billy also like strawberry and don't see any reason for not choosing that flavor instead.

## Consent: A Cornerstone of Self-Organizing

Once everyone on the team has a defined role, the next practice of self-organizing is decision-making. Many would argue it is the most important of all organizational practices.

In traditional organizations, decisions usually fall to managers. The bigger the decision, the higher up the hierarchy the decision moves. Rather than relying on a rigid hierarchy and centralized decisions, self-managing teams depend on strong decision-making processes.

Three decision-making methods tend to rule within most traditional organizations: autocratic, delegation (usually the passing of autocratic decision-making from one person to another) and consensus. At one end is autocratic decision-making where one person decides and informs everyone else. It's typically a HiPPO — highest-paid person's opinion. This style of decision-making can be useful when fast action is the primary driver.

On the other end of the spectrum are consensus decisions. Consensus decisions often happen when no one has power over others, such as in cross-functional groups of peers. These decisions are characterized by lots of discussion. Done well, these decisions are egalitarian and elicit engagement. They also often require a lot of time. Done poorly, they frustrate everyone, lead to the lowest-common-denominator decision and breed stagnation.

The third type of decision-making in most organizations is delegation, which typically, though not always, falls on the autocratic end of the spectrum. A decision is put in the hands of someone positioned to make the best decision or who can learn from the experience. Things can move fast when delegation is done well and can run into trouble when the person delegated to doesn't hold context or seek proper input.

Most self-managing teams rely primarily on two different decision-making tools, both in the family of consent-based decision-making: advice process and generative decision-making. These approaches marry the best aspects of autocratic and consensus decision-making without the related downsides. But they do require leaders to embrace two beliefs:

**Decision-making needs to be distributed** In traditional organizations, decision rights are held by the people at the top of the pyramid. This approach made sense when those at the top had the most knowledge and relevant experience. In today's fast-moving world, these assumptions no longer hold and therefore we need to reconsider how we make decisions.

**Intervening in decisions develops learned helplessness** When decisions can always be overruled, an attitude of learned helplessness emerges. People start taking less responsibility because someone is always looking over their shoulder. They aren't truly responsible for their choices. Senior leaders will bemoan that people aren't taking more responsibility while, at the same time, unintentionally fostering this learned helplessness. Senior leaders regularly insert their opinion with the intention of adding value and without appreciating the impact of their intervention. To help bring this belief to practice, the partners at Seattle-based TGB Architects decided they "reserve the right to jump in on decisions that pose an existential threat to the business." Outside that, the team owns their decisions.

Assuming decision-making authority is sufficiently distributed and won't be unnecessarily overruled, your team can start experimenting with the advice process and generative decision-making. In their truest forms, these two approaches enable team members to initiate a decision in any area not otherwise assigned to an individual or role. Let's explore in more detail how these two processes work.

## The Advice Process

The advice process declares one person as the owner of a particular decision—most often the person who recognizes a problem, holds the related accountability or is closest to the problem. The decision owner starts by seeking input and advice from two groups: those who will be affected by the decision and those with subject-matter expertise.

This process assumes that people trust their colleagues to make decisions in the best interest of the collective, and that people's input will be sought when appropriate. After seeking input, the decision owner proceeds in a way they deem best for the organization. They do not need to act on all advice provided. Seeking approval or announcing their decision in advance of acting is not required, although we recommend making the decision public. For more important decisions, sharing the advice received throughout the process boosts transparency.

Equal Experts, a multinational software and agile consultancy of around 1,000 people, has adopted the advice process as its primary method for making decisions. They started using it two and a half years ago when the company was half its current size, beginning with the goal to change the culture so everyone treats their colleagues like the grown-ups they are. The team started small, experimenting with the advice process in just one group. The advice process is now the dominant form of decision-making throughout the organization. They have even published their specific flavor of the process as a playbook.

Equal Experts has devised methods to make the advice process work at a scale across more than a dozen offices. For instance, frequent questions, such as how much spending is acceptable when attending a conference, have been turned into common advice that everyone can reference. Team members need to seek advice only when going outside these standard suggestions.

The advice process elicits a sense of personal responsibility, which leads to increased engagement. Dave Hewett, a partner at

Equal Experts, notes that decisions coming out of the advice process have generated many more ideas and unleashed an untold amount of creativity. Now, instead of a central leadership team responsible for all the idea generation, everyone is involved. The senior people on the team apply a minimal amount of constraint so individual excellence can thrive.

The advice process relies on the power of adult conversation. The bigger the decision, the wider the net is cast for advice. For small decisions, one additional perspective may be all that's needed. At times, advice from external advisors, industry experts or board members may be appropriate. Another notable piece of Equal Expert's implementation of the advice process clarifies who the decision maker should be. If the spend is under £6,000, it's a personal decision. Between £6,000 and £20,000, the decision falls to the business unit lead to confirm the decision maker. If it impacts multiple business units or it's above £20,000, then someone on the executive team confirms who becomes the decision maker.

The team at Equal Experts publishes the results of every advice process to a Slack channel either before or after the decision is made. In Dave's words, "People aren't typically shy about offering their opinions around here, so it's useful to be clear whether you want more input or not."[3]

*The Decision Maker* by Dennis Bakke is a quick read and does an excellent job of explaining the advice process in detail.[4] He outlines how leaders who have traditionally been the prime decision maker become the person choosing who is best positioned to be a decision owner in a given situation. Using an online tool like Loomio or Cloverpop can bring speed and transparency to the advice process. These tools are also excellent for making decisions across distributed teams. We go into more detail about these tools a bit later.

The advice process can be applied simply in most groups. To get started:

- Choose a group that is open to experimentation.

- Explain the advice process to team members and cocreate a "safe enough to try" experiment. For instance, use the advice process for four weeks and then complete a retrospective. (See chapter 13 to learn more about retrospectives.)

- Iterate as needed until the team feels comfortable using the process.

- Share your learnings with colleagues outside the initial group. If the advice process works well for the first group, other groups will be interested in what you are doing. Over time, the advice process will spread through the organization.

Maintaining the integrity of the process is critical. For example, to facilitate a more honest discussion, if you are the decision owner, state your biases up front to provide full transparency. The advice process fails when a decision owner acts disingenuously by excluding people who are likely to disagree with their preferred decision. Going through the steps without seeking diverse perspectives or while ignoring important input quickly destroys trust. One organization grappling with a market-driven product change needed a different set of skills than those held by the person in the customer support role. The product manager initiated an advice process and solicited advice from other members of the team, but to avoid confrontation, they consciously excluded the person who would be affected most by the change. At the end of the process, the customer support person was told their skills no longer fit the role and that they should therefore leave the company. Trust was severely compromised across the entire organization. A better approach would have been to include them in the process, giving them all the information to allow them to identify possible solutions or alternatives.

## Generative Decision-Making

Compared with the advice process, generative decision-making is more structured. The generative decision-making methodology was created by the team at Percolab as an improvement on a process called integrated decision-making and is best used in a live (in-person or remote) meeting with everyone relevant to the decision present. Two key elements make generative decision-making powerful. First, there is no single decision owner. Whoever makes the first proposal becomes the proposal holder. Their job is to onboard and integrate feedback from other meeting participants until a final decision emerges. This process may result in a decision that diverges completely from the initial proposal. Second, participants may only object to a proposal if they feel it will "cause harm or move us backward."

Having a better idea is not a sufficient reason to object. That's where traditional consensus-based processes often fail. Many discussions stall as individuals offer what they believe to be better solutions and rally others to see their points of view. The search for the best option can drag on endlessly. Generative decision-making operates on the agile principle of "good enough for now, safe enough to try" and is rooted in the belief that movement—an imperfect experiment completed quickly—is far superior to a prolonged or watered-down decision. With generative decision-making, once a decision is arrived at, experiments provide additional data, and decisions can be revisited and improved in the future.

Generative decision-making involves several steps.

### Recognize the right time
Is the time right to make a decision on this? Do people have the right context? If not, could a conversation help the group move toward a decision?

## Create a proposal

Anyone can start the process by describing a problem they see and proposing a solution, making that person the proposal holder. Someone volunteers to facilitate the decision-making process and ideally removes themselves as an active contributor to the decision. The facilitator's main role is to keep the process moving and to help test objections for validity. (More on objection testing shortly.)

## Ask clarifying questions

Anyone can ask the proposal holder clarifying questions. The proposal holder provides an answer to each question or states that they haven't yet contemplated an answer. No reaction or dialogue is permitted at this point. It's the role of the facilitator to ensure questions are for the purpose of clarifying the proposal and don't drift into sharing opinions or reactions.

## Express reactions

One by one, each person (except the proposal holder) responds to the proposal as they see fit. No additional discussion is permitted. During this phase, the proposal holder may want to keep notes about what they are hearing.

## Amend and clarify

Once the reaction round is complete, the proposal holder can choose to clarify or amend the proposal based on what was heard in the last two steps. Once again, no discussion is permitted.

## Invite objections

The facilitator invites objections by asking each person in turn, "Do you see any reason why adopting this proposal would cause harm or move us backward?" For an objection to be valid, it must meet at least one of the following criteria: 1. The proposal, if adopted, would move the team backward in its capacity to deliver on its purpose. 2. A problem that doesn't already exist will immediately be caused by this proposal. 3. A significant future problem can be predicted based on this proposal and there will not be sufficient time to react.

Having a better idea, believing that the current proposal is not useful or that it's not a current priority are not valid objections. For these reasons, many objections tend to melt away during the objection round. If no valid objections surface, the proposal is adopted. Perhaps the most challenging and necessary part of the facilitator's role is assessing the validity of an objection and rejecting invalid objections.

## Integrate objections

If a valid objection is raised, the proposal holder is responsible for crafting a revised proposal free of valid objections while continuing to address the original problem. The proposal holder focuses on each objection, one at a time. Once resolutions to all objections are integrated into the revised proposal, another objection round is completed. This process continues until a solution is adopted.

## Confirm visually

The final step in the process is a visual confirmation that everyone is ready to move forward with the final proposal. It's not until every participant in the decision process gives a thumbs-up that the proposal is officially adopted. Even after all resolutions to objections have been successfully integrated into the proposal, it's not unusual for a participant to resist the final adoption. Surfacing and discussing these points of resistance are critical before moving on.

Once teams are proficient in the use of generative decision-making, the process can move from proposal to adoption in seconds if everyone is ready to give a thumbs-up to the proposal without further discussion. With the whole Percolab team trained on the methodology, they can rapidly move through important decisions. Their record is nineteen quality decisions in sixty minutes.

Start applying generative decision-making with choices that warrant a live full-group discussion. We recommend engaging an outside facilitator or having a member of your team trained in it when you are first learning how to use generative decision-making. The process is not complicated but does require strong facilitation to be effective. Generative decision-making works best when the majority of the meeting participants are familiar with the structure. If necessary, take time at the beginning of the meeting to go over the process flow. Like most new things, you may need to move slowly to learn the new process before reaping its rewards.

## Tips for Effective Decision-Making

In addition to the advice process and generative decision-making, there are several other tips and tools that will strengthen and speed up your decision-making processes.

### Name the decision maker/decision process

The simple process of naming who is deciding and how the decision will be made may seem obvious but is far too often overlooked.

Once Again Nut Butter is a 100 percent employee-owned food manufacturing company with eighty employee-owners. As owners, employees expected to have a voice in company decisions, but no explicit structure was in place for including them. After a controversial decision was made about opening a new facility, a governance committee was set up to create more clarity around decision-making. The committee, with the help of the Sociocracy Consulting Group, identified four categories of decisions: financial, personnel, operations and corporate organization/governance. For each type of decision, they determined the decision maker, from whom the decision maker must seek input and who, if anyone, must ratify the decision.[5]

You can leverage this approach even if you aren't the decision maker. Just ask for clarity into how a decision will be made to bring attention to the need for transparency.

## Capture decisions

What exactly has been decided? Until a decision is captured in writing and shared with everyone who needs to know, assume misunderstanding. Written decisions provide a reference for everyone long after the decision has been made. You've probably experienced the pain of revisiting a key decision many months after the fact only to realize no one understands what exactly was intended.

Loomio is an online tool that fosters discussion and supports the various decision-making paradigms discussed here. Most important, it captures both the process and the outcome of the decision along with who was involved, which makes it easy to go back and review.

Cloverpop offers a standalone decision platform and a Slack integration. Both simplify and support good decision practices, enabling companies to scale those practices across their organizations. Cloverpop enables quick communication of decisions to stakeholders and the receipt of feedback when people aren't aligned.

## Make decisions faster

Many decisions should be made sooner with less or imperfect information. Having two-thirds of the information you wish you had is likely enough. When you wait until you have 90 percent or more, in most cases, you've waited too long. Just as fruit is best consumed when it is ripe, rather than under- or overripe, decisions should be made at just the right time.

## Review key decisions

If you make important decisions without all the data, information will be coming in as you act on the decision. But decisions don't need to be final. As new information surfaces, you can make new decisions. Setting reminders to reflect on decisions or blocking review time in recurring meetings can bring your focus back for a quick check-in.

### Delay the commitment

In *Lean Software Development: An Agile Toolkit*, Mary and Tom Poppendieck describe a counterintuitive technique for making better decisions: "Delay commitment until the last responsible moment, that is, the moment at which failing to make a decision eliminates an important alternative. If commitments are delayed beyond the last responsible moment, then decisions are made by default, which is generally not a good approach to making decisions."[6]

This is different from procrastinating. Cofounder of Stack Overflow and Discourse Jeff Atwood calls it "inspired laziness": "Decisions made too early in a project are hugely risky."[7] There is a natural tension in an organization between leaving options open and moving things forward. Getting the balance right involves knowing your natural tendency and adjusting to meet the needs of others.

### Dot vote

"Teams increase positive results by six times and cut failure rates in half when they double the number of choices considered before deciding," according to research by Cloverpop.[8] With multiple options, narrowing the list quickly can be challenging. In dot voting, each participant gets a set number of dots, typically between three and five, to place by the ideas that resonate most for them. One variation allows people to place more than one dot on an idea. Once dot voting is complete, you can quickly see which ideas resonate with the group or if opinions diverge.

### Try fist to five

This simple tool offers a great way of checking the level of agreement across a group. It starts when someone says, "Shall we do a fist to five?" Much like in a game of rock, paper, scissors, on the count of three, everyone responds to a proposal in unison by holding up between zero and five fingers:

- A closed fist means "I don't support. I'm blocking."

- One finger means "I see *major* issues we need to resolve before I'll agree."

- Two fingers means "I see *minor* issues we need to resolve before I'll agree."

- Three fingers means "I see minor issues we can resolve later. Let's proceed."

- Four fingers means "I'm fine with this proposal as is. Let's proceed."

- Five fingers means "I love this proposal and will help champion it."

If everyone is a three or higher, with at least some fours or fives, the group accepts the proposal and moves on. If anyone shows a two or lower, the proposer pauses to listen to the concerns with the goal of resolving those concerns and completing another fist to five. Much like dot voting, this tool provides a quick temperature check on alignment and avoids group discussions that go longer than needed.

## Disagree and commit

This idea, attributed to Intel's Andy Grove, builds on the concept of fist to five as well as the advice process and generative decision-making. For a team to move forward, sometimes people must commit even if a decision does not line up with their personal preferences. If a team embraces the disagree and commit philosophy, once a decision has been made, everyone works proactively for its success. Without this intention, only those who agree with the idea get on board while others may disregard or quietly sabotage successful implementation of the decision. In today's interconnected workforce, this leads to predictable challenges of good ideas falling flat in execution.

Fist to five and disagree and commit both rely on the idea that our range of tolerance is much larger than our personal preference.

Our personal preference would rate a five on the fist to five; things still in our range of tolerance would be a three or four. We often advocate strongly for our personal preference, which can be useful to a point. It's less productive when it's time for a group to converge toward a single path forward. A better frame is asking whether you can tolerate this path forward even if it's not your personal preference. Generative decision-making and the advice process also rely on trust and tolerance to be successful.

## Do it if it is safe enough to try

Decisions can be categorized into two categories: type 1 (or one-way door) and type 2 (or two-way door). Type 1 decisions are consequential and irreversible, or nearly irreversible. If we walk through that door, we can't return. Most decisions are type 2, or can be divided into type 2 decisions. "Safe enough to try" is a concept that promotes moving forward quickly on type 2 decisions. If a proposal is safe enough to try, then allow it to proceed.

In a 200-person consultancy, a team member wanted to change the performance review process. This change would ripple throughout the organization. To start, the team member and their immediate colleagues experimented with a new process for one review cycle, thereby limiting the scope tremendously. In this way, what was originally a type 1 decision scaled down to a safe-enough-to-try type 2.

## Promote the phrase "I intend to..."

When people ask for and receive well-meaning input from those with more seniority or context, learned helplessness often sets in. An ask might start with "Do you think we should..." or "Could we..." or "What do you think about..." Most leaders naturally take the bait and answer the question.

In his book *Turn the Ship Around!*, David Marquet shares his real-life account of being captain of the submarine USS *Santa Fe*. During his tenure, he transformed the submarine from the worst performer to the best performer in the US Navy. He attributes the success primarily to one seemingly small change. He instilled a culture where crew members were expected to present solutions by saying "I intend to . . ." These three words led to a big shift in the team's personal sense of responsibility and ownership, transferring the onus for decisions to individuals. Captain Marquet responded to them either with "Proceed" or with questions. So the next time someone comes asking for advice, ask them first what they intend to do.

## Open multiple channels and increase bandwidth

When gathering input on key decisions, open multiple communication channels online and in person, both from local and geographically dispersed locations. Consciously try to improve the experience for everyone by proactively facilitating the decision-making process. Pay special attention to voices that might be softer or less heard. And when differing opinions come up, increase the bandwidth of discussion. Bandwidth is simply the amount of communication being interpreted, including non-verbal communication. Enspiral uses these techniques and when more bandwidth is needed, they move from Loomio to Slack, Slack to video, video to one-on-one conversations, often via Zoom, and one-on-one conversations to mediated discussion. Once resolved, they report outcomes back to the group.

WHEREVER YOUR team is on its journey, there is undoubtedly room to strengthen decision-making skills and processes. Try out consent-based decision-making by picking an approach that feels most appropriate for your circumstances. Effective decision-making can be a strategic advantage for scaling your business. You will make progress by experimenting and learning. Invest time now to reap benefits long into the future.

# 13

# Feedback

Create Information
Loops That Flow
through the System

"Feedback refers to the signaling mechanism in living systems, including organisations, by which they draw upon the collective intelligence of the whole, emerging from the specific local knowledge of the parts."

**GEORGE PÓR**[1]

SELF-MANAGING ORGANIZATIONS ARE inspired by natural ecosystems. For natural ecosystems to survive, they need feedback loops—information flowing through the system so the system can adapt. In workplaces, the best feedback loop is often individuals noticing patterns of how specific actions influence the system. If decision-making is the most important of all self-managing practices, understanding the impact of decisions on the system is a close second. Anyone working within a successful organization will name effective feedback as a cornerstone of their success.

We'll pause here to highlight the difference between natural feedback loops and structured feedback in a business context. The feedback loops in natural systems *just are*. They have evolved over time to enable stasis, growth or regeneration. Traditional management systems hold the idea that certain individuals can define "good" on behalf of everyone else in the system. This belief, often called meritocracy, has influenced everything from recruitment to performance management to strategy creation. Certain individuals decide on behalf of everyone how we should communicate, how reports should be written and how feedback on a person's work should be shared. This implies there is a best practice that should be followed by all.

In predictable systems, tried and true methods can be codified as best practice. Elements of your business are obviously served by applying tried and true methodology. If you know the specific outcome you are after, following the blueprint will improve your chances of getting your desired result. But human organizing is not predictable, and the danger of treating it as such is to limit its potential. Every human being on your team is unique, each bringing their own will, experience, personality, ego and more. That's the beauty and also the undeniable complexity of human systems.

Whenever we give feedback for anything other than the execution of a set of exacting steps, that feedback is subjective. Workers on an assembly line know there is one right way to do their job. The processes are intended for an absolutely consistent outcome. Companies that aren't designed to output the same exact thing over and over have an inherent opportunity for innovation and development. How then do we avoid limiting our organizations by assuming or imposing a hierarchical version of good? The answer lies in allowing everyone on the team to ask for what they need in both giving and receiving feedback.

We've all worked on teams where we've felt disappointed by the performance of a colleague in comparison to either our own or the collective consensus of what is right or useful. It could be the way they speak to others or perhaps variability in the quality of what they produce. It could be that they consistently miss deadlines. These performance issues become especially noticeable when they affect our own work. In response our reactive thoughts may include versions of "They don't know what they are doing!" or "I can't believe they get paid more than me!" or "Ugh, again?" or "They are pulling us all down." Which one of these thoughts is true? Are any of them? When we respond to our reactive thoughts, we often default to avoidance, hostility, passive-aggressive behavior or even bullying. Our ability to jump to fast conclusions and blame is astounding. The alternative to assuming and judging is to become curious instead.

## Going Beyond Feedback to Mutual Curiosity

Feedback methodologies and approaches have changed significantly over the past few decades. Bosses delivering feedback in a more humane way was a huge advancement. The book *The One Minute Manager*, published in 1982 and with over 13 million copies in print, popularized the feedback practice colloquially known as "the shit sandwich": say something nice first (compliment), then give the critical feedback and end by saying something nice (appreciation). Whatever you might think about that approach today, it was revelatory at the time.

A few years ago, impact feedback gained popularity as a way to help us talk about hurt feelings or the consequences one person's behavior has on another. Models like SBI (Situation-Behavior-Impact) aim to take the emotion out of how we describe a situation that caused us pain and state the impact as fact from the perspective of the wronged person. The issue with this approach is that hurt feelings often have little to do with a specific action, and much to do with our lifetime of experience—a reflection on our own confirmation bias and old wounds. Even in teams that commit to the belief that everything is done with good intention, relying on strategies like impact feedback can unintentionally bring immense subjectivity into feedback.

If a colleague doesn't meet a commitment that you depended on, and you share the impact on you as "I felt disrespected" or "I had to miss my daughter's soccer match," you imply that there was a clear understanding and that the person doing the harm should have known better. But when you take on a feeling of hurt, you disregard all other possibilities. Had your colleague been up all night caring for their sick child? Are they distracted by a tricky home situation or an unmet bill? We make ourselves the center of our universe and can so quickly place the blame for our reactions on others. We wind ourselves into such balls of aggravation because all of these external forces are causing us to look bad or feel bad, taking away our liberty or our autonomy or our choice. In reality, we are saying, "I have to tell you what you did and how it made me feel, and I want you to take responsibility for it because I need to ensure it never happens again." This is one approach, but is it really any better than the shit sandwich?

We could instead simply be curious. Instead of saying, "When you don't invite me to that meeting, it makes me feel invisible and unworthy," try "I'm curious about why I've been left off the meeting invite lately, and I'm noticing that I'm reading all sorts of things into it. Can we explore that together?" Another example: "It's frustrating to me that you are not meeting your commitments. When you say at our daily team stand-up meeting that you are going to have this piece of work complete and that there are no blocks, I leave the meeting expecting you will deliver. I'm curious about why the work is not yet complete and perhaps what I'm not understanding. Can we talk about it?"

If we really aspire to peerdom, we need to practice not ascribing blame, victimhood or falling into a parent-child or passive-aggressive stance. We need to commit to exploring together.

## It's about Consent

Despite the impassioned critique above, as we have said throughout this book, there are many different approaches to working together. Many books and models exist for improving how you give and receive feedback, which may be totally appropriate for your team. The only opinion we hold staunchly on this subject is that there should be mutual consent between individuals.

Radical responsibility requires that you each take responsibility for asking for what you need, and feedback is a great place to practice this skill. When Susan worked with the blockchain software technology company ConsenSys, she helped create an experiment based on the simple mandate that every team member engage in some sort of feedback process. The approach was simple: don't assume that there is one right way, and don't conjoin feedback to performance. The culture team at ConsenSys created a template for what they called DIY feedback. Through research and a design process, the team identified multiple feedback personas and then condensed these to three personas. Each person identified their unique feedback-receiving personality, for example:

**Radical** "Give it to me! I want as much feedback as I can get, and make it as unfiltered as possible!"

**Not helpful** "I'm suspicious of feedback because it's so often not relevant. The people providing it don't have enough context about what the project, the system or I need to make it useful."

**Averse/traumatized** "Feedback is a weapon to judge/shame/change me."

Next the feedback giver was to consider the context of the feedback relationship: Was the feedback for someone they worked with regularly in a team? Was it with someone they'd just started working with? Or was the feedback coming from something they'd noticed from afar?

For each of these contexts, different practices were identified and tested out. Every practice required mutual agreement between the giver and receiver, transparency up front about each participant's feedback persona and a commitment to work within those boundaries. The focus here was on the invitation, not just crafting an invitation with a subtext or as a lure, but honestly and clearly being curious and inviting others into conversation about what you'd genuinely like to better understand.

## Practices for radical feedback lovers

If you identify as someone who thrives on giving or receiving radical feedback, your invitations to a curious conversation could look like this:

**For those you work with regularly** "Let's grab a virtual coffee and go for it [give each other radical feedback]. Are you game?"

**When working on a new project together** "I thrive on feedback and hope you'll be open to doing a round after each work session together. Would this work for you?"

The delivery step can be as simple as a partner retrospective, where you explore together what's working, what's not and what you'd like to be doing differently going forward. The explicit step of exploring together clarifies that this is a mutual process of learning, along with a commitment to reflect together and agree on the next steps.

## Practices for those suspicious of feedback

If you identify as someone who generally doesn't find feedback useful, your invitations to a curious conversation could look like this:

**For those you work with regularly** "I'm noticing a pattern that I'd like to get your insights on. Can we grab coffee and explore together?"

**When working on a new project together** "I'm sensing that we might be repeating patterns I've seen in other projects. Can we take some time to test that hypothesis and learn from each other?"

## Practices for the feedback-averse

If you are feedback averse, invite someone you trust to practice with you. It can be as simple as practicing reframing reactions to feelings of hurt or perceived judgment. Frameworks like SBI can be useful in helping us understand when this is happening: noticing, owning and naming our reactions are often enough. Instead of saying, "Oh, there you go again with your passionate arguments. Do you have any idea how that impacts me? Well, clearly not, so let me tell you in detail..." try a simple reframe: "I noticed I had a strong reaction during that conversation. Could we talk it through?"

## Illuminating Blind Spots

We don't see ourselves as others do. If we believe that everything is subjective, how do we navigate potential blind spots without falling into the trap of projection?

One practice that can work across all personas and situations is a peer development triad. This simple process begins with a round of the question "What are you noticing in the system?" to de-personalize feedback loops and to practice scanning the broader environment as a team. In a second round, each person shares one thing they've been working on improving. Mary might be seeking to improve her facilitation skills. She shares what she's been trying, and then asks you and the other participant in the triad if you have additional ideas or advice that illuminates opportunities she hasn't yet seen. Mary knows that she wants to improve her facilitation. She can feel it and doesn't need anyone to tell her that her skills aren't quite up to par. By giving Mary space to own her own development needs, she can cultivate skills in ways that are unique to her, rather than trying to adopt a best practice defined by someone else.

## Team Learning

Retrospectives are the practice of pausing to learn, often at the end of a project. The retrospective is a team meeting with a defined, limited duration set in advance, usually between thirty minutes and two hours. The meeting focuses on making the next work segment more enjoyable and productive by both improving the team's processes and helping individuals develop.

Retrospectives range in scope and approach. With a larger and more dispersed team, more formality is useful in setting up your retrospective. David Horowitz is the CEO and cofounder of Retrium, a company providing software to simplify the retrospective process. As you would expect, David and his team use retrospectives religiously and have discovered a series of side bene-fits as a result. Through repetition, the team built an indispensable set of skills related to process improvement and providing feed-back. On the formal side, Retrium offers a variety of approaches. The 4Ls is one example that, with a few modifications, works well with teams of any size.

To begin, participants work on their own to create a list of responses in each of the following four categories (below, X stands for the time period or project under review):

- What I *liked* about X is…
- What I *learned* from X is…
- My own performance during X *lacked* with respect to…
- What I *longed for* during X is…

Responses are then compiled and the group picks one to three areas to focus on improving for the next block of work. Next, the group creates plans to address the challenges and ways to mea-sure improvements, either quantitatively or qualitatively. Lastly, someone is appointed to oversee these adjustments. At the next retrospective, the team reviews progress. Other items from the last retrospective can be examined as a way to jump-start the next cycle.

There are many types of retrospectives you can undertake. All retrospectives have a few key ingredients that create a shared understanding. They highlight what's going well and should therefore be continued or amplified. Retrospectives also recog-nize that many problems have multiple causes and are systemic in nature. Little to no time is spent discussing who caused indi-vidual problems. Some people worry that this can promote a lack of accountability, but the opposite tends to be true. When the team comes together and feels collectively accountable for results, it becomes clear who isn't meeting the team's shared agreements and expectations.

## What, So What, Now What?

Another tool for creating a feedback loop and understanding what a system needs next is the Liberating Structure (see chapter 15) of What, So What, Now What?—a practice in which participants answer three questions in a defined order.

Think of each question as a rung on a ladder: answering the first one helps you climb up to the second. The first question asks, "What is the data?" In answering it, your team collectively surfaces facts and data free of personal opinions or assumptions using your five senses, most often what you can see or hear. What exactly was said? What are the numbers? What specific behavior occurred?

Next comes "So what?" This question acknowledges that, on top of each fact, you individually and collectively infer what those facts mean. It's here that you each attach your own interpretation to the data: "I interpreted what was said to mean...," "My perspective on the numbers is...," "I assumed that your crossed arms meant..."

Lastly, the group answers the question "Now what?" You cocreate a plan by testing proposals, suggesting experiments and surfacing new ideas: "Based on what we've learned, I propose that...," "Now that I have the benefit of everyone's insights, I have an idea...," "Perhaps, going forward, we can experiment with..."

Using this process in place of a free-flowing conversation helps prevent assumption-making and leads to actionable next steps. The process reveals that even with unassailable data, we each in our own way make assumptions about and attach meaning to data.

Consider using these three questions to frame any form of feedback. Each time you are drawn to tell someone what you think about their work, start at the bottom of the ladder and work your way up. By doing so, you will unpack your inferences and be better positioned to enter into productive dialogue.

WHEN WE practice together, it's easier to understand and identify our tendencies and biases as we make sense of information.
Whether we are engaged in a feedback loop at the system or individual level, we have an opportunity to explore with curiosity and
avoid proceeding on the basis of our reactive thoughts. We build
our awareness and choose how to share what we are learning in
generative, potential-inducing ways.

# 14

# Interpersonal Tensions

Move from Conflict
Avoidance to Conflict
Transformation

"Conflict is resolved not through compromise, but through invention."

**MARY PARKER FOLLETT**[1]

S HORTLY AFTER REBECCA joined a new team, tensions
started to rise with her colleague Phil. Rebecca is a petite
thirty-five-year-old Asian American. Phil is a tall, boister-
ous white man, a bit older than Rebecca. Both Rebecca and
Phil are strong contributors to the team and committed to the team's
work. Phil's direct power-over approach and inappropriate jokes
have led Rebecca to become abrupt with Phil. Nasty emails are fly-
ing back and forth, and an escalating dispute is underway. Rebecca
feels disrespected and unsafe. Phil believes Rebecca is incompetent.

Jill and Shruthi work together at a consulting firm. Jill is a senior
consultant, highly experienced and driven. Shruthi recently grad-
uated college and is new to the consulting world. Shruthi agreed
to support Jill on an important client deliverable and, from Jill's
perspective, failed to deliver. Shruthi believes there was a miscommunication. Jill ended up using two days of her vacation to finish
up the project and no longer wants to work with Shruthi.

The names and a few details have been changed, but Rebecca,
Phil, Jill and Shruthi are real people working in companies transitioning to self-management. The tensions and associated emotions
are deep and personal. Both Rebecca and Jill shared their frustrations with the leaders of their respective organizations in hopes
something would be done to fix the problem.

Many tensions that arise don't start out as emotionally charged
as the two examples above. Chris Ashworth is the founder and
CEO at Figure 53, a company making software that controls media

playback in live performances. In Chris's team, tension most often arises from the daily business of managing communication with each other. In his words, "It is very common—certainly weekly and often daily—for teammates here to spend time and energy on recognizing and then discussing behavior that creates issues in small ways. This isn't big stuff but rather issues of tone, or excess negativity, or any other of the many little ways that humans can cause each other to feel unheard, or upset, or anxious, or not validated."[2]

When resolving these small yet important incidents, the skills of knowing when to take a break or slow down a conversation or be more explicit about intention help. Engaging more consciously with even minor issues on a daily basis is important to ensuring they never turn into bigger issues.

## Owning Tension

Think of an elastic band. In its natural state, it is tension free. But as soon as you start pulling at its ends, tension forms. The more you pull, the greater the tension becomes. When you let go, the band flies—how far depends on how much tension was stored up.

Your body behaves similarly. When all is good in your world, you probably hold little to no tension, moving through your days with relative ease. But if something comes up that makes life more difficult or uncomfortable, tensions start to build. It could be something small, such as discovering that someone has reorganized the kitchen so it's harder for you to complete your morning routine. Or it could be something big, like finding out your customer is upset because one of your colleagues didn't deliver on a commitment. Whatever the source of the tension, it's real. You feel it. The longer you hold the tension inside, the more intense it feels. Learning to notice and then name tensions are key skills for building productive and healthy self-managing teams.

The leaders of teams on the journey to self-management are often asked—or feel compelled—to get involved in resolving tensions between team members. Over time, Simon Wakeman from Deeson learned that tensions need to be owned by those involved: "Leaders can end up sitting in a room going, 'Right, well, Fred, you said this, and Paul, you said that.' At Deeson, we no longer get involved in that kind of conversation because those people need to sort things out themselves. If I get involved, I take away their responsibility and the next time they'll come straight to me."[3]

Instead, Simon ensures both individuals have different coaches who they can talk things through with. Neither he nor the coaches intervene directly. He adheres to the underlying principle that responsibility needs to remain with the individuals. Everything is about pushing responsibility to those individuals and then coaching them, equipping them and helping them to find resolutions that work. The team at Enspiral has a similar philosophy, which they refer to as a steward model. Every new contributor on the Enspiral team is matched with a steward. When a conflict emerges, each participant's steward is there to look after the health and well-being of the individual throughout the conflict.

Many tensions are easily resolved through quick conversation. This is especially true in teams where trust is high. When tensions become more intense, so can the emotions for all involved. Our ability to think clearly and rationally declines. The simplest of conversations to agree on a path forward become difficult, if not impossible. For these reasons, it's critical to have a common understanding of how tensions and disagreements will be managed before they arise.

Linda Alvarez, author of *Discovering Agreement*, refers to these pre-agreements as touchstones. They provide the place everyone goes in order to find a path forward. Touchstones for resolving tensions and disagreements can fall under social agreements (see chapter 10) or legal agreements (see chapter 26). In this chapter, we provide ideas for how you may wish to shape and document a common tension-resolution understanding within your company.

## Language

The language you use while resolving tensions directly impacts the speed and effectiveness of resolution. When you use offender and victim language, you shape a toxic dynamic, firmly rooting both parties in defensiveness. The named offender needs to defend their goodness and their rightness. The named victim needs to protect themselves. We all know these roles well. We've played them many times.

A better alternative focuses on an action or collection of actions. Someone was the author of the action(s) and someone was the receiver. This language allows us to anchor to the action rather than the person. Consider Rebecca and Phil's story. We could easily cast Phil as the bad guy based on his power-over approach and inappropriate jokes. Likewise, Rebecca fits the typical role of victim, feeling disrespected and unsafe. With this framing, it's not difficult to imagine emotionally charged conversations erupting between the two. If instead Phil was the author of a series of actions and Rebecca was the receiver, what type of conversations could be possible?

## Space for Pain and Grief

Many traditional employment contracts use *grievance* to reference a conflict, usually between employer and employee. At the heart of a grievance is grief, a sense of loss. The tensions and disagreements—or grievances—we experience are best served when we remember and reflect on the unmet need that conjures that sense of loss. Only then can we address the loss in conversation with empathy and understanding and mutual comprehension.

The author of a tension-triggering act isn't a bad person; they did something that made sense to them from their perspective. With this in mind, it's helpful to look at that context and see how everyone involved may take self-responsibility rather than foisting blame on an accused party. Blame is more likely to inspire retribution or coercion rather than a healing conversation.

In the book *Crucial Conversations* (which we highly recommend), Al Switzler, Joseph Grenny, Kerry Patterson and Ron McMillan encourage each of us to start with heart and avoid the sucker's choice. Often we find ourselves justifying our own sordid behavior because we see only two options: we can either be honest and attack the other person, or we can be kind and withhold the truth... a sucker's choice. A third option exists. We can start with heart, avoiding assumptions and clarifying feelings, including those of pain and grief. When Shruthi agreed to support Jill on an important client deliverable and then failed to deliver, Jill found herself gravitating to a sucker's choice. Does she let loose on Shruthi with all of the anger she has bottled up? Or does she keep the peace by staying silent? The third option is to recognize that the anger she's holding originated from the grief about lost time with family and the feeling of hurt from a belief that Shruthi didn't care. Only when Jill can name and acknowledge her sense of loss will she be able to shift into a space of healthy resolution.

## Processes for Resolving Interpersonal Tensions

The tension-resolution process followed by the team at Morning Star has become a template for many self-managing teams. Their principle of direct communication and gaining agreement applies to any type of disagreement. The process flows as follows:

1. One person asks another to gain agreement.

2. The two sit together and try to sort out their tension privately. In doing so, the initiator has to make a clear request (not a judgment or demand), and the other person has to respond clearly to the request (with a yes, no or counterproposal).

3. If they can't find an agreeable solution, through nomination they identify a colleague whom they both trust to act as a mediator. The colleague's role is to support the parties in finding agreement and not to impose a resolution.

4. If the mediation fails, a panel of topic-relevant colleagues is convened. The panel's role is to listen and help shape an agreement. The panel cannot force a decision but usually carries enough moral weight for matters to come to a conclusion.

5. Only after the first four steps are complete can the founder and president of Morning Star be called into the panel to further reinforce the panel's moral weight.[4]

Since the disagreement is private, all parties are expected to respect confidentiality during and after the processes. The two people at the heart of the conflict must resolve their disagreement between themselves and are discouraged from spreading the conflict by enlisting support and building rival factions.

Other organizations have built on this process and added their own flavors.

In a majority of cases, a tension is exacerbated by the parties feeling unheard and misunderstood. Often, a gentle process of working in trios with a team member may be enough. This team member can help each party stay relaxed and nonreactive so as to truly hear and understand the other's position. The practice of checking in with the other members of the trio for understanding is simple and can unearth unintended assumptions and conclusions.

# Reflect and Act Using Nonviolent Communication

Nonviolent communication (NVC) is a useful tool for resolving interpersonal tensions. To explore NVC in more detail, *Nonviolent Communication* by Marshall Rosenberg is a helpful read.[5]

**Step 1:** Reflect on what occurred and write down what you didn't like.

- List the behaviors about the other person that really bother you.

- Explore the judgments and whatever comes up. The more honest the better.

- Separate behaviors (things observable by a camera) and judgments (all the thoughts and stories you tell yourself about what the behaviors mean).

**Step 2:** Explore your feelings and needs.

- From your initial statements, work to identify your feelings (emotions) with the universal needs that underlie those emotions. For example, when I feel disappointed, it shows me my need for effectiveness isn't being met. For help naming your emotions or needs, type "NVC feelings and needs" into your favorite search engine.

**Step 3:** Prepare to shift your frame of reference.

- Ask yourself, "Am I ready to consider what the other person might be observing, feeling and needing?" Proceed only if the answer is a definite yes! If you do not feel ready, go back to step 1 with the new question: "What do I feel when I think about empathizing with this person?"

**Step 4:** Find empathy for the other person.

- Ask yourself, "What might they be observing, feeling and needing?" Consider why they have reason to feel hurt, fearful and/or anxious? What universal needs might those feelings point to?

**Step 5:** Reconsider your position.

- Notice if your perspective has changed. If so, you may now be on much better footing to have the conversation.

- With this new understanding, how might you best engage with someone who feels and needs what this person might?

## Using interpersonal tension coaches

It can be challenging to resolve an interpersonal tension when emotions are high. Bringing in a neutral, trained third party is a good option. At ET Group, the team selected a few of their most trusted colleagues to be interpersonal tension coaches. Those individuals received additional training in conflict resolution. There are also two members of the team with significantly more training who act as senior interpersonal tension coaches in more challenging scenarios.

## Engaging a senior mediator

In traditional organizations, the most fraught disagreements tend to land in the lap of the team's most senior leader, such as the founder or CEO. In self-managing organizations, the role of senior issue resolver can be assigned to anyone. The team at the Ian Martin Group has replaced the role of the founder and president in step 5 of the Morning Star process with a senior mediator. If the disagreement makes it through steps 1 to 4 without resolution, the senior mediator becomes the steward of a final decision. Any conflict can be escalated immediately to the senior mediator if someone feels a colleague's actions breaks the law, violates an Ian Martin Group conduct rule, demonstrates a refusal to earnestly engage in this process or if the colleague continues destructive behavior. The senior mediator, not the company president, becomes the final decision maker.

### Calling a review board

Another alternative is a review board. At Figure 53, if individuals are unable to resolve conflicts alone, the option exists to call a review board. Its role is to devise a response to the incident or problem that considers the best interests of the company and all involved. The review board is made up of three or four colleagues: one chosen by the founder, one chosen by each individual whose actions are the subject of the board and one chosen by the rest of the team.

## How to Be a Helpful Coach

When friends and colleagues ask for help, many of us jump to problem-solving mode. Based on our own experiences, how would *we* tackle this challenge? To be most helpful, you need to resist this urge. If you become the problem solver, you disempower the individual and remove their responsibility. More importantly, you waste an awesome learning opportunity. Instead of being a problem solver, the best coaches play a supporting role by:

- Helping your colleague turn the lens inward and supporting the skills of self-awareness and self-management.

- Firmly anchoring conversations in behaviors and experiences (author and receiver language) rather than labels (offender and victim language).

- Helping unpack and identify the core emotions at play. (For example, is anger a secondary emotion to fear, sadness, worry, loss, disappointment or discouragement?)

- Creating space between your colleague's experience and their initial emotional response, thereby providing the opportunity for reflection and choice.

- Offering strategies and teaching skills without prescribing a solution.

The role of facilitator (also referred to as a mediator in the Morning Star process) is similar to that of a coach. Rather than supporting one person, facilitators create a safe space for all involved, again while staying out of problem-solving mode.

Becoming an exceptional coach or facilitator requires time, training and practice. For those organizations on the journey to self-management, building coaching and facilitation skills on the team are worthwhile investments. Until those skills are adequately established, engaging outside practitioners is a good alternative.

# 15

# Meaningful Meetings

## Design Gatherings That People Want to Attend

"Meetings should be like salt—a spice sprinkled carefully to enhance a dish, not poured recklessly over every forkful."

**JASON FRIED**[1]

WITH SO MANY of us more practiced than ever in remote working, we rely on meetings as a way to do everything from share information to gain context to synchronize next steps. As a result, the way we structure meetings has taken on a whole new level of importance.

Meetings don't have to be terribly draining or a waste of time. They can provide some of the best opportunities for connection, coherence building and deliberate development. The way meetings are structured and facilitated is critical. This doesn't mean you can never have a meeting without an agenda, but you should never have a meeting without everyone knowing its objective. Consider invoking the law of two feet: "If at any point during our time together, you find yourself neither learning nor contributing nor strengthening relationships, use your two feet and go someplace else." How would your meetings change if this rule was in place and being lived?

Meetings serve a multitude of needs for us and our teams. The COVID-19 pandemic saw so many more of us moving our traditional in-person meetings to the virtual world. One result has been a greater focus on rethinking what meetings are for and how they can be most useful.

Different types of meetings serve different purposes. The team at Percolab distilled four reasons for meetings:

1. announcements and the one-way dissemination of information;

2. feedback, where information is shared for which the sharer seeks a response in real time;

3. cocreation, or doing work together in the moment, such as working on strategy and

4. proposals and decisions, that benefit from being done synchronously.

For their weekly management meeting, they use what they call a wise meeting agenda template, which lives in a shared drive and is populated during the week. It's a simple process of adding your name and topic under one of the four categories listed above, along with the number of minutes needed. This process helps in two ways: it keeps the person with the need accountable for not taking up more time than they request, and it allows the facilitator to triage and ask for help in prioritizing if the time allocated is oversubscribed.

Many organizations use the Holacracy practices of tactical and governance meetings, either in their pure form or in an adapted form. (Guides for running such meetings can be found online.) Enspiral uses a riff on the tactical meeting template for its board meetings and as a persistent place for meeting minutes. It's a simple spreadsheet with five tabs: checklist, actions, metrics, agenda and roles.

## Facilitation Is a Craft

Whether in person or online, the role of meeting facilitator is crucial. More often than not, meetings are chaired by the most senior person, or a delegate thereof. Susan worked at a multinational that held biweekly meetings for major project status updates. These were hour-long meetings with twenty-plus people in two conference rooms on either side of the country. The project manager hosting the meeting always picked the projects with the fewest issues because he knew that the CEO would blow a gasket if things weren't on track. This is not the kind of facilitation we are advocating.

Great facilitators ensure that the objective of the meeting is met. They have the capacity and mandate to read the room (in person or virtually) and guide its energy. It's best if the facilitator is not always the person with the greatest perceived power, as that consolidates too much power within one person. Kate Beecroft from Greaterthan shares tips for facilitation:

> Always have an objective for each meeting or intervention, even if that objective is to let the group explore. A guiding objective gives the group a place to go if things get off course.
>
> Be prepared by creating an agenda, but don't necessarily stick to it. Have a loose plan, even if the discussion needs to go somewhere else. As you gain experience, you'll be able to judge when staying on a certain topic is a better use of time than following the agenda.
>
> Get consent to facilitate. Attempting to facilitate otherwise can be at worst coercive (unfair to the group) and dangerous (unfair to the facilitator). Without consent, the facilitator might face resistance and the group (and discussion) will be confused.
>
> After receiving the mandate, the facilitator has a responsibility to the group. Facilitators will spend more time talking than others and must direct the group's attention; however, this must be done in service to the group.[2]

Well-run meetings can benefit from additional supporting roles, for example a timekeeper (who keeps the time for timeboxed items on the agenda or ensures the meeting starts and finishes on time), a scribe or harvester (who captures important notes and action items throughout the meeting) and a logistics person (who sends out invitations, the agenda or pre-work and sets up the meeting space, including arranging any snacks or meals). Unless decided otherwise, the facilitator's job is to ensure these roles are filled. Consider rotating them so that everyone takes a turn; doing so balances power dynamics in the meeting and allows everyone to understand how challenging it can be to fill these roles.

## Tips for Running Great Remote Meetings

Remote meetings present unique challenges that many of us have limited experience managing. It wasn't long ago that video conferencing was limited to specially equipped meeting rooms. Hosting virtual meetings is now an everyday occurrence for many. Here are some questions to think about and steps to take to deliver the best possible meeting experience.

### Prepare the tech

First you must choose a platform. Which is best for your group and the meeting's purpose? Do participants need to create an account or download anything in advance? Does your company's firewall allow it? What's your backup if you encounter last-minute difficulties with your preferred platform?

You also need to provide technical guidelines and an opportunity for troubleshooting. Could users do a test call to check that their audio and video is working? Do you have a tip sheet, or do you offer a brief call to introduce the technology for those who need it? You also need to sort out how people can join. Is by phone okay, or do you want to mandate computer-only participation to maximize interactive functions like video and live chat? What's the protocol for late joiners?

### Prepare for facilitating

Decide in advance if you want to prepare an agenda or if you will cocreate it live during the call. Either way, make sure to share any links to agenda, reference, support or visual documents ahead of time (and watch those sharing permissions).

To guide you as you facilitate, make a cheat sheet and a run sheet (agenda items along with purpose, timing and so on), written instructions for any interactive elements (such as question prompts, check-in questions, interaction scripts) and links to synchronous work documents (such as Google Docs or Slides, Mural, relevant resources and so on). Again, check that the sharing/editing permissions are correct so people can contribute as needed.

Check that your tech is working by testing your audio and video. Practice any maneuvers (like breakout rooms) beforehand if you're new to them.

## Overcome arrival awkwardness

In the first five minutes, people will be arriving in the online meeting space, troubleshooting their tech or waiting for the meeting to begin. Instead of that awkward silence or stilted small talk, you can support people to connect and orient themselves. For example, you might welcome people as they arrive, saying hello and checking that each participant's audio and video is working. Remind people to select gallery view, instead of speaker view, so they can see everyone, and make sure their display name is correct and visible. While you wait for the full group to arrive, you might consider an introductory activity like getting people to change their display name to add their location (if you're a globally distributed team), or something more fun like your superhero name. Or have them answer a simple question in the chat.

## Check in

If your group size is smaller than twelve people, a great practice for fostering connectedness and focus is to do a check-in round: ask a question or offer a conversation prompt to help people arrive, be present and connect to one another. The check-in question can be as simple as "How are you feeling in this moment?" Try experimenting with different questions, depending on whether you want to deepen the connection or introduce a bit of fun, energy or humor. Because you can't create a physical circle to do a round, either the facilitator can read out names in the order they appear on screen, or each person can volunteer the next person following their own check-in. You could also ask everyone to join in a minute of silence or to take three deep breaths together.

If your group is larger than twelve people, a check-in round takes too long (although you might decide in some cases it's worth the time investment). With a larger group, in order to have people interact from the start, try a structure such as 1-2-4-All from Liberating Structures (a series of thirty-three practical methods for meeting, planning, deciding and relating to one another), set up breakout rooms in pairs or trios for checking in or have them type an answer to a check-in question in the chat.

## Clarify roles and responsibilities

Facilitating and taking care of the tech simultaneously can be tricky. Beforehand or on the fly, consider asking for volunteers to fill these two additional roles: a tech facilitator to manage breakout rooms and tech issues, and a live blogger to share highlights and important soundbites from the spoken conversation in the live chat, along with links, terms or resources mentioned.

## Foster engagement during the meeting

In remote meetings where it's harder to pick up on the nuances of microexpressions, it's even more important to intentionally foster engagement and full participation. For example, you might try "roomio" (a riff on the online voting platform Loomio), when voting in response to a proposal (for example, "Shall we record this call?"):

· Thumbs-up means "I agree." (I want the proposal to go ahead.)

· Thumb to the side means "I abstain." (I am happy for the group to decide.)

- Thumbs-down means "I disagree." (I think we can do better.)

- Hand up means "I block." (I veto the decision.)

You can also use fist to five (as described in chapter 12) to gauge people's resonance with an idea, and encourage other hand gestures to amplify reactions without taking up time or audio space, for example, "sparkle fingers" to show appreciation or enthusiasm when someone is talking.

## Check out

Leaving a remote meeting can feel a bit abrupt, so it's valuable to do something as a group to check out. You could do a check-out round (if manageable for the group's size), where each person responds to a question or a prompt, or you could do something synchronous to check out, such as a gesture or typing a comment in the chat.

TAKE TIME to really consider and understand the objective for your meetings, and keep practicing these techniques together. Review the effectiveness and energy of your meetings regularly with retrospectives. Consider a pulse check or a fist to five at the end of each meeting to avoid complacency. At their best, meetings provide the space to connect and deepen relationships as well as build coherence, again and again.

# 16

# Personal Growth

Intentionally
Develop Yourself
and Your Team

"The minute we separate development from how we do things every day, this gets us into trouble—culture is operations, operations is culture."

**BRYAN UNGARD**[1]

A S WITH MANY topics in this book, we begin here with awareness—the willingness to step back and notice what is actually happening in our companies. When we were in school, it was expected we'd learn skills and facts that would be useful in life. It was also assumed that we'd learn how to develop relationships, friendships, partnerships and teamwork. This is what humans do: we form and nurture relationships, and those relationships help us grow. We work through the messiness of complex problems and relationship dynamics in school, and we do so in our families. Why is it that we so often avoid the difficult work of enhancing our "being human" skills in the workplace? What more would be possible if we not only recognized but really leaned into the messiness of humans coming together to work, learn and grow?

Most workplaces prioritize the mechanics of the work above all else while relationship building is pushed aside, so much so that we've forgotten how to integrate it into our days. Whether the "relationship stuff" takes five minutes or five hours, it's treated as not integral, integrated or valuable to the work, but as separate, a waste of time, not useful, soft.

Practicing these skills doesn't need to be complicated or time-consuming. For example, many teams use check-ins to start every meeting. The simple practice of gathering a bit of information about each other builds connection: "I'm a little tired today, still recovering from a cold." "I'm really distracted because I'm behind on the report I'm writing." "I'm fired up! I've had a breakthrough in the last few days so I'm feeling super energized."

This is all useful information about whether the team can go fast or needs to be more mindful, whether the team is firing on all cylinders or needs to reprioritize. This is also human relationship data. When we pretend to be "on" all the time, we are enacting a farce. We all ride our own physical, mental and emotional roller coasters. When we tune in to how we are feeling and share that information, a powerful interdependence emerges.

This is not to say that the check-in is the holy grail. It's merely one practice. How you use it and what question you ask will lead to varying experiences thanks to the uniqueness of your team. Practices such as this one are tactically simple to implement. But until a strong leader—like you—chances trying something out of the norm, nothing new can emerge.

## Deliberately Developmental Organizations

For many years, leaders have invested time, energy and effort into attracting, recruiting and retaining the "best" people—the most knowledgeable or the most experienced—and have continually searched for those who they believe will ensure the organization succeeds. This approach is anchored in a belief that a small percentage of the workforce—primarily those with leadership potential—is worth the investment.

But a growing movement of organizations operates with a deliberate focus on, and commitment to, the ongoing development of all team members. These companies base their cultures on the premise that within everyday operations it's possible to support and encourage people's ongoing development.

Deliberately developmental organizations (DDOs) support all team members in exploring their own growth, establishing their own development goals and finding opportunities within the business to develop. This differs from the annual appraisal philosophy, where an employee is given feedback and agrees to improve in a particular area. Instead, DDOs focus on self-directed growth and exploration, providing opportunities for development. This simple yet profound approach is producing incredible results around the world.

A DDO's focus is firmly rooted in developing the capacities of all employees using the culture and operations of the business as the classroom. DDOs operate on the foundational assumptions that adults can grow through a combination of challenge and support and that the workplace is a perfect place to do this learning. A simple example is sharing a desire you have to be a proficient public speaker as well as your terror at the thought. Together with colleagues, you would then find everyday opportunities to practice, such as in team meetings or low-risk presentations. Another example is declaring that you and your team have no idea how to articulate a strategy, being willing to share this reality openly, then exploring together how to develop this capability.

In addition to having a mission statement or purpose statement, DDOs also have developmental principles that live through employee's actions and behaviors. In a strong developmental culture, principles are discussed, debated, applied, revised, posted; in short, they are ever present and play an active daily role. One DDO has a principle that it is okay to make a mistake, but unacceptable not to identify, analyze and learn from it.

Like all businesses, DDOs need to monitor their bottom line and productivity, but they see productivity and human development as interlinked, not mutually exclusive. Bold business aspirations such as high profitability and the development of people are seen as parts of a single whole.

## A Multifaceted DDO

Decurion employs approximately 1,100 people in California. It cultivates the conditions for the business to flourish *and* for people to flourish by enabling people to self-direct their own lives and their own contributions within the Decurion community. Decurion demonstrates the deliberate aspect of a DDO by routinely encouraging people to consider what they themselves and their teams don't yet know how to do and to identify what they need in order to develop.

Within Decurion's ArcLight Cinemas, there is a senior role dedicated to supporting the operations and culture of each cinema. As the individual in this role becomes competent at leading their cinema and their teams, their personal growth is supported. They may be asked to move to a different cinema or another part of the business so they can experience a new challenge. To remain merely competent in one role does not provide the opportunity to grow and develop.

Personal development is alive at Decurion's Hollybrook Senior Living facility too. A survey completed by colleagues surfaced what skills would help caregivers in their personal and professional lives. These included assertiveness, budgeting and self-regulation skills. Open workshops provide training in the areas each individual identifies for their growth and development, with the support of their colleagues provided along the way.

Bryan Ungard, Decurion's chief purpose officer, says, "Development can be a tough process sometimes; it's full of ambiguity, anxiety and confusion. Decurion's role is to actively sit alongside people and to support their growth and development in a way that makes sense to them."[2]

## Start Small

Introducing the notion that all adults can grow—and that our workplace is a great environment to do so—is a perfect place to start. Think about your organization as a community where all of the elements of the business exist to provide opportunities for individuals' ongoing development. Start with yourself and expand to your immediate team. Over time, the concept will catch on. Introduce new questions into conversations that invite shared vulnerability and exploration:

- What outcome do I/we/you desire that has not yet been achieved?

- Where do I/we/you need to develop to achieve this outcome?

- What new thing do I/we/you want to work on and learn about together?

- How does this area of development link to the business and support it to flourish?

- How can our colleagues support me/you/us in deliberately finding places to practice this?

- In what ways do I/you/we need to be supported?

Practices like peer development triads (introduced in chapter 13) and working out loud circles bring colleagues together for thirty- to sixty-minute practice sessions per week for personal and professional development. In working out loud circles, designed by John Stepper, colleagues commit to meet for an hour per week for twelve weeks. He explains, "A working out loud circle is a small peer support group in which you pick a goal and build a network of relationships that can help you with that goal... By the end of your twelve weeks in a circle, you'll have developed a larger, more diverse network and a set of habits you can apply toward any goal."[3]

# Reflect and Act on Your Development

How much time do you invest in your own development? How much do you support others with theirs? Meet regularly and intentionally to hold yourself and your peers accountable to development goals. The more we identify our needs and aspirations collectively, the more we learn how to encourage one another from a place of peerdom as opposed to projection or coercion. Radical accountability encourages each of us to plow through the resistance and know we have each other's backs. Here are four questions to help you reflect on your own development:

- What is the next development area or learning goal I have set for myself?

- What resistance will I need to plow through?

- Who is my accountability partner?

- Have I given that person permission to hold me to account and let them know how best to do so?

# Transparency

Determine When,
How and Why
to Share Information

"If you want people to make the same decisions that you would make, but in a more scalable way, you have to give them the same information you have."

**KEITH RABOIS**[1]

I N OUR FAST-PACED world, members of our teams need to make increasingly complex decisions more often. Transparency ensures everyone has the information to make good decisions and it requires more than just the free flow of data. Decision-making requires the capacity to turn information into meaningful, actionable insights. Done well, transparency can boost business results, breed trust, help with innovation and support learning.

Transparency clarifies where power lies and where the action happens. One of the best moves to increase transparency is to ensure every team member knows how each decision is made, whether by an individual, a group or through a process. At employee-owned Once Again Nut Butter, after transparency issues arose regarding how decisions were made, the process was made explicitly clear, resulting in improved communication and collaboration at all levels of the company.[2]

Agile teams have long relied on multiple tools and systems to support transparency. Kanban boards, software sprint boards and burndown charts are examples of physical and electronic tools to make information visible and dispel assumptions. Everyone can see the good, the bad and the ugly.

Our willingness to work transparently—or not—comes from our beliefs. Are others capable of handling the ambiguity and anxiety that often accompanies the "burden of knowledge"? Can the team work through provocative conversations without getting distracted by information not immediately relevant? Do our colleagues have the skill to manage challenging or even confidential information appropriately?

Moving toward transparency allows a team to grow its capacity. If we prioritize creating more transparency, teams learn to deal with higher degrees of ambiguity, develop the skills to have challenging conversations and build capacity to focus on relevant information. All of these skills are useful in many teams and essential in self-managing teams.

## Where to Start

Transparency within an organization is not binary—information is never fully hidden from or fully available to everyone. Even when attempting to operate transparently, there is always more to share. The criteria for what and how widely to share varies from team to team. To start, you can open up previously confidential internal communications to more team members. Internal messaging apps, such as Slack, are great tools for doing just that. On the more extreme end of the spectrum, you can open up salary and financial information to the entire world. Some companies are attaining excellent business results from extreme transparency.

The social media platform Buffer has set the bar on transparency. On its website you can find the entire team's salaries, stock options, perks and benefits as well as pricing, revenue, profit, expenses, diversity data, log of internal communication, source code for much of their product and more.[3] In a *Harvard Business Review* article, Ryan Buell talks about the value of operational transparency, or showing your customers where their money is being spent.[4] Buffer puts this into practice by sharing the breakdown of expenses that go into delivering the product. How do you feel knowing Buffer spends 65 percent of every dollar you give them on salaries, 95 percent of which is focused on product and support? Do you have any pause over the 4 percent profit that they take so their business can be more sustainable and therefore guarantees they'll be available as a supplier for longer? Ryan found this sort of operational transparency not only increases sales but also people's trust and satisfaction.

Consider sharing the following more broadly:

- Details of your team's culture, which might include vision, mission, values or some combination thereof (see nearsoft.com/blog)

- Your internal communications channels (see the SideFX story below)

- Your internal handbook or playbook (see handbook.etgroup.ca)

- Your pricing model (see open.buffer.com/transparent-pricing-buffer)

- Portions of your source code (see sylius.com)

- Your product roadmap (see api.slack.com/roadmap)

- Your entire customer base (see bullfrogpower.com/bullfrog-community)

- Your complete hiring process (see deeson.co.uk/careers)

- Your financials, including revenue, costs, salaries, stock options and so on. Tools such as Baremetrics make this easy and increasingly common.

When the team at SideFX implemented Slack as a tool for boosting efficient and effective communication, they used many closed channels, meaning conversations within that channel were available only to those specifically granted access. After some experimentation, the team decided to open most channels to full company access. The result? While participation in each channel remained relatively unchanged, everyone was able to browse conversations at will. By removing an unnecessary level of secrecy, the team was no longer left wondering what their colleagues were up to.

To decide if you're ready for more transparency, here are a few questions you might ask yourself:

- When looking at the causes of slow or inaccurate decision-making, how much can be attributed to the lack of transparent data?

- Do your colleagues have sufficient training to turn data into actionable next steps? For example, do they know how to interpret financial data in ways that help them make decisions?

- Do you and your team share information frequently and fully in a timely manner? Data gets stale quickly. Partial data leaves colleagues guessing and leads to assumption-making.

- Does the team have sufficient experience with the difficult conversations that might arise from increased transparency?

- Are you looking for and leaving yourself time to see the positives that come from transparency? Any shift in a system creates new challenges. The benefits of having a more informed team accrue over time.

## Potential Challenges

On the other side of the coin, there may be valid reasons for limiting transparency. Let's separate out the valid reasons from the fear-based ones. Some data may need to remain confidential, including the data your clients entrust to you, sensitive personal information related to team members, such as social security numbers and health records, and any other information that is not yours to share, such as data protected under an NDA. You may convince yourself that other data needs to remain secret. There are four common stories we tell ourselves when it comes to minimizing transparency: that revealed proprietary information may be used against us; that sharing too much information decreases team focus with distractions and ambiguity; that hoarding information makes us more powerful, and we enjoy that power; and that transparency leads to difficult and uncomfortable conversations that we'd prefer to avoid.

Let's explore these four stories one at a time.

## Proprietary information

Joel Gascoigne of Buffer says transparency breeds trust. Duncan Oyevaar, founding partner of OpenBook.Works, agrees, "The main concern most people have when it comes to transparency is whether... it will be shared with the competition. Experience shows when you give someone trust, you will receive trust in return."[5] It's true that some information may need to remain confidential. That said, Buffer's extensive experiment with transparency is a case study in how sharing information can build trust with customers without exposing a company to undue risk. If you decide to share information more broadly, start slowly to build confidence, then expand. If a colleague shares too much, handle that case directly rather than withdrawing from transparency altogether.

## Decreased team focus

In today's information-rich world, we can become overwhelmed with too much data. To counteract the risk of overwhelm, create transparency first around information that matters and is actionable. Your colleagues will spend the time to understand things that matter. Building the capacity to handle ambiguity is a critical skill for surviving and thriving in business today. Introduce transparency at a pace that allows team members to strengthen that muscle. Younger generations are becoming accustomed to sorting through large amounts of information quickly.

## Maintaining power

Power can be addictive; sometimes our addiction to it comes from a desire to control. Just as often, it comes from a place of fear. Increasing transparency can create a great deal of angst at the start, especially for those who have held power. Understanding and inviting this fear into the conversation is part of the learning journey. Ask what others need. Share your own needs. You may be surprised by what you learn and how you grow.

## Uncomfortable conversations

The ability to manage interpersonal tension is another critical skill in the sphere of self-management. It's a capacity that needs to be built and nurtured. Exposing more information can naturally lead to increased tension and more difficult conversations. Don't let this fear hold you or your colleagues back. As the saying goes, "Feel the fear and do it anyway"—while developing the necessary skills in the process.

## Tools for Transparency

Technology changes quickly. Undoubtedly there will be new tools available before this book goes to print. Here are some of our current favorites for creating a more transparent workplace. Each allows more visibility around works-in-progress and real-time status updates across teams. Keep your eyes open for new and better options as they emerge:

**G Suite or Microsoft Office 365** Both tool sets offer powerful and easy ways to share working documents. We wrote and edited this book together in real time from different places around the world using Google Docs. Especially helpful are the commenting and suggesting modes.

**Google Drive, Dropbox or Box** These shared storage spaces are great for sharing documents and files created in your organization. Keeping these spaces well organized is critical for the data to be useful.

**Trello, Asana or Monday.com** These web-based task lists are incredible tools for sharing and prioritizing work. We used Trello for coordinating our individual work while writing this book.

**Slack or Microsoft Teams** These communication tools can supplement or even supplant internal email. As many discovered while working from home during the COVID-19 outbreak, these tools are especially great for remote teams. One big advantage is the ability to add people to a thread, which allows them to see the conversation history while keeping their individual inboxes clear.

**Loomio or Cloverpop** Both of these apps simplify the decision-making process and make it transparent.

**Zoom, GoToMeeting or Google Meet** Teams using video conferencing tools such as Zoom can record meetings and make those recordings available to the entire team.

**Scrum or Kanban boards** These physical (preferably) or virtual boards track the progress of things to be done, typically using categories like planned, doing, done and launched. They are excellent for visualizing and prioritizing work and making it broadly transparent.

Transparency is not about overwhelming colleagues with mass amounts of unnecessary and unhelpful data or tools. It is about removing barriers to effective contributions and increasing psychological safety. Traditionally, when in doubt, we keep information confidential. As you step further into leadership within a self-managing context, we encourage you to experiment with the idea of "When in doubt, share it out." Help your organization make transparency the norm.

# 18

# **Compensation**

Consider a Fresh
Perspective on
Value Exchange

"Because money is still (one of) the most taboo subjects in society, it's the perfect place for us to hide our shadows."

**PETER KOENIG**[1]

EADING ABOUT organizations with transparent salaries can feel at once transformative and salacious. Discovering what your colleagues earn elicits all sorts of emotions and may become fodder for gossip and judgment. Is it equitable pay for equitable work? How is equitable work measured? Are the measures objective and fair? Meritocracy, as decided by those in power, is not the answer. At its root is a system of value judgments made from a limited perspective.

Compensation traditionally consists of three pillars: salary, variable compensation and equity. Salaries intend to fairly value an individual's day-to-day contributions. Processes to set salaries are usually regimented, inflexible formulas or kept confidential to hide discrepancies and avoid difficult conversations. Variable compensation is most often used as a carrot-and-stick approach to influence performance. It also mitigates the risk of expenses outpacing revenues. Ownership and equity aim to reward risk-taking, build a sense of personal connection and retain team members. Although this is logical in theory, you may sense how these three compensation pillars feel out of step with many of the concepts we've been exploring in previous chapters. The traditional approach to compensation is deeply rooted in putting human resources into boxes to be measured and priced.

## Self-Managed Compensation

In self-managed organizations, setting compensation tends to rely much more on transparency, crowdsourced data and negotiation. Some progressive organizations have removed bonus plans altogether, choosing instead to use company-wide profit sharing. Company ownership becomes rebalanced to better represent both individual contributions and risk, with greater fairness applied in determining how the pie gets sliced. Your team needs to create a compensation system that works best for your organization. Here we share examples of compensation approaches that challenge the status quo.

### Salary change proposals

Morning Star uses a system where, at the end of the calendar year, each colleague associated with a factory approaches a representative compensation committee of factory peers and shares their colleague letter of understanding (as outlined in chapter 10) and performance measures for the previous year (called Steppingstones). If the colleague desires a pay increase above the official government cost of living increase for the upcoming year, they present a business case for the increase and negotiate the request with the committee. If the colleague chooses not to present a business case for an increase, then they can expect to receive only the cost of living adjustment.[2]

### Capability mapping

Another option is to set compensation based on an individual's relevant capabilities. The team at innovation design firm The Moment is internally transparent with compensation and embraces many other progressive philosophies. As the team expanded, a project was launched to design a scalable compensation approach. The team developed a comprehensive competency rubric consisting of twenty-six different measures that allows each team member to plot their personal development, both as a consultant and a contributor to the business. Individuals complete a self-assessment against the twenty-six measures and ask three colleagues for input. The four colleagues then meet, share reflections and discuss the ratings. At their own discretion, the individual then updates their self-assessment based on the feedback received. The final ratings map to a compensation matrix. All final self-ratings are made visible to the entire team.

In the first attempt to use this open compensation framework, the founders were uncomfortable with the final ratings, realizing team members had differing interpretations of the rubric. Rather than using the data directly, the founders made final compensation decisions using the ratings as a significant input. Erika Bailey, current leader of The Moment, says, "This wasn't a great moment for us. From a team member point of view, it was tough to participate and then not participate. This shook trust a bit."[3] The first pass through the process was a bit clunky and each iteration has helped bring more sophistication and refinement. The founders now participate as equal team members and are no longer involved in a decision-making capacity. As a result, the process is more true to its promise of self-set compensation.

In reflection, cofounder Greg Judelman says, "Designing a scalable compensation approach has taken us more time than anticipated and required personal courage by everyone involved. But it's been worth it—we've grown and jelled as a team and have a clear sense of the collective values that we're working and living for."[4]

## Collaborative salary setting

With collaboration, transparency and trust being critical elements in practicing Teal, all team members at Fitzii—a company within the Ian Martin Group—know one another's salaries, and detailed company financials are available for review each month. After their first year with the company, each team member is eligible to participate in a compensation advice process (CAP), during which they seek the advice of their peers, investigate the market and understand how their compensation fits within the budget. Equipped with that information, individuals decide on their salary and publish their reasoning in a proposal that uses the consent process. Interestingly, team members routinely pay themselves less (not more) than they would have asked for from a boss.

## Fully transparent compensation

As a beacon of transparency in everything it does, Buffer published an instructive article on its website about how it calculates team salaries, using factors such as market data, location, cost of living, role value, experience, loyalty and risk tolerance. This system makes salary calculations fair and transparent. It also provides team members direct visibility on how they can increase their compensation.

## Needs-based compensation

In early stage companies where revenue is unpredictable, leaders can show care by understanding and meeting each team member's base financial needs, which is often also a necessity for the organization's survival.

At Enspiral, small teams known as livelihood pods have open conversations about personal needs. Based on the concept of abundance, everyone requests and receives the minimum they need to sustain themselves. Two examples of livelihood pods are Root Systems (software developers) and Golden Pandas (facilitators, consultants and teachers). As revenues generated by the livelihood pods increase, compensation conversations follow. The Root Systems livelihood pod calculates a month's pay by adding a business viability bonus and a performance bonus to a base income. Base income is the monthly amount a core member will always receive, no matter how many hours they work. The business viability bonus is an additional amount paid based on how sustainable the team perceives the business to be. A performance bonus is added based on work that brings money to the organization. How exactly these different amounts are calculated depends on the team's current financial buffer and the activity types conducted during the month.

## Crowdsourced compensation

Crowdsourcing provides insights to make well-informed decisions. HolacracyOne is the consulting and training company behind Holacracy, which we explore further in chapter 25. In the early days at HolacracyOne, coworkers filled out a survey about all their colleagues with only two ratings: this person contributes (much) more or (much) less than me (on a scale from +3 to -3), and this person has a good basis to evaluate me (on a scale of 1 to 5). An algorithm was used to process the data collected, and colleagues were grouped into salary buckets. In a system like this, "The more experienced, knowledgeable and hard-working people land in the higher buckets that earn bigger salaries; the more junior, less experienced colleagues naturally gravitate toward buckets with lower salaries."[5] Because the team at HolacracyOne has grown, this early approach reached its limits so the team began experimenting with different approaches. They now use a method similar to Fitzii's, where anyone can propose the amount of their compensation, and a vetting process, which involves many of their colleagues, follows. Those involved in the vetting have to answer a simple question: "If this person didn't already work here, would you advocate for hiring them at their proposed new compensation level?" All compensation amounts in the company are transparent internally, so each team member can triangulate on an appropriate compensation level for themselves by internal comparison, in addition to using external market data. This system has proven quite effective and scalable for the company and has been copied by many other organizations as well.

## Centralized compensation team

A centralized team to help with compensation decisions provides consistency. At software company Valve, a designated group of employees (which changes over time) interviews everyone in the company annually. They ask for feedback on each individual the interviewee has worked with over the past year. The information collected is used primarily for constructive feedback. They also ask the individual to rank each member of their own project or product group on four metrics: skill level/technical ability, productivity/output, group contribution and product contribution. Each of these metrics is given equal weight in compiling a stack ranking of all employees and is used to determine compensation.[6]

## Compensation sponsorship

For many, championing our own compensation increase feels uncomfortable. It's an area where we have little experience or expertise. In Miovision's early days and prior to the team developing more sophisticated compensation processes, each member of the team had a sponsor for their compensation. It was up to the compensation sponsors to ensure team members were paid fairly. In this model, when compensation issues arise, the sponsor works through the issue with a shared responsibility to the company and the individual.

## Allocating project budgets

The team at consulting firm Greaterthan has been using the Happy Money Story game, developed by Charles Davies, to decide how to distribute team budgets.[7] At its core, the game is a playful way to openly discuss how to distribute money among a group. The most important rule is that everyone must leave the conversation feeling happy about the result. In multiple rounds, team members propose how to split the money with a story about why. A Happy Money Story is as much an opportunity to describe the project from multiple perspectives as it is to distribute the money. For example, a globally distributed team may find it hard to discern the effort team members put in, beyond client delivery. A team member might say, "I think Elena should be recognized for the time it took to redo the documentation after the last retro," which is work that may not have been seen by the entire team. Participants keep going around until a story is shared that everyone feels happy with.

For Francesca Pick, a partner at Greaterthan, there are several reasons why this is a great practice. "It builds a lot of trust with teams around a subject that can feel scary or confronting; it enables you to build shared vocabulary around money and value and it also helps each participant become more aware of what money represents to themselves in different situations."[8]

## Sales compensation

The above compensation mechanisms work well in many organizations, but can they work for sales teams? Sales compensation is usually designed with the belief that sellers need the opportunity to earn commission to stay motivated. Several companies have proven this assumption wrong.

Culture Amp is a fast-growing, San Francisco–based software-as-a-service (SaaS) company that focuses on measuring company cultures over time. They are privy to a mass amount of data and came to realize that compensation wasn't a driver of engagement, including for those in sales roles. They found that salespeople want the same things as most other professionals: career development, challenges, meaningful work and a good team. At Culture Amp, everyone is paid a salary appropriate to their role and experience.[9]

Recognition is a big driver of engagement. Culture Amp celebrates sales wins and shares recognition using clever puns. The puns are so funny and engaging that most members of the company read them. The puns include anyone who contributed meaningfully to the deal. It's quite an honor to get a shout-out in a pun. Despite not having a sales commission plan, sellers still have quotas. Quotas provide a useful measure in determining who may be ready for advancement or need additional support. The quotas also show up on a scoreboard as a way of encouraging friendly competition. However, Culture Amp doesn't experience the selfish actions that happen in organizations where personal sales success directly affects take-home pay. Instead, people are more than willing to lend a hand, share expertise and help close business to benefit the overall team. Customers also benefit through increased trust in working with a company where nobody is protective of the customer relationship to the exclusion of others.

This model isn't a universal elixir. Not everyone is a great fit for this sort of role. Hiring needs to be intentional. Some top-performing sales recruits will be hesitant to give up the chance to win big. For those who prioritize team atmosphere, intentional development and great product work, this approach will resonate. The results at Culture Amp speak for themselves: sales tripled over eighteen months, the sales team grew to more than eighty people and they only lost three sellers in three years. These stats are impressive since the average tenure for SaaS salespeople at many companies in Silicon Valley is only twelve months.

## On Ownership

When a team consists of the right people who communicate openly, make commitments to one another and support each other's growth, there is the possibility of a different sort of relationship to risk and ownership. If a founder believes in the importance and value of nurturing a creative spirit and energy—their own and others'—their philosophy on ownership can play an important role. We can't ignore or discount the emotional labor most founders endure when building an organization—and the feeling of responsibility and accountability they have for the livelihoods of their colleagues.

Entrepreneur, author and lecturer Mike Moyer has written extensively about a philosophy for fairly distributing equity. *Slicing Pie* offers a simple formula based on the principle that a person's percent share of the equity should always be equal to that person's share of the at-risk contributions.[10] At-risk contributions include time, money, ideas, relationships, supplies, equipment, facilities or anything else someone provides without full payment of its fair market value. This means anyone who risks more, such as a founder whose salary goes unpaid early on, would be compensated over time with a greater share of equity and/or profit. This approach provides ways to accommodate colleagues with differing risk profiles. It also allows people to evolve their equity agreements when their risk profiles shift due to life changes.

DISCUSSING COMPENSATION is challenging, even in teams where psychological safety is well established. If you are ready to start exploring new and different compensation approaches, here are some suggestions for the journey:

- Invite input from everyone impacted.

- Make sure to get expert input around compliance and legal issues.

- Be clear about who the decision maker is for any change.

- Be transparent about the decision-making process and provide updates each step of the way.

- Establish guiding principles for compensation design.

- Provide ample time for the process to unfold without undue pressure.

- Tune in to how easily old compensation paradigms can influence thinking.

- Consider using a third-party facilitator to help guide the process.

# 19

# Diversity and Inclusion

Break Free from
Bias and the Failure
of Meritocracy

"Our ability to reach unity in diversity
will be the beauty and the test of our
civilization."

**MAHATMA GANDHI**[1]

F OR AS "WOKE" as we imagine ourselves to be, bias is hard-wired into all of us. As Nicholas Kristof writes in the *New York Times*, "The human brain seems to be wired so that it categorizes people by race in the first one-fifth of a second after seeing a face... Even when people are told to sort people by gender, the brain still groups people by race. Racial bias also begins astonishingly early: even infants often show a preference for their own racial group."[2]

It's a lovely aspiration that a more diverse and inclusive workplace will allow people to contribute their unique brilliance to the challenges we face together. But we need to be honest—it's an aspiration rarely realized. Admitting we are all biased is not enough. If we really want to build a diverse and inclusive workplace, we need to prepare ourselves for a challenging journey.

In most organizations, responsibility for diversity and inclusion is relegated to the HR department, first and foremost as a compliance and legal issue. Rather than being an important human aspiration, it devolves into just another element to measure. A diverse and inclusive workplace is supposedly better for business and championing the cause makes companies look good.

We coauthors had many contentious discussions about whether or not to include this chapter. We strongly questioned whether it's appropriate for us as people of relative privilege to purport to tell our readers, especially those from underrepresented groups, what they should do. Acknowledging that we do not have the experience or perspective of an underrepresented person is important. Knowing what is appropriate to do next is not always clear.

Many people find it obvious that a diverse team is of tremendous value for its breadth of experience and opinion. In the recent past, it was broadly espoused mostly, if you look, by white men that the workplace can and should be a meritocracy where the best ideas rise to the top. But if privileged people at the top decide the criteria for what makes a good idea, true meritocracy isn't actually present.

A 2010 study, "The Paradox of Meritocracy in Organizations," found that in cultures espousing meritocracy, managers may in fact "show greater bias in favor of men over equally performing women."[3] In a series of three experiments, the researchers presented participants with profiles of similarly performing individuals and asked them to award bonuses. The researchers found that telling participants that their company valued merit-based decisions only increased the likelihood of their giving higher bonuses to the men. The facts are crystal clear: equal pay for equal work is not a reality. The pay gap may be narrowing, but it still exists.

The biggest privilege of privilege is not having to see or acknowledge privilege. As with everything we've shared in this book, awareness and discernment is at the heart of all change. If we aspire to a truly diverse and inclusive workplace, we must acknowledge that we are not playing on an even field. By unpacking our own inherent biases and acknowledging the systems that have been passed down to us from earlier generations, we can begin to redress past mistakes. A good start is to ask others what they think and need rather than assuming we know best and imposing our own version of good. If, as leaders, we intend to change, this is the place to do our most significant work.

When thinking about diversity, people often consider gender, ethnicity and sexual orientation first. Diversity includes many kinds of differences. Introverts and extroverts have different styles of processing information and communicating. People of different ages relate more to particular customer groups and issues. People with different experiences of ability have valuable perspectives on usability. People from different geographies bring differing cultural values and an understanding of different markets. There are opportunities to think about and seek diversity in many ways.

## Fix the System

Inclusion means creating conditions in which everyone feels welcome and valued—that they belong. This may sound obvious and easy; it's not. The systems of organizing that we've accepted, lived in and perpetuated are, by design, not inclusive. Think of a playground at a primary school: there are the cool kids and the shy kids, the kids considered high performers, the teacher's pet, the sporty girls and the artsy boys. Map that onto a workplace; labels and cliques can persist. In most places, exclusivity is less obvious than it used to be—not as many managers have offices—but even not-so-subtle changes send a message about remaining gaps in inclusion.

Belonging is a human need, not only in the sense that we are included in the things that matter, but that we bring something of value to the group. A lack of belonging is a manifestation of what psychologists call social pain, which Naomi Eisenberger of UCLA found activates the same area of the brain that's related to physical injury.[4]

According to Liz Guthridge, who wrote on this topic in *Forbes* in 2017:

> The signs and consequences of inclusion and exclusion are universal to people everywhere. When you feel excluded, even if you're part of the majority group, such as a white male in a corporation, you can react in some or all of these six ways:
>
> •   Experience a drop in your intelligence and reasoning skills.

- Become unwilling to cooperate and show other pro-social behavior toward colleagues, family and friends.

- Have greater challenges regulating your emotions, such as being civil when angered or provoked.

- Face difficulties in making healthy choices regarding eating, time management and leisure activities.

- Feel defensive and start to lack a sense of purpose.

- Suffer from impaired sleep, depression and other health problems.[5]

It's up to us to change or modify our systems to accommodate this knowledge. When we name and acknowledge the systems or assumptions that increase exclusion, we can work to change them. What are the subtle and insidious ways we perpetuate exclusion? What can we do instead? Many things, big and small, can be done to become a more inclusive organization. If you don't know where to start, here are some practices to consider.

## Be intentional

Some of your colleagues are comfortable and confident speakers who think fast and debate effectively. Others are not. Often extroverts, experts and elders do most of the talking. The knowledge and experience of quieter members aren't considered because they're not heard. New group members offer fresh insights. Every member of the team shares the responsibility of ensuring balance within conversations. A few expressions you might choose to adopt:

- "Now that we've heard Sam's perspective, I'd love to hear what others are thinking about this topic."

- "I've been talking for a while. Let me stop and see what you are thinking about this. Do you agree or do you have other ideas we should explore?"

- "I'm noticing three of us are doing most of the talking. Let's give everyone else a few minutes to chime in with other ideas."

- "Nadir, I'd really like to hear what you think about this topic."

## Do rounds

Rounds are a simple procedure where a group goes around the physical or virtual room with each person sharing their opinion on a topic without cross-talk. No one speaks for a second time until everyone has been heard. It's a quick way to get every voice into the room.

## Create understanding of differences

Take opportunities to explore human differences and the gifts embedded in these differences. Personality instruments like Myers-Briggs, StrengthsFinder, Enneagram or McQuaig all show how everyone brings different—and often invisible—natural abilities to the team. Seeing other people's differences as gifts starts to shift our perspective on how those differences strengthen the team.

## Up the ante

After trying out the practices above, raise the stakes by focusing more on issues that are getting in the way of a diverse and inclusive environment. Create safe spaces for conversations about each team member's lived experience to foster both understanding and connection. Doing so may expose unintentional systems and processes that are unhelpful for certain groups within your organization. These conversations are more likely to cause emotional reactions. Talking about our experiences and feeling valued matter.

## Ask for help

When awareness of discrimination, a persistent lack of diversity or a general desire to improve in this area emerges, consider seeking help rather than going it alone. These are challenging topics that may be best served by engaging external experts who can help you create the changes that will shift the system.

## Bring Diversity to Recruiting

The hiring process is where diversity begins. We can be blind to the impact small decisions in the recruiting process can have on how diverse, or not, our pool of candidates will be. Let's look at some practices that bring diversity to recruitment.

### Prioritize culture contribution over culture fit

It's common to look for a good cultural fit when hiring someone to join the team. We are strong believers that hiring for fit is important. However, well-intentioned cultural initiatives can negatively impact diversity. A popular cultural filter is to ask ourselves questions like, "Would I want to have a drink with this person after work?" or "Would I enjoy taking a long car ride with this person?" We tend to socialize with those most similar to us, so filters like these lead us to reduce rather than increase diversity.

Instead, consider the question "Could this person contribute something new and helpful to the culture here?" By using the organization's values as a guide, you can evaluate how someone can contribute something new, while still being a great fit for the organization.

### Pay attention to language

Look at the demographics of your applicants. Are you getting a good variety of applicants based on your broadest possible candidate pool and the communities your company serves? If not, then you're likely missing an opportunity. Studies have shown that certain words appeal more to certain genders, for example. Buffer realized that women represented less than 2 percent of their developer candidates. They took several steps to attract more women, including removing words from their job requirements such as *rock star*, *ninja*, and *dominate*, which tend to resonate more with men.

Be aware of the signals you may be sending, both consciously and unconsciously, to various groups. Notice where you might be losing a particular pool of applicants at different steps of the recruiting process and get curious about the potential causes. Small tweaks can lead to big changes.

## Hire to bring out genius

Menlo Innovations, a software consultancy in Ann Arbor, Michigan, has a unique hiring practice. They have found that hiring people who have good "kindergarten skills" is key to their success and their growth. They bring people in for large group interviews and evaluate whether people work well together and bring out each other's genius. Given that focus, it may be no surprise that Menlo Innovations employs double the national average of women in technology roles, at 40 percent. The top seven of Menlo's most senior and highest-paid team members are women.

WHO ARE you surrounding yourself with? Are those around you invited to fully contribute their unique gifts in their unique ways? Building the strongest teams requires diversity of thought—a diversity that we're not likely to create without conscious intention. With the perspective that everyone can be a leader in self-managed teams, what leadership role will you take in boosting the inclusion of diverse thought on your team?

# 20

# Future Colleagues

Recruit a Team
That Will Build
the Organization

"Great vision without great people is irrelevant."

**JIM COLLINS**[1]

**A**RE SELF-MANAGED, agile organizations for everyone? The simple answer is no. Self-organizing teams tend to operate with considerable ambiguity and require a willingness to embrace radical responsibility. For some, that ambiguity and level of responsibility can be too challenging and feel unsafe. Being transparent about your unique environment and spreading the word widely allow those drawn to this new way of working to find you.

First, let's look at some characteristics that make people successful in self-managed organizations. In "21st-Century Talent Spotting," Claudio Fernández-Aráoz shares five indicators of an individual's potential.[2] Although not specific to self-managed companies, these attributes are indicators for the high level of independence required to operate in these environments:

**Motivation** The ambition to excel in the pursuit of unselfish, collective goals; deep personal humility and a focus on self-improvement.

**Curiosity** The instinct to seek new experiences, knowledge and feedback with an openness to learning and change.

**Insight** The ability to gather and make sense of information that suggests new possibilities.

**Engagement** The capacity to use emotion and reason to communicate a persuasive vision and connect with people.

**Determination** The ability to fight for difficult goals despite challenges.

Doug Kirkpatrick, cofounder of the Morning Star Self-Management Institute, has ample experience recruiting individuals to join self-managing organizations.[3] He seeks out people who are not particularly sensitive to power distance and therefore willing to talk to anyone at any time about anything. Grit, the willingness to persevere despite obstacles, is another big success factor he calls out. Since not everything runs smoothly in self-managed environments, it can take time and effort to line up stakeholders and help people buy into new ideas. A willingness to negotiate terms of engagement with peers and follow those terms is critical. Doug also encourages teams to look for potential colleagues with an internal locus of control—the sense that they are responsible for themselves and their choices—paired with a sufficient level of self-awareness.

In addition to these self-management competencies, your team's purpose and values play a role in determining fit. Do one or more of the candidate's personal purposes align with your team's purpose? Is there a good overlap between your team's values or principles and theirs?

## Practices for Recruiting

Team-based self-reflection and experimentation will help you identify the most appropriate indicators for fit with your team. For inspiration, we've collected recruiting practices from eight different organizations.

### Trial collaboration

The typical recruiting process is short in duration, often leaving many questions unanswered. Trial collaboration, as the name suggests, is an opportunity to work together for a defined period of time and test the fit.

The team at Percolab places high value on sharing experiences with potential candidates in advance of any hiring decisions, usually beginning with a candidate attending Percolab's weekly tactical meeting, which is open to the public. Since Percolab's meeting style differs from most organizations', a guest experiences how team members relate to one another and what they value. If it feels like a fit for both parties, they might collaborate on a project. No promises or commitments are made beyond seeing how the collaboration feels and works.

If the first project works out well, and if the individual desires a more formal and committed relationship, they are invited to write a letter to the team expressing their intentions.

Thereafter, in an online space (Loomio), each person in the team shares their honest thoughts and feelings about this new person joining. Once everyone has spoken, they decide whether to bring in the person. If there are no objections, a contract is prepared. The candidate chooses three people from the team to sign the contract. The signatories clarify the final details, such as transitioning out of current commitments or working around planned travel. Once the contract is signed, the joiner has full access to the Loomio conversation discussing their hiring. This establishes a transparent culture and puts the developmental process into motion.

## Group recruiting

Since interviewing potential candidates one at a time can be slow, arduous and inefficient, the candidate pool is often narrowed through a résumé review—which can eliminate potentially great candidates. Group recruiting overcomes that problem.

Menlo Innovations aims to maximize quality and project agility with integrated project teams. The company hires via large group auditions; the interviewers do not look at résumés in advance. Interviewees are paired during three twenty-minute exercises to evaluate culture fit. Those who pass this initial audition are invited back for a full-day interview.

All software development and user experience design work at Menlo is done in pairs, so candidates spend the day doing paired projects, coding or designing with Menlo team members. The paired approach allows the team to assess a large volume of candidates in a single day and means Menlo can double the size of its team within weeks if needed. Plus, anyone selected to join Menlo already has a meaningful team experience and the start of personal relationships.

As we mentioned in the previous chapter, Menlo looks for "good kindergarten skills"—the abilities to learn, grow and play together. Unlike most tech companies, Menlo isn't hiring for specific technical skills. They believe software development requires constant learning. Following the interview day, the team collectively decides who they'd like to consider further. Those individuals are invited back for three weeks of paid work. If the team feels their initial assessment still holds, the relationship is extended to full-time employment.

Because no one looks at résumés before the interview, Menlo has much greater diversity on its team than other tech companies. For example, their team includes people with degrees in philosophy, astronomy, physics and early childhood education. Menlo's experimental approach has proven that removing traditional résumé bias increases the diversity of new hires.

## Values-based recruitment

In values-based recruiting, someone's fit is measured against company values. As we've previously outlined, values alignment is critical in some Teal organizations. Nowhere is this truer than in community support organizations like Wellbeing Teams. Wellbeing Teams operates using small, self-managing, neighborhood-based groups that support people to live well at home in their communities. Tasks and challenges are used in the team's values-based recruitment process to identify recruits who have the values, attitudes and aspirations necessary for work in health care. Examples of their values and associated recruiting processes include:

**Self-management** Wellbeing Teams looks for individuals who can work effectively in a team without traditional management structures. During recruitment, candidates give each other feedback to demonstrate their skill and approach; candidates "reverse interview" representatives of the organization about the role to demonstrate their curiosity in seeking out valuable information and candidates contribute to the recruitment day by, for example, bringing food and participating in a shared lunch. This allows the team to see the individual's approach to sharing and teamwork.

**Authenticity** Care and support roles benefit from people bringing their whole, authentic self to work, rather than a sanitized work persona. Recruitment exercises include: crafting a "Could this be you?" role description that goes far beyond qualifications and experience, which invites people to bring their life experiences into the process; sharing with the candidate whole-self personal profiles of team members involved in the recruiting process and, at the beginning of the process, playing a human bingo game that invites candidates to learn personal and professional information about the interviewers and others they meet along the way.

**A person-centered outlook** Successful candidates need to value care and compassion and to demonstrate these values in their work. Candidates are asked to identify what really matters to others in the room, as well as to demonstrate physicality, comfort and readiness to engage with others through hand massage.

## Creating your own job
You can apply the concept of radical responsibility to freelancer recruiting. Enspiral turns recruitment on its head by imagining a world of work where potential team members exercise their agency in identifying opportunities and proposing relationships. Since Enspiral doesn't employ anybody, it's up to individual freelancers to negotiate a way in and find their place. Where can they do their best work and make their best contribution? In this way, the very

idea of recruitment doesn't exist. Potential contributors navigate, propose and ultimately decide. They need to put in the requisite effort to understand where and with whom they choose to do that work. It's a big leap in the traditional sense of recruiting but a reality for many freelancers.

## Full transparency

For candidates applying to traditional organizations, the recruiting process is often shrouded in mystery. Many Teal organizations choose to be fully transparent about their processes. The team at Deeson believes that they can teach people how to work the Deeson way if there is a values fit, and so they use identified behaviors and core values to guide their three-stage selection process.

The first stage is a half-hour phone or video conversation with Simon Wakeman, the managing director. Simon asks a scripted list of questions designed to provide evidence of values and make sure the candidate has enough of the required professional skills. Next the candidate comes in for an interactive exercise with some future peers. This step is about testing their skills and ability to collaborate. Is there chemistry with the group? Following the exercise, the candidate joins a randomly selected group from the team, none of whom are decision makers in the recruitment process, for a conversation. Simon tells the candidate, "You have this time to talk with Fred, a developer, and Jane, a designer. Ask them what you'd like. I won't ask them for any feedback. This is your opportunity to find out what it's like to work at Deeson and whether you think you'd be suitable for it." Lastly, the candidate meets with the other company director. Deeson is completely transparent about this process, which is described on their website.

## Interviewing for fit

An assessment of fit is important in any recruiting process, particularly if your organization would be an unusual fit for some, as with self-managed companies. Since Fitzii operates as a fully self-managing team, they work hard throughout the interview process to expose candidates to what life at Fitzii is really like. Matt McKenna from the Fitzii team describes the interview process as being radically open: "We are open and vulnerable about ourselves and our experience here. Our own challenges and failures are shared. Candidates interviewing with us will find the typical sheen that is characteristic of most interviews is conspicuously absent. We also ask the candidates to show higher levels of openness than they typically would. This helps the candidate see and experience what it's like at Fitzii, and helps us sense if there's a fit there. We've found that people who have struggled with this interview style have not thrived in our group."[4] Interviewees also get directed to blog posts written by the team. The team uses these first interactions to gauge the candidate's level of interest and buy-in to Teal concepts. Are they excited about working in different ways because they recognize the old way of doing business is broken?

During the interview, the team assesses whether Fitzii's goals and work align with the candidate's purpose, whether the candidate is likely to succeed in a self-managed environment and if the candidate has the skills, knowledge and qualifications needed for the role.

The traditional interview process only goes so far in educating prospective team members and determining fit. In the words of a new joiner to the team, "I really thought I understood how comprehensive Teal was. But it's one thing to read about it and sign on. Living it really calls into question a lot about how you work, think and communicate. If you're going to bring your whole self to work, you have to learn how that whole self impacts the team and the business."

As a result of this learning, the Fitzii team now explicitly tells candidates that the first three months will serve to determine the overall mutual fit, especially for working in a Teal environment. After the first three months, they decide whether the candidate will continue as a full-fledged team member.

## Veto rights

When it comes to deciding who can join your organization, consider giving everyone on the team the right to veto any candidate who they don't believe is a fit. That's how they do it at Cyberclick. The founder, David Tomás, usually completes the first intake interview by phone. The candidate then comes to the office to meet members of the team, after which a test is given to assess the candidate's skills. On a second trip to the office, the candidate meets and interviews with people from other parts of the company. Team members then go out for coffee with the candidate. Anyone can say, "I don't think that person is a culture fit." Even if David or others love the candidate, other team members can block the hire.

## Attracting diverse candidates

As we talked about in the last chapter, there are a multitude of reasons to prioritize reaching out to a diverse candidate pool. The team at Buffer spends time sculpting a role description because, as Courtney Seiter describes on Buffer's website: "We believe starting out this way creates a fairer hiring process because it sets the stage for candidates to be assessed for the same skills, traits, values and qualifications. This helps mitigate interviewer bias and enable consistent candidate evaluation so we can make evidence-based decisions."[5] After sharing the role internally and before sending out the description externally, the team uses Textio—AI software that analyzes language, including job descriptions, and highlights jargon, boring bits and words that could come across as particularly masculine or feminine—to evaluate their job listing. Textio makes listings more gender neutral, inclusive, clear and attractive to qualified candidates.

Buffer has worked hard at crafting a transparent, appealing culture and receives lots of applications as a result. To reach the largest and most diverse talent pool possible, Buffer uses its candidate mailing list of over 15,000 people and its social media, as well as contacts groups that are underrepresented in its industry, including via diversity-in-tech organizations.

## Put It into Practice

Only you and your team can decide the best recruiting style for your organization. Our invitation is for you to view recruitment through a broader lens than many traditional, mechanical processes. Get curious about your process and seek feedback from recent joiners. What are the routines and rituals you use now? What do they tell candidates about your values as a company? How will you invite candidates to interact with your company? How can you meaningfully test for fit and allow candidates to do the same? Recruiting is a never-ending journey of discovery, with each new role and candidate offering an opportunity to experiment.

# 21

# The New Joiner Experience

Skillfully Onboard
New Team Members

"It takes courage to grow up and become who you really are."

**E.E. CUMMINGS**[1]

T HERE'S NO BETTER way to unintentionally say "We don't really care about you" than a minimal investment in onboarding new team members. On the flip side, an awesome onboarding experience pays dividends to everyone involved. How you choose to recruit people will influence how you shape onboarding. If you embrace the trial period approach, recruiting and onboarding are intertwined. If your recruitment process has a traditional start date, onboarding is more distinct. The content of this chapter applies to both scenarios and is written with the two-phase approach in mind: recruiting, followed by onboarding. Onboarding into cultures that are markedly different from what most new joiners are used to takes special care and attention. The stakes are higher when asking someone to learn a new job, a new company and a new way of working.

## Awesome Onboarding

Onboarding is a tactical list of tasks and experiences that gives newcomers what they need to get started. When it is done well, individuals understand expectations, company culture, the various elements of their work and how things get done day-to-day. It's a celebration. Transitioning into a new company is rife with uncertainty for the new team member: "Did I make the right decision?

Do I like these people? Do they like me? Am I competent in this role? Am I seen as worthy?" How will you know if you've delivered an awesome onboarding process? Proactively setting the bar high is key. Compare these two examples:

1. Our onboarding process ensures every new team member has the supplies they need, understands their job and integrates into the team by the end of their first week.

2. By the end of our onboarding process, every new joiner believes they are fulfilling a unique role in our organization. They are fully participating, contributing and meeting commitments. They feel like they've found their community.

Can you feel the difference? Traditionally we think of onboarding as an *integration*. How fast can we integrate the newbie into our team? How fast can we get this person to think and work like us? A more powerful approach is to ask, "How fast can we create an environment for new team members to be fully contributing as *themselves*?" When everyone is willing to fully be themselves— sharing fears, weaknesses and uncertainties—the whole team is free of unnecessary distractions. You create space for faster personal and team development.

## The Pre-onboarding Phase

Onboarding is often viewed as a one-day or one-week event that begins when new team members show up for their first day. In reality, the experience begins with the first interaction a candidate has with your company. This could be reading published content, such as your website, or having an introductory conversation. In those early interactions, the joiner forms impressions and mental images. They will use these expectations to evaluate their first week at your company. Exceed those expectations and all is good. Unfortunately, we often unintentionally oversell, and within a joiner's first week, things start going sideways and disappointments mount.

With attention and good planning of the pre-onboarding phase, new joiners will feel fully valued and pleased with their decision to become part of your team. Meetings and conversations with candidates are a goldmine of information that can shape an awesome onboarding experience. Pay attention to what the person enjoys and values, and you can incorporate these passions into the process. If your new team member is a sports fanatic, consider scheduling a lunch with a team member who shares this passion. Each team within the company can create unique experiences in bonding with their new peers.

The window of time between when someone commits to joining and actually joins is fertile with opportunities for positive interactions. Send a welcome package to the joiner and their family. Have their new colleagues reach out by phone or schedule coffee. Write a personal note. A few simple actions go a long way in over delivering on expectations. Marc Mandeltort, the CEO of Marco Specialties, a pinball parts manufacturer, makes it a point to take a new potential hire and their spouse out to dinner. He says Marco Specialties is like a family and so invests in building relationships.

## Onboarding to Self-Management

Joining a self-managing company for the first time can be a real shock. New joiners may have read about self-management during the interview process and asked good questions along the way, but it's not until they're submersed in a self-managing environment that they appreciate how different it is.

There are four essential onboarding tools in self-management: a role description, an onboarding checklist, new joiner buddies and self-management learning.

It's important new joiners understand what success looks like, so they need a **role description**. Percolab's role format, as shared in chapter II, offers a template. Sharing and shaping this document with the new joiner during the recruiting and onboarding phases ensures ongoing alignment.

An **onboarding checklist** is an essential tool. Experiment with creating a comprehensive master onboarding checklist that covers every new joiner. Include a time frame column for each task. Begin by creating a list for a specific individual; for subsequent hires, use the same templated list and add any new items. In the time frame column, use a label such as "not required" for items critical for previous joiners but not for the current individual or remove those items altogether. Repeat this process every time you onboard someone new. In no time, you will have a single onboarding checklist that can be customized in minutes. As an added bonus, each new joiner will gain an appreciation for what other team members needed to learn.

In preparing checklist content, consider incorporating four distinct components:

**Education** What does the individual need to learn, and how will they, to quickly become a wildly successful contributor?

**Observation** How can the joiner benefit by observing others? Many people learn best by watching others in action.

**Activation** What exactly does the person need to do, experience or complete to build their own competence and confidence?

**Demonstration** What does the team need from the individual to build trust in their new colleague's capabilities?

Consider the example of a new joiner entering a sales role:

**Education** The joiner will first need to learn about the company's products and services by reading specific company documents, reviewing previous sales presentations and asking questions of their colleagues.

**Observation** As a next step, the joiner will shadow one or more colleagues in a few prospect meetings.

**Activation** Before leading their first prospect meeting, the individual will complete several role plays.

**Demonstration** Lastly, the person will be joined in their first sales calls by a colleague who will observe and provide coaching. Once the colleague is comfortable, the new joiner is ready to move forward on their own.

The checklist could be created in a spreadsheet or document, or in a tool such as Trello or Asana to help create transparency and simplify updating and versioning.

Many companies assign a **new joiner buddy** to help people during their first few weeks. Unfortunately, this role often doesn't get the attention it deserves. In organizations using self-management principles, the buddy role is critical. The team at Fitzii assigns a sponsor for each new hire. That person is 100 percent responsible for the success and engagement of their new joiner.

Rather than assigning a single buddy, Buffer uses a triad: a leader buddy, a role buddy and a culture buddy. The leader buddy, an experienced member of the team, can have effective, tough conversations about living Buffer's values. The role buddy understands the new joiner's role. The culture buddy is an experienced member of the team who has shown a consistent ability to give praise around the culture fit of new and existing team members. Praising culture fit is a far more effective way to help others feel integrated than pointing out missteps.

Who owns the onboarding process in a self-managing company? We advocate having the joiner take charge of the process with the support of buddies. No one cares more about the joiner's onboarding than they do. Hand the checklist to the joiner on day one and explain that the ultimate responsibility to complete it falls to them. The buddy acts as an accountability partner and can raise a red flag if the process starts slipping.

The onboarding process should also include a phased approach to **learning self-management** and experiencing self-management practices. Shortly after team members join ET Group, they are invited to a ninety-minute introduction to Teal, during which they learn about the organization's evolution into self-management and the associated practices, called the ET Group Way. They are also matched with one of three self-management coaches. New joiners to Ian Martin Group are introduced to a Trello board called Teal U that includes a list of self-management topics and practices to be learned over time.

## Tips for Top-Notch Onboarding

Developing a solid and effective onboarding process is a minimal requirement. An absolutely knock-it-out-of-the-park process separates top-performing companies from the rest. Here are a few examples to prime your thinking as you consider the best approach for your unique circumstances.

### Make first impressions memorable

How do you make a new joiner's early impressions positive and memorable? The first thing anyone joining Ian Martin Group does on their first day is to go desk to desk with their sponsor, delivering tasty treats and taking selfies with their new friends that are then published on the internal messaging system. Cloud computing company Rackspace populates its onboarding effort with "games, skits, costumes, thumping music and a limbo bar."[2] What could be more memorable than that?

### Share company history

Every company has a history and origin story. That history has shaped the team and is worthy of sharing. Ray Cao, the CEO of marketing services company Exact Media, wrote a letter to all team members sharing his personal history and experiences from the early days of building the company. During his tenure, all joiners received that letter in their first week. A one-on-one chat with Ray followed shortly thereafter to talk about the history of the company in more detail. Tech firm Bazaarvoice organized a weeklong scavenger hunt to educate new joiners on company culture and terminology.[3] Jeroen in 't Veld, cofounder of Dutch consultancy firm Rebel Group, facilitates an onboarding module in which he shares the complete history of the company, including how he's learned from mistakes along the way.[4]

## Practice the core building blocks

Working in a self-managing environment requires specific skills— core building blocks—that most new joiners have not yet learned. In their first week at Salesforce implementation company EMPAUA, new joiners practice the two primary Holacratic meeting structures (tactical and governance) as well as learn and practice nonviolent communication.[5] The team at nutrition coaching and certification company Precision Nutrition uses modeling and notice-and-name practices to help new joiners recognize unhelpful behaviors and learn better options.

## Teach the core business

It's not unusual to join a company without fully understanding or having experienced its core offering. Exceptional customer service is at the heart of accounting software company FreshBooks' business. The company is an example of how prioritizing values in the onboarding process takes commitment. Every new member of the FreshBooks team spends a full month working in customer support before jumping into their actual role. The company is unwavering in this element of the onboarding process. The result is an award-winning customer service orientation that permeates the whole company.

At FAVI, an organization specializing in pressure die-casting, newly hired engineers and administrative team members are trained to operate at least one machine on the shop floor so they have a shared experience with the machine operators. New joiners to recruiting agency Bee Talents receive the company's financial statements to better understand the financial operations of the company.[6]

## Close out the onboarding process

Fitzii uses the concept of a three-month graduation period, with a celebration ritual at the end. This period can be extended if someone is struggling. The ritual includes asking the new joiner to share why they want to be part of the team, what they are leaving behind from their past and how they want to grow and be in the new team.

At the end of green-energy provider Bullfrog Power's twelve-week onboarding process, new joiners have a wrap-up meeting with the onboarding process owner to share learnings and help improve the experience for future joiners. At FAVI, joiners end their onboarding process by writing a free-format open letter to their group of colleagues, sharing thoughts about their experience and expressing gratitude to those who helped them along the way.

HOW DO you rate the effectiveness of your onboarding process on a scale of zero to ten? How do your recent joiners rate it? How about the colleagues working with the new joiners? If it's not a solid and consistent eight or more, consider investing in stepping up the awesomeness by a notch or two. Experiment with a few additions to the process. Invite the team to get creative. Learn from each onboarding to improve the next. Before long, your investment will pay dividends.

# 22

# Exiting Colleagues

Learn Brave New
Ways for Moving On

"I realize there's something incredibly honest about trees in winter, how they're experts at letting things go."

**JEFFREY MCDANIEL**[1]

**R**AJ WAS the third person to join an organization founded eight years ago. The team began the shift to self-management two years ago and has since grown to twenty-five people. Everyone on the team is excited about the shift and eager to make it work... everyone, that is, except Raj. From a hierarchical perspective, Raj is one of the three most senior members of the team. While his colleagues embrace self-management, Raj is holding firm to his positional authority and traditional views of how things should run. The rest of the team is fed up and ready to ask Raj to leave.

Much-repeated advice from the world of meritocracy suggests we should hire slowly and fire fast. In a self-managed organization, who decides who gets to stay and who goes? Is it okay to ask team members like Raj to leave because their approach is different? Is it even an option in this new way of working?

The exit of a team member is an emotional experience. Every step of the process is fraught with uncertainty. New self-managed teams frequently struggle in this area.

## Three Well-Traveled Paths

Using the story of Raj, let's walk along three traditional paths for exiting team members. You will likely recognize these and may see your own past footprints along the way.

## Path 1: Move fast

Raj's colleagues have put up with his power-oriented behaviors for years. Since the shift to self-management, tolerance for those behaviors has dwindled. Everyone is waiting for Carol, the most senior member of the team, to decide it's time for Raj to go. In one particularly bad week, Raj's actions angered four different people on the team, including Carol. Over the years, Carol has had a few conversations with Raj about his behavior and she has no desire to have another one.

After two sleepless nights, Carol decides it's time for Raj to leave. She prepares the paperwork, calls Raj into her office and notifies him of her decision. Raj is angry and feels blindsided. He has worked incredibly hard to build the organization to where it is today. He leaves the meeting fuming. A letter from his lawyer arrives a few days later.

The team is happy Raj is gone. Carol moves on, while harboring her own inner feelings of doubt, disappointment and discouragement about how things turned out.

## Path 2: Move slow

Raj's behaviors have become like a pebble in his colleagues' shoes. No single word or behavior is outrageous. He cares deeply about the success of the team. Every two or three months someone is frustrated enough to pull Raj aside and give him feedback. He adjusts his behavior for a week or two, then slips back into old patterns. This cycle has repeated itself for years. This week has been particularly maddening for Carol so she has yet another difficult conversation with Raj, knowing that nothing will change in the long run.

This pattern continues until Carol or someone else senior on the team can't take it anymore. Eventually it becomes an "either Raj goes or I go" dilemma.

### Path 3: Attempt to fix the person

A few members of Raj's team have concluded that his behavior patterns point to bigger underlying issues. There are some things Raj needs to learn for his own good and for the sanity of the team. If Raj is to stay, his patterns need to change. It's time to let him know exactly what's wrong and how he should go about fixing himself. Two of Raj's colleagues decide to stage an intervention.

The intervention seems to go okay. The colleagues confront Raj with the intention of demonstrating personal care while also challenging him. It's hard for Raj to hear, but he agrees to work with a coach. He does this work for six months, but progress is slow. He becomes more resentful that he has to change when no one else in the organization is being asked to do so. Others become discouraged by Raj's slow progress. Over time, he gravitates back to his previous beliefs, now with an extra layer of defensiveness.

## A Different Path

Self-management does not invite fast exits, slow exits or interventions. Instead, it invites clear agreements, honest communication and personal choice. The following principles and practices offer options for bringing clarity to how and when individuals leave self-managed organizations.

### It's not full-time happiness

Self-management does not equal full-time happiness. It's natural to seek happiness in our work. When someone comes along who disrupts our flow by injecting frustration, debate or challenging views, our happy life feels like it's under attack. Our fight (fire or fix that person) or flight (ignore that person and hope they go away) responses kick in. Start by looking inward and asking, "What exactly is going on for me? What emotions are triggered? What part of this experience do I need to own?"

## Agitators add value

Agitators play a role in making a system better. Too many teams are conflict avoidant until issues become so big that avoidance is no longer an option. Healthy debate most often leads to better solutions. What difficult conversations need to be embraced?

## Gaps in understanding happen

Most interpersonal conflicts can be attributed to an expectation-to-reality gap. One person has an expectation of what another will do and how they will do it. When actions fall short of expectations, a gap is created. To prevent that gap from growing, establish shared agreements and role definitions. If a gap exists, pause to reach and document a common agreement. Become accustomed to asking, "Can I check something with you?" as a way of testing shared understanding.

## Gaps in values and social contracts exist

As we explored in chapter 10, social contracts exist in every organization. Some are documented, many are not. These are the rules of how we choose to coexist as a team. Friction builds when people live by different social contracts or embrace conflicting values within the same team. What social contracts are causing friction because they are unnamed, undocumented or not fully adopted? Try pausing and getting curious: "I'm wondering if you and I have different expectations about how to work as a team. What's your perspective on this situation?"

## Full-blown disagreements can be managed

If I'm 100 percent certain we should choose blue and you are 100 percent certain we should choose green, what color do we choose? In self-managed teams, these types of disagreements come up from time to time and require a path to resolution beyond exiting the dissenting voice. In chapter 12, we introduced tools for decision-making. Chapter 14 covers managing tensions and disagreements. Does your team have effective agreements about how decisions are made and disagreements unpacked? Follow those processes to their conclusions and see if disagreements resolve themselves.

## Integrity can be maintained

Once a final decision has been made, you need to maintain integrity. Having shared values, agreements, roles and social contracts in place isn't enough. You need to maintain the integrity of those artifacts by doing your best to honor them and helping others honor them too. In chapter 21, we mentioned an approach used by Precision Nutrition called notice and name. Noticing when someone is not living up to a pre-agreed behavior and having the courage to name what we've noticed can go a long way to bringing behaviors back into integrity. In doing so, we make no assumptions nor do we place judgment. We simply say, "I'm noticing that our shared agreement on this isn't at the forefront right now, and I'd like to invite us to reflect on that agreement before going any further."

## Early and frequent conversations help

Every time we notice an unhealthy behavior and allow that behavior to go unnamed, we are being unhelpful or insincere in our actions. By failing to speak into your tension and challenge your colleague directly, you conceal valuable information that can help your colleague improve. The longer you wait and the more you conceal, the bigger the expectation-to-reality gap becomes. The bigger the gap, the more intense the emotions.

## You can balance polarities

Along with the freedom and responsibility inherent within self-managing organizations are two important polarities (opposite ends of the same string). The first is acceptance versus accountability. We each have the right to be accepted for who we are and how we choose to work while also delivering on our commitments and role accountabilities. The second is individual versus group. Making decisions about exits requires balancing the needs of individuals with the needs of the group. Simply being conscious of these polarities and naming them can go a long way in making good decisions.

### Exit compensation can be determined up front

We each have our own relationship with money. For some, $100 is a lot of money; to others, it's trivial. To minimize any expectation-to-reality gap related to exit compensation, declare and document an agreement up front. How much are team members paid when leaving your organization? Is it a set amount? Is there a formula? Is it open to negotiation? Is the negotiation and/or final amount transparent to the team?

## How Exits Work

Sometimes it's best that someone leaves a team and therefore we should prepare in advance for those situations. In traditional organizations, the termination process is commonly understood. If someone with more power than me doesn't want me around anymore, I'll be asked to leave with or without prior warning. Like so many elements of self-management, every organization needs to decide, document and adopt its own clear exit process. Who decides? How is the decision made? Who communicates the decision? How is the exiting team member involved? What shared expectations exist for the process?

The Ian Martin Group relies heavily on its role advice process (see chapter 11) in helping individuals decide to stay or leave. When it becomes clear to the team that someone isn't likely to fit in the long term (usually due to underdelivery on role responsibilities), one or more seasoned members of the team have the following conversation with the individual: "Here's feedback we have for you. Reflecting on this feedback, we think it is best if you leave the organization. If you choose to leave, here's the package the orga- nization will give you to support your transition to something new. You also have the opportunity to go through a role advice process to see if options other than exiting the company exist. We expect you will receive feedback and advice similar to what we've shared with you today." The invitation to go through a role advice process over the following two weeks is genuine and the decision lies with the individual.

Menlo employs team decision-making. With so much of its work done in groups, the team has a big say in who they work with. The team makes the hiring decisions and takes it as their collec- tive responsibility to make sure that person has every opportunity to succeed. If one team member doesn't work well with another, senior team members encourage the two colleagues to discuss and resolve the issues. Sometimes the result is a break from working together for a while. If a critical mass of people prefer not being paired with the same person, it becomes clear they may not be a fit for Menlo. A subset of team members then speak with that person about any interpersonal or technical skills that could be improved. This process is usually slow and thoughtful to ensure time for prog- ress. Often, if things are not working out, the person in question initiates a separation. If, however, the team wants to let someone go, a few team members consult with the founders about it.

Everyone at Menlo knows job separation is painful. Their processes are shaped humanely and with the knowledge that self- worth is often connected to our work. As soon as they decide to let someone go, a subset of the team lets the person know. They take care not to surprise the person with this decision, and they focus on being compassionate and helping the individual find a more suitable job. It's not uncommon for previous team members to have had such a good experience that they bring projects to Menlo from their future companies.

You may recall from chapter 3 that new members to the Counter team take on the role of New Counterpart. Once the individual has learned and embraced self-management philosophies, they become a Counterpart Friend and possibly Counterpart-ner. Counter is now experimenting with an Exiting Counterpart role. Outside any egregious behavior, the Counter team does not fire team members in the traditional sense. Similar to the Ian Martin Group, people make their own choices about departure, usually after a series of difficult discussions. Once it's determined that someone will be leaving Counter, that individual shifts into the Exiting Counterpart role, which has clearly outlined expectations such as ensuring work is professionally transitioned and sharing how the team can make their exit the best exit ever. The Counter team makes no guarantees but has the intention of doing everything possible to honor the requests of their exiting colleague. So far, they've found that doing so has been fairly easy.

## An Alternative to Exiting in Tough Financial Times

The COVID-19 pandemic provided an interesting window into how companies can handle incredibly challenging financial times. Organizations were impacted in a variety of ways. Gravity Payments, a payments processing company, saw revenue plummet. In one week, it lost about 50 percent of its $4 million monthly revenue. Instead of jumping to layoffs to save the company, CEO Dan Price was open and honest with everyone about the magnitude of the challenge. He had forty small group conversations with the more-than-200-person team. He decided to cut his own salary to zero. Ten other employees volunteered to work for free temporarily and two dozen more gave up half or more of their paychecks. In the end, 98 percent of people volunteered for a pay reduction, giving the company a total of $2 million in savings.[2]

This level of candor is possible because Gravity Payments engages in many of the trust-building practices we've shared throughout this book. It has a level of psychological safety and team cohesion already in place. Dan had confidence that, given the right information, the team could and would pull together in a way that worked for everyone. He had to position himself not as someone who had the answers but who needed help from everyone. By doing so, he was able to address a financial shock that claimed many companies in a very challenging time.

AS YOU experiment with your team, we invite you to bring three elements into your exit process: clear agreements, honest communication and personal choice. Where there is a lack of clarity or alignment, invest in creating and documenting agreements. When agreements are not being lived, be honest with yourself and open with others in noticing and naming your tensions. Lastly, make choices for yourself and create an environment where others have everything they need to make their own informed choices.

# 23

# Bold Strategy

Sense and Respond
in a Fast-Paced World

"Traditional planning is dead. The increasing speed of technological innovation, as well as the shift to more open styles of production and organization, are forcing everyone to rethink how we go about setting, executing on and measuring performance against goals."

**JIM WHITEHURST**[1]

ORGANIZATIONS PLAN in two ways: predicting the future and then aiming to control outcomes or sensing what's changing and responding accordingly. The former continues to rule the day, but progressive leaders see that predictions have become less reliable. With this knowledge, they are shifting how their organizations set strategy.

The predict and control approach aims to create certainty where unknowns exist. We don't know what our revenue will be for this year and we won't know until the year is done. Based on past experience, we predict year-end revenue, create detailed plans and targets, then do our best to control the outcome so our prediction proves accurate. When change was knowable or minimal from year to year, the predict-and-control strategy was helpful.

Change is increasing rapidly. The average lifespan of an S&P 500 company exceeded sixty years in 1958. In 2012 it was under twenty years and it's forecasted to shrink to just twelve years in the current decade (by 2027).[2] That's a 50 percent decrease in ten years. Each company on the S&P 500 shapes our world and the shortening tenure of these companies suggests a correlated decline in predictability. We humans don't like uncertainty and work hard to avoid dealing with it. Hence the continuing prevalence of predict-and-control approaches to planning. The problem lies in overplanning and then believing too much in plans based on imperfect predictions.

A sense-and-respond approach acknowledges and embraces uncertainty. Instead of trying to control an unknowable future, organizations using this approach do much less forward planning since they know it will likely be irrelevant or wrong. Instead, they tune in to what's true today. When something changes, they decide how to respond. The result is much tighter loops of feedback, reflection and calibration. The role of space holder, which we discussed in chapter 1, is critical for sensing in fast, complex environments. You must be able to rest in ambiguity, stay grounded in the organization's purpose and engage with what is happening rather than try to control it. You still plan, but the time and energy spent is less intensive and more frequent than in the predict-and-control world.

## Three Elements of the Strategic Process

Every strategic planning approach has three core components: sensing, aggregating and planning. Sensing is the process of collecting data and becoming aware of what's going on in the world around us. "What do our customers need? How are those needs changing over time? How well are we serving those needs? Who else is serving those needs?" Sensing is primarily an individual activity completed by various members of a team. Once sensing is complete, it's time to aggregate individual knowledge and experiences to create a collective understanding. "What have we each learned? How do these pieces fit together? What big messages emerge? What is this information telling us?" Lastly, it's time to plan. "What action do we need to take? Where will we go from here?"

Both predict-and-control and sense-and-respond approaches include these three components. As the following table shows, how each is completed and how much time is allocated differs significantly between the two.

|  | Predict and Control | Sense and Respond |
|---|---|---|
| Cadence | Completed annually, usually with quarterly checkpoints | Initiated when the team senses a need, sometimes prompted by semiregular gatherings |
| Sensing | A small amount of time and effort by a handful of senior team members | A large group from across the organization (often everyone) investing meaningful amounts of time and energy |
| Aggregating | Completed by the same small group and affected by associated biases | Completed by the same large group with less opportunity for individual biases to affect group outcomes |
| Planning | Significant time invested, first by a small group and then cascaded throughout the organization in the form of extensive metrics | Limited to the smallest, lightest plans necessary based on current sensing and aggregating, often with no longer-term plans required |

If you believe the world has shifted to the point where predict-and-control methods are no longer appropriate, how do you bring sense and respond to life in your organization? By now, you can appreciate how the two approaches to strategy are markedly different. Effective sensing and responding requires skill along with shared practices. Before discarding any predict-and-control processes in place, build the muscles of collective agreement-making, shared decision-making and radical responsibility. If you move away from predict and control before the team's sense-and-respond muscles have been developed, your organization may find itself ill-equipped to handle challenges.

## Sensing

Let's say a group is hiking together and goes off trail. They are in uncharted territory and don't know what's ahead. Is there a marsh blocking their path they can't yet see? For Jo, the newest hiker in the group, the question isn't top of mind. Meanwhile Justina, the most seasoned of the group, has been tracking water flows since beginning the hike and senses a potential obstacle ahead. She pauses and suggests the group find a spot to get a broader view.

Certain people are better at noticing emerging opportunities and challenges. Like Justina, these individuals can call attention to the need for sensing and strategic thinking. That strategic thinking may or may not need to evolve into a strategic plan. External shifts in the marketplace, new technology or investment opportunities may suggest it's time for your organization to do some strategic thinking. An internal lack of clarity or alignment is another good reason. Whatever the prompt, your team needs to get curious.

An important mechanism to unleash collective intelligence at Fitzii has been its inkling practice. When anyone on the team senses a problem or opportunity, they share their inkling on Fitzii's internal communication platform or in a meeting. From there, people with energy rally around those issues and address them. Topics generating little-to-no energy from the team are left to rest. This practice has sparked new projects, shifts in strategy and ways of working together.

Once the sensing process begins, it becomes a team activity. No single individual owns it in a way that makes their voice more important than any other. That said, one person might become a sensing coordinator with an objective such as to get as many team members as possible interviewing a wide variety of people both out in the world and internally. Open-ended questions such as the following can be helpful: "What question, if answered by our customers and prospects, could make the most difference to shaping the future of our organization?" or "What opportunities are you seeing now?" or "What assumptions are we holding that we need to test or challenge?" or "Who is holding very different beliefs than we are and what would they say about what we should do next?"

Karn Manhas, the founder of Terramera, a Vancouver-based sustainable agriculture cleantech company, views asking questions as a continual practice for sensing new opportunities rather than staying anchored to current thinking:

> Questions don't occur in isolation. Answering one simply opens the door to asking another. If you follow this line of inquiry, you can utterly transform your business. My company aims to change how we grow food for the world, and I've spent a lot of time thinking about how we introduce our organization. Usually people do this sort of thing with a statement about their purpose, but I find the standard mission-statement format to be stagnant, abstract and even dictatorial. Questions, on the other hand, are alive. They spark curiosity, inspire continuous engagement from your team, and they can even transform your corporate identity.[3]

## Aggregating

Once sufficient sensing is complete, it's time to aggregate. The team at Cyberclick gets together twice yearly for this purpose. Much of their retreat time is dedicated to deciding where the team is heading next. In preparation for this conversation, everyone on the team is asked to respond to questions like, "What do you think our priorities should be? What is working? What's not working? What are you noticing? What opportunities do you see?" The responses are collected together and organized. The team then has a discussion about priorities and where they want to go next. Everyone on the team, even interns, participates in determining the direction and priorities of the company.

Aggregation is best done in as large a group as possible. Structures for large group conversations such as 1-2-4-All, Wicked Questions and Ecocycle Planning from the Liberating Structures toolkit can make this experience of consolidating thoughts both quick and fun. In the process of aggregating, we often overemphasize the head (intellectual) at the expense of the heart and gut (feelings and intuition). The best sense-and-respond cycles look at things from all three angles.

An example of aggregation in action is Nulogy's semiannual Open Space gathering of its entire 150-person team. Open Space is an approach for hosting meetings that focus on a specific, important purpose or task. Gatherings start without any formal agenda beyond an overall theme. In this way, any topic, idea, opportunity or challenge can be raised. Meeting participants vote with their feet by attending and choosing to stay in the conversations most energizing for them. Notes are collected and compiled from each meeting as a tool for aggregating thoughts and actions.

Swarming is a technique that puts the process of sensing and aggregating on steroids by sourcing the wisdom of crowds. It's based on research that shows that average estimates collected from a large group are almost always more accurate than individual estimates made by members of the group. Swarming provides an equal voice to everyone on a team, in an organization or across a large community. If you're interested in learning more, check out swarm.ai.

## Hold Plans Lightly

As you strip away predict-and-control activities, you may be surprised by how little planning, measuring and budgeting you actually need to do. In a sense-and-respond world, you hold lightly any plans or targets that you create. Every strategy document is alive, constantly revisited and revised.

Planning is nothing more than a set of choices—what we do and don't do—and the resulting actions. When done well, the sensing-and-aggregating steps surface choices and associated actions. For everything else, carry on as is. Likewise, we've gotten into the habit of measuring everything. When something goes wrong, our knee-jerk reaction is to add another measure. Shifting away from target-heavy predict-and-control planning means we're going to measure less... a lot less. That said, getting rid of all targets goes too far.

There are two primary purposes of measurements: to allow a system to self-correct, and to assure external stakeholders that everything is okay. For some, goals also support self-motivation and provide a way of staying on track. That said, the harm caused by goal setting is often overlooked. Anchoring yourself to goals can narrow your focus, leading you to take your eyes off the bigger picture, work counter to your values or take excessive risk. Many of the elements of good work can't be measured. What is the minimum you need to know to work effectively? What does the nature of the work demand? What does the team need in order to opt in? Whatever measures are set, when conditions change, so should the associated measures.

Budgets are a specific type of prediction. Budget setting is a painful annual ritual in many organizations. Do you still need them in a sense-and-respond world? Marco Specialties was facing a dilemma about how to effectively use budgeting. Specifically, they were looking to budget for initiatives to improve sales. They initially considered a plan that included sales training and a six- to twelve-month effort. Before proceeding, they discovered a better option. They had recently implemented new sales reporting with results being published on a weekly basis instead of only quarterly. This allowed the team to completely rethink how they approached their sales challenge. Instead of investing in a big sales-training effort with hopes of seeing increases in sales many months ahead, they could instead try small training experiments and see the result in the following week's data. They quickly learned that while training offered some improvements, better inventory tracking made an even bigger difference. Through sensing and responding, they were able to make a more agile, more effective and less expensive decision.

Creating opportunities for more people to participate in sensing and aggregating is likely to surface more and better ideas. Start
by asking good open-ended questions, using participatory facilitation tools and leveraging emerging technology. Pay close attention
to what portion of the overall process is being spent on sensing,
aggregating and planning. Whatever plans you do create, revisit
them regularly. Experiment, learn and iterate to create a strategy
process that works best in your environment.

# 24

# Rituals

Sustain the Routines
That Matter Most

"We cannot be fully human in organizations that have few rituals and little space for stillness, silence, sadness."

**TIM LEBERECHT AND
GIANPIERO PETRIGLIERI**[1]

RITUALS ARE the tools of purposeful habit building. By doing something intentionally and routinely, we build muscle memory. We also reinforce what is most important to us. Things that may initially feel unnatural and awkward become habitual and even comfortable.

You will have experienced the power of habit. If you get up at the same time each morning, brush your teeth, meditate or do some journaling, exercise and drink a smoothie, those activities become habits forming your healthy morning routine. You might just as easily fall into an unhealthy morning routine of sleeping in, skipping the gym and quickly grabbing a croissant.

Organizations can build unhealthy habits too, which are hard to break once in place. Alternatively, rituals can create healthy habits to sustain successful company cultures. In a 2017 study, "The Psychology of Rituals: An Integrative Review and Process-Based Framework," the authors define a ritual as "predefined sequences characterized by rigidity, formality and repetition that are embedded in a larger system of symbolism and meaning, which partially lack direct instrumental purpose."[2]

Steven Handel, creator of the Emotion Machine website, suggests that rituals:

- are symbolic and meaningful;
- are internally motivated;
- require full engagement;

- are anchored in celebration;
- tell a story;
- bring a sense of belonging; and
- focus on the performance of tasks.[3]

Rituals range from traditional and practical to unique and outrageous. Rituals, and the resulting habits, are anchor points of social connection. Many rituals are anchored in food—regular team lunches, celebratory meals or feedback feasts. These rituals bring people together and break down social hierarchies. They can be created intentionally or can emerge naturally. They often begin when an action, story or phrase is embraced and repeated by the team. Other times, significant planning goes into developing a ritual and its associated cadence. One ritual, which may seem silly but helps participants leave video meetings with a smile, is having an "I'm out" action. The Enspiral Foundation's Catalyst team ends meetings with a victorious arm gesture, while the Golden Pandas team makes panda ears.

In organizations where colleagues are autonomous and self-select how and with whom to work, explicitly communicated routines and rituals take on a heightened level of importance.

## Simple and Powerful Rituals

Two of the easiest, most common and powerful rituals—first introduced in chapter 4—are meeting check-ins and check-outs. The idea is simple: each time you are with a new group of people throughout the day, a check-in welcomes everyone into the space and provides an opportunity for important things to be said. Check-ins are usually completed by going around the physical or virtual room, with each person speaking about what's top of mind. Responses may include statements like, "I'm looking forward to this meeting," or "I'm not sure why I'm at this meeting," or "I just had a frustrating call and I'm distracted." For shorter meetings, a check-in can be as simple as each person saying green, yellow or red to express their emotional tenor.

Sharing your state of mind is important not only to the speaker but also to others in the space. Although people sometimes say what they think the group wants or needs to hear, over time, this practice creates an environment where everyone feels comfortable being authentic and opens the possibility for more trust and honesty. It's also additional data—knowing who has energy and who might be tired or distracted can be very useful in calibrating expectations. Research by Dr. Matthew Lieberman has also shown that naming our emotions can reduce their impact.[4] Emotions are often our body trying to send us information. Sometimes a simple acknowledgment allows things to shift.

Questions asked in check-in circles can be used to both lighten the mood and allow you to get to know the other attendees better. Here are examples of great check-in questions, published by Buffer[5] and by collaboration specialist Amanda Fenton[6]:

- What's the best thing that happened to you today?

- What are you most excited about right now?

- What's the last picture you took on your phone?

- What habit or improvement are you working on?

- What problem do you wish you could solve?

- What's one new and interesting thing you've been thinking about lately?

- What is your personal weather status (cloudy, foggy, sunny and so on)?

- What's one thing you're really proud of that you'd like to share with the group?

- Why did you accept the invitation to join this gathering?

- What are you seeking to learn and contribute?

Check-outs are similar and provide a way to close a meeting with a quick parting thought. A frequently used check-out question when time is tight is "What's one word to describe how you are leaving this meeting?" When there is more time, invite a round where each participant recognizes the contributions of someone else on the team or try the question "What, if anything, has been left unsaid and needs to be shared?"

The daily stand-up meeting, a ritual from the agile community, happens every day in the same place at the same time. As a quick connection point, it allows everyone on the team to understand what's happening day-to-day. Everyone stands and everyone participates, whether attending in person or virtually. One person at a time answers these three questions: What did you do yesterday? What are you going to do today? What are the impediments that could prevent you from delivering? These meetings are not for dialogue, problem-solving or lengthy sharing. When done well, stand-ups take no more than fifteen to twenty minutes, regardless of the group size. Standing reminds everyone not to get too comfortable or talk too long.

With a little planning, the daily stand-up or other meeting rituals can be readily adapted for virtual teams. Use technology for more inclusive meetings, like working together in a Google Doc or on enhanced whiteboard software such as Mural.co, or creating a "cameras always on" video culture. For teams spread across multiple locations, it's possible to use a tool like Slack to do stand-ups asynchronously, allowing everyone to share and get updates when it fits their schedule.

## Cadence

Cadence is the flow or rhythm of events. It's like the pulse of the organization, bringing predictability to an otherwise chaotic environment. Cadence creates a regular schedule for showing work and delivering value. Agile processes work in two-week iterations or sprints. In contrast, bulkier multistage projects traditionally rely on milestones with little sense of cadence.

Let's look at a few examples of how cadence plays a key role in various teams' rituals.

The entire Percolab team meets for two hours every Tuesday at ten a.m. Their meetings are open to anybody, including the public. The check-in, agenda building, approach to decision-making and check-out are all rituals within the weekly meeting routine. The Enspiral Foundation Catalysts use a two-week rhythm of scrum sprints—regular, repeatable work cycles—to manage their work and communicate progress to the network. The predictable heartbeat and consistent flow of the sprints allows individuals to jump in and out of work commitments according to their availability and energy. In addition, the partially distributed team at Enspiral comes together in its entirety for a retreat twice a year for deeper connection. Within the retreats are rituals, like story circles, Open Space and shared meals.

Some rituals are tied to a specific event or a milestone. At SideFX, the morning after a software build breaks, the developer responsible for the error brings in enough doughnuts for the whole department. Over the years, the bringing of doughnuts has become a fun and meaningful ritual. It sends the message that messing with live code is a big deal, that smart people make mistakes and that learning is an ongoing process worth celebrating. Similarly, many teams schedule celebrations when major objectives are achieved.

The Corporate Rebels, a future of work research firm and blog publisher, documented a light structure for their otherwise structureless team, which they posted publicly. Over time, they've developed a way of working based on a weekly and monthly cadence. On the first Monday of every month, the team sits together. It's a day focused on team building, learning, sharing knowledge and helping each other out. They move through the following topics:

**Monthly goals** We use Trello to keep track of who's working on what. We review last month, and then discuss next month's goals. It helps to focus on what matters most at a particular point in time. And it helps us to say no a lot more! It's a great way to create transparency on who does what. It helps us keep track of progress. It's a simple way to practice result-based working.

**Provide feedback** If needed, we take a moment to reflect and provide each other with feedback. Sometimes we use the simple stop, start, continue method that Netflix uses. Other times we follow no specific structure at all.

**Celebrate achievements and fuck-ups** We take some time to reflect on the big achievements and fuck-ups of the past month. It helps us to value the cool things we're doing. We're better at completing this step than we were in the past, and it still needs improving. We're working on that at the moment.

**Community growth** Each month we look at numbers that help us know if we're growing our impact. We use community stats from [social media] and website stats from Google Analytics. It's a way to check the pulse of community involvement.

**Finances** We review important financial documents—the income statement and the cash-flow forecast. Everyone is then aware of current finances. No secrets, no surprises.[7]

In addition to the monthly review, each Monday, the Corporate Rebels team walks through the upcoming week to share who is up to what. It's a sneak peek into one another's main activities and a great way to get excited about the week ahead. Every Friday afternoon, the team meets for a social activity (in real life or virtually) to close the working week.

## Retreats

Rituals are often attached to events, such as retreats. Retreats are not the same as off-site meetings, although they may include similar elements. These events might focus on a particular topic, or may be checkpoints in your organization's ongoing journey. Retreats tend to offer extra time and space for colleagues to be together, relax, play and relate away from the confines of normal routine.

Depending on the group and the intention of the gathering, retreats can be anything from camping trips to catered stays at purpose-built venues. The key is for the group to be together for an uninterrupted, extended time. Szabolcs Emich, an agile coach and facilitator from Hungary, believes in this idea so much that his consulting practice sells three-month residential innovation retreats to multinational companies. His results show that all measures of happiness and performance rise when teammates work and live together.[8] We aren't suggesting this level of intensity or time commitment is possible or necessary for everyone, merely that extended retreats are an option worth consideration.

As a globally distributed team of digital nomads, Greaterthan has ritualized a pattern of seven- to ten-day, in-person work sprints four to six times per year. The six-person team temporarily lives and works together in amazing locations to become invigorated by collective focus and flow. They assert that the recharge from these intense collaborations easily gets them through the next quarter of working solo and in different time zones.

As you plan your first retreats, rituals may need to be defined by making agreements. Will attendance for sessions be optional or mandatory? Will there be alcohol at your retreat? Are laptops and smartphones permitted? Over time these agreements become part of the rhythm. At Enspiral, for example, there is an agreement that story circles happen with no alcohol or substance use before or during this ritual. This act of sanctifying the space offers a level of safety that those substances can sometimes disrupt.

## Beware of Mechanical Rituals

Rituals, especially unnecessary ones, are best not unnaturally forced. If your team's first retreat was a massive success and unlocked all sorts of new ideas, but the second and third did not, then it may be time to experiment with something different to adapt to current needs. Francesca Pick from Greaterthan describes the process of emergent (or minimum viable) rituals:

> We've sort of been learning by doing and adding new rituals and practices as we go. Our general principle is minimum viable bureaucracy. What we've been doing is trying to create this process of letting a behavior or a practice emerge and then writing it down—documenting it and then letting it be taken again into practice where it may get updated again. If you create them as you go, you can keep the creativity and spontaneity. If you create rituals too early, you restrain the energy and they might end up feeling like constraints.[9]

Rituals are different from bureaucracy. They are human and personal. Take care that you are not ritualizing things that need to remain flexible or emergent. You have to be prepared to adapt or even stop rituals if they cease to be useful or the organization has evolved in such a way that something else is more appropriate. In some respects, the commitment to having and appreciating rituals may be more important than the ritual itself.

You can also adapt your organization's default rituals to reflect a new way of working. Blogger Tim Casasola invites us to tweak rituals, for example, by changing the name of a weekly *staff* meeting to a weekly *action* meeting for a different vibe.[10] The ritual of having the meeting doesn't change, but that ritual adapts to reflect its new purpose.

When routines and rituals outlive their purpose, it's time to say goodbye. This is especially true for meetings that have been engraved into the culture for a long time. Ending meetings can be hard because they feel like part of running the business. Try a trial separation. Stop the meeting for three weeks and then ask, "What can we no longer do that we used to be able to?" Letting go of old rituals can free up energy and space for more important and powerful ones to emerge in their place.

## Find Opportunities to Experiment

Humans are creatures of habit. When we leave it to chance, we stumble into both good and bad routines. Our invitation is for you to become more intentional in the habits you and your colleagues create together.

Small, simple rituals can have a significant reinforcing effect on individual and team behaviors. Some rituals may emerge from an intentional social contract, such as having lunch together every Thursday or blocking Monday mornings for a team planning session. Other rituals drift into playful or whimsical territory: "If you're at work on your birthday, you will be invited to spend the day wearing an adult-sized banana onesie."

Notice your organization's cultural patterns. What rituals and routines already exist, even if unnamed? Which ones are important enough to name, emphasize and proactively support? Perhaps you'll notice some patterns you want to let go. Allow space for a range of ideas, including fun and silly ones, to take on a life of their own.

# 25

# Operating Systems

Design Your Organization

"Theories are like scaffolding: they are not the house, but you cannot build the house without them."

**CONSTANCE FENIMORE WOOLSON**[1]

T HROUGHOUT THE BOOK, we have shared ideas based on an agile, ecosystem approach to organizing. Each philosophy or tool is powerful on its own and offers opportunities for you to experiment. We have saved the most significant and deeply rooted element of traditional business for the end. Despite the effectiveness of everything we've shared, real change will be elusive if your organization's structure is a rigid hierarchy.

Traditional hierarchies are old school. They are useful in reducing variation and creating repeatability by centralizing information and restricting innovation. Despite the compelling reasons to abandon hierarchical structures, young organizations often start pyramid-building without considering other options.

Progressive leaders have experimented with a variety of alternatives, replacing rigid pyramids with agile structures. These experiments have resulted in some clever and effective systems embraced by organizations around the world. Three different approaches have stood the test of time, with most of the teams profiled in this book relying on one of the three: parallel teams, webs of individual contracting or nested teams.[2]

Hierarchy still exists on each of these paths, but it is dynamic rather than static. Today you may be best qualified to lead a specific project or part of your company while being led by someone else in other areas. Next month, a different configuration might make more sense.

**Parallel teams** are small groups within a larger organization with each group doing work similar to the next. Buurtzorg, a Dutch home-care organization, has many autonomous teams of around a dozen nurses that take care of different neighborhoods. Parallel teams are best for large organizations with a short value chain, such as retail or service-based businesses. When a small number of people can deliver the full value chain to a customer with little coordination needed between groups, parallel teams provide a lean, efficient and customer-centric approach. Parallel teams often rely on coaches to teach people how to work in a self-organized way. A small centralized group of specialized resources may also support the teams in areas such as IT and finance.

In **webs of individual contracting**, people or microenterprises negotiate between themselves to create agreements. Haier, the world's largest appliance maker, with 75,000 employees, uses this model. In Haier's case, a microenterprise—a small group of people within the larger organization—could be a team that has decided to bring a smart refrigerator to market. That microenterprise might hire other microenterprises from within Haier to help with sales, manufacturing, marketing and finance. Webs of individual contracting function best for long, simple value chains that do not change often, such as food or chemical processing and lengthy assembly lines. Rather than relying on a predesigned structure, team members in these organizations establish contracts with each other that determine accountabilities, agreements and associated goals. It's a peer-to-peer process that creates a web of relationships and accountabilities, instead of relying on centralized control or a chain of command.

**Nested teams** offers the most flexible model of the three. Nested teams consist of circles or groups within other groups. This model is most similar to traditional hierarchies, with a few notable exceptions. First, circles have a hierarchy of purpose rather than a hierarchy of authority. Team members commonly fill roles in multiple circles at different levels within the structure. Second, there are defined ways for circles to interact with each other. Nested teams work best for long, complex value chains, such as banking, software and hardware product development or aerospace. When a value chain is long, complex and dynamic, nested teams subdivide the organization's purpose and related work into roles and smaller subcircles. Roles connect subcircles with pre-established rules, keeping things running smoothly. The three most popular nested team operating systems are sociocracy, Holacracy and sociocracy 3.0. A fourth derivative system called Organic Organizations is also emerging.

## Sociocracy

The word *sociocracy* was coined by French philosopher Auguste Comte in the 1850s to describe a new way for people to organize themselves into social systems and for governments to govern. Over the next 120 years, Auguste's initial concepts developed further, resulting in Gerard Endenburg's Sociocratic Circle Organization Method. Gerard's system, now commonly known as sociocracy, consists of a hierarchy of circles with links between each circle that form feedback loops throughout an organization. Four principles are core to sociocracy:

**Consent** Consent governs policy decision-making. Decisions are made when there are no remaining paramount objections, that is, when all participants give informed consent.

**Hierarchy of purpose and focus** A hierarchy of semiautonomous circles composes the organization. The hierarchy does not constitute a power structure but rather different scopes of purpose and focus.

**Linked circles** One individual within each circle is a full member in the decision-making of both their own circle and the next higher circle, creating a link between circles.

**Elected roles** Individuals are elected to roles and responsibilities through open discussion, using the same informed consent criteria as for other policy decisions.

The Sociocracy Group (founded by Gerard), the Sociocracy Consulting Group, Sociocracy for All and other organizations provide support to companies adopting and practicing sociocracy.

## Holacracy by HolacracyOne

Holacracy is an operating system born out of the experiences of Brian Robertson. Brian founded Ternary Software in 2001. The start-up software company became a laboratory for experiments designed to answer the question "What gets in the way of people working together as effectively and efficiently as possible?" As the system evolved through trial and error, it became known as Holacracy. Brian then partnered with entrepreneur Tom Thomison to further evolve the system for more general use and bring it to other organizations.

Holacracy allows each organization to customize its set of processes, roles and rules, using structured steps that facilitate continued customization and evolution. The company's website describes the framework as bringing "structure and discipline to a peer-to-peer workplace." It is designed to offer an agile organizational structure, efficient meeting formats, increased autonomy to teams and individuals and a unique "meta-process" for changing any other process in the organization. The key aspects of Holacracy include:

**A fundamental power shift** Everyone works under the same concrete, actionable set of rules on a level playing field and within a framework that helps each organization customize the specific roles and processes for their unique circumstances.

**Clearly defined roles** Each team defines clear roles and responsibilities, with roles defined around the work rather than titles and status. Some roles may have a broader scope of authority than others.

**A governance process** Each team has its own governance process in support of a decentralized learning environment that allows the organization's structure to change as soon as a need for improvement is sensed.

**Operational practices** Operational practices, including tactical meetings, help teams be efficient, result in actionable outputs with clear ownership and support high levels of autonomy.

The greatest benefits of Holacracy are role and process clarity, especially in the early stages of organizational transformation. When executed well, there is little ambiguity about how things are to run and how decisions are to be made. It is an efficient system. Some argue that the efficiency of Holacracy comes at the expense of the human element. Others disagree. The team at Evolution at Work has developed the Symbiotic Enterprise and associated Language of Spaces frameworks to increase the human element in Holacracy's organization context.

A debate about whether Holacracy is scalable beyond mid-sized organizations is raging. Zappos, once a scrappy scale-up and now an Amazon subsidiary, has developed a reputation for testing out radical ideas. In March 2015, the company's CEO, Tony Hsieh, announced the company was shifting to Holacracy. Since then, the 1,500-employee company has become an ongoing case study on the pros and cons of this new way of working.

HolacracyOne provides a software platform called GlassFrog to administer Holacracy's structures and meetings. Certified Holacracy consultants are available to assist with implementations and ongoing coaching.

## Sociocracy 3.0

Sociocracy 3.0 (S3) is a framework developed by Bernhard Bockel-brink and James Priest based on the methodologies of sociocracy, Holacracy and agile. S3 centers on seven basic principles:

**Effectiveness** Devote time only to what brings you closer to achieving your objectives.

**Consent** Do things in the absence of reasons not to.

**Empiricism** Test all assumptions through experiments, continuous revision and falsification.

**Continuous improvement** Change incrementally to accommodate steady, empirical learning.

**Equivalence** People affected by decisions influence and change them on the basis of reasons to do so.

**Transparency** All information is available to everyone in an organization, unless there is a reason for confidentiality.

**Accountability** Respond when something is needed, do what you agreed to and take ownership for the course of the organization.[3]

S3 is an open source framework shared via a Creative Commons free cultural works license, allowing anyone to use and apply the philosophies. The S3 team is available for consulting, learning facilitation, coaching and mentoring.

## Organic Organizations

The Organic Organizations (O2) operating system is being developed by Target Teal in Brazil. Similar to the Holacracy constitution, O2 offers a set of essential rules, or meta-agreements, all organizations are encouraged to follow. Building on the work of sociocracy and S3, it also offers a library of patterns that teams can leverage. O2 incorporates an element not contained in the Holacracy system that is often called out by critics as missing: tribal space. Tribal space acknowledges the need and provides the time for people to connect human to human. It's for soul-to-soul connection and distinct from the role-to-role interactions that dominate most work. By defining a space separate and distinct from the more tactical elements of the operating system, O2 highlights the importance of caring for relationships. In doing so, it aims to develop communication, recognize individual needs and nurture openness among members.

The team at Target Teal runs workshops in Brazil and globally to support organizations in adopting their approach to organizing and working together.

## Reflect and Act on Your Journey

Many of the practices shared throughout these pages can stand on their own as independent experiments in one-on-one relationships and small-team settings. As we explore bringing everything together within a unifying structure and operating system, now is a good time to check in with yourself:

- How am I feeling about shifting from traditional hierarchy to embrace the Teal paradigm?

- What have I tried so far? What holds me back?

- How have my perspectives on leadership evolved?

- Where have I encountered resistance within myself? With others?

- What potential benefits are exciting me?

- What additional support do I need to begin or keep going with the journey?

Everyone's journey is unique. Transforming your organizational structure will be appealing to some and completely off the table for others. Only you and your colleagues can decide if and when the time is right for this type of big experiment. As you may recall us saying in chapter 12, fruit is best eaten when it's ripe, and by the time we have all the information we'd like, decisions are usually beyond ripe. Every self-managing team we've supported as they embraced the Teal paradigm longed for more examples or more data, but over time they came to appreciate that it's only after jumping in with both feet and experiencing true immersion that the learning truly began. What do you need to jump into with both feet?

## Choose a Path

Organizations have adopted the aforementioned methodologies in different ways. Some have taken a system as is, while others have followed the path of Kurtis McBride at Miovision. Kurtis read about and researched many different philosophies and then customized an approach for his company.

You may also need to try out a few different approaches, learning and iterating until you land on what works best for your organization. The team at Deeson went through a few models before finding the best structure. They started with what they called pods, popularized by the team at Spotify, in a variation on the parallel teams approach. Each pod had a group of clients to work with. Conceptually it made sense and people could get their heads around it, but it became an operational nightmare. One pod would have too much work, while another would not have enough. It evolved into a system where the pods were lending people back and forth. In the end, the team realized the pod approach didn't work well in their context.

For their second experiment, the team members were grouped around projects and given autonomy to serve the needs of their respective projects without extensive policies or organizational units—a web of individual contracting. The team has since moved to a loose matrix structure, in which people belong to what they call a chapter, based on disciplines such as technical, design or user experience. They belong to the chapter, with the bulk of their day-to-day engagement and measurements of success tied to specific projects. The team has been working this way for three years now. With a few minor tweaks, it continues working well and has scaled nicely.

Our intention is not to advocate for one approach over another but rather to invite you to explore beyond traditional hierarchy. That said, the operating systems outlined here have been tried and tested by many companies. Building your own system from scratch may lead to years of work and result in a mess. Having made it this far into the book, you must already believe there is much to be learned from those who have come before you.

Whatever path you choose, we offer one last piece of advice: when shifting to any new system or approach outside of a traditional hierarchy, recognize that it will be a journey. There is no guaranteed path to success. Limit the challenges by learning from others, investing in training and coaching and celebrating progress. Enjoy the journey; it is a gift in and of itself.

# 26

# Legal Agreements

Take a Values-Based
Approach

"If you're not going to take the time to translate values from ideals to behaviors … it's better not to profess any values at all. They become a joke. A cat poster. Total BS."

**BRENÉ BROWN**[1]

P ERHAPS THE BEST test of lived values can be found in your legal agreements. What messages do those agreements convey about you and your team? Is it okay to say you value human connection and collaboration yet ask new members to sign a cold, templated employment agreement? We have been well conditioned to write and sign lengthy, impersonal legal documents filled with language never used in any other context. We draft agreements from a place of fear, worrying that we'll be burned in the future. Can you feel the dissonance between the values held by leaders profiled throughout this book and traditional legalese? As we shared in chapter 4, language matters.

How did the typical legal agreement get to be verbose and hard to read? The answer lies in centuries of cultural evolution. The law as we know it today in the English-speaking world has its roots in the Roman Empire. Legal tradition changed as territories were conquered and then conquered again. Old English, Anglo-Norman French, Medieval Latin, French and English all took turns as official languages for contract law. In the medieval era, lawyers used a mixture of Latin, French and English in contracts. Sometimes for clarity or to provide greater emphasis, lawyers paired words from different languages and eventually those pairings became stylistic habits. For example, *will and testament* is a combination of English and Latin.

So here we are, anchored in outdated language. In the words of Stewart Levine, author of *The Book of Agreement* and former deputy attorney for the state of New Jersey, "Most legalese is left over from the past and of no significance... In some ways, legalese demonstrates laziness about cleaning up old language."[2] Following decades of experience practicing and teaching law, Stewart has moved away from traditional legal language. His perspective is that "if an [agreement] contains a promise by one person to do something by a certain date, for a certain amount and the promised performance can be measured, then it is a legally enforceable agreement."

## Values-Based Agreements

Rather than from a place of fear and scarcity, values-based agreements are rooted in abundance and opportunity. They put in place values-aligned approaches for addressing future changes, conflicts and crises. Easy to understand, these documents are human-centered, providing certainty and safety. Kim Wright is a lawyer who specializes in values-based agreements. For Kim, this values-aligned approach starts at the very beginning, when a company is forming. The founding documents create a conscious foundation for the organization.

A values-based agreement doesn't start with a document; the facilitated process ends with one. From Kim's experience, "It starts with people who've come together representing their entities. They've had conversations and sorted out what's really important to them. That's the foundation upon which they're going to work. They've seen what they appreciate about each other and that's why they're making this agreement with each other."[3] The written document follows this organically structured conversation and exploration. The end-to-end process helps you figure out who you are entering into an agreement with. When they push back, why are they pushing back? In the traditional system, the inability to come to agreement is considered a failure. In the values-based agreement process, a contract that doesn't happen because values don't align is a gift. It's better to find out in advance that the match isn't there.

Fred Schneider and Von Coven cofounded Breyting Community Roaster, a coffee roasting company in Florida. At the heart of their roastery is an ambition to contribute to economic, social and environmental progress, using the coffee business to fund other collaborative projects. Von and Fred realized their commitment to change needed to encompass how they engage contractually with each other and with others. They reached out to Kim Wright for help. For Von, embracing values-based contracts was "kinda life changing." At first, it took him a while to get comfortable with the approach. He came to appreciate that he wasn't used to being so vulnerable in a business context:

> In previous business relationships, I didn't ask or answer the right questions. I didn't understand my business partner's goals and he didn't understand mine. When starting Breyting, we had the hard discussions up front. We really got into things... "What do you value? What do I value? What if you die? What if I die? What if there's a shortage of money? How will we handle disgruntled employees?" Now we feel really confident. If we ever need to go in front of a judge, it will be to uphold our original agreement that we spent so much time creating.[4]

Breyting has gone on to use values-based contracts in many different contexts. Every agreement they sign embraces their values and beliefs.

## Traditional Contracts versus Values-Based Agreements

Let's take a look at common elements of traditional contracts compared to those found in values-based agreements. In which column do your current agreements reside? What's your intention for the future?

| Traditional Contracts | Values-Based Agreements |
|---|---|
| Shaped with a protectionist and competitive mindset that assumes participants will be future adversaries | Starts with the belief that participants are partners in cocreating their desired future and therefore invites creativity and collaboration |
| Conflict resolution goes unaddressed or includes grievance clauses that move parties immediately to investigations, mediation and/or litigation | Conflict is anticipated and invited with clear, values-aligned steps for addressing changes and engaging disagreement while restoring comfort, collegiality and alignment |
| Designed to be interpreted by others in the legal profession and written in formal legalese using words like *heretofore, indemnification, warrant* and *force majeure* | Written in everyday, conversational language ("I agree I am responsible for," "I promise to," "I agree to pay") so the documents can be read and understood by those using them |
| Created from a comprehensive template covering a broad set of potential risks | Personalized and customized to suit the specific participants and their unique situations |
| Rely on rules in an attempt to minimize the need for trust | Anchored in purpose, values and transparency to maintain ongoing alignment and trust |

FX Agency is a corporate communications firm based in the Netherlands. Its employment agreement fits on one sheet of paper and is written in plain, easy-to-read language with an attractive graphic layout. The left-hand side shows what the team is offering, including the job title, contract duration, salary, pension, paid leave and travel expenses. The right-hand side shows what's expected in return in the form of the team's shared values. The back contains four simple legal paragraphs, which integrate it with the conventional legal system. Simple, effective and legally binding. In the words of the company's founder, Peter Zijlstra, "We have had nothing but compliments from all the colleagues who have joined us since we started using this employment contract. It provides a warm welcome as they start their career with us."[5]

In *The Book of Agreement*, Stewart outlines ten essential elements that should be included in every agreement:

- intent and vision
- roles
- promises
- time and values
- measurements of satisfaction
- concerns, risks and fears
- renegotiation/dissolution
- consequences
- conflict resolution
- a final confirmation that an agreement has been reached[6]

He provides thirty-one examples of agreements that span a wide set of situations. Each one is written in simple language and short enough to fit on one page. We recommend picking up a copy of Stewart's book and transforming how you draft your next agreement.

## Harmony and Dispute Resolution

Instituting a clear conflict-resolution mechanism long before disagreements emerge is key. What steps will you take to find resolution? What restorative questions will you work through together? Who will you trust to help you navigate more challenging or emotionally charged disagreements? What principles will guide you in returning to alignment? Linda Alvarez is a US-based lawyer and author of *Discovering Agreement*. In Linda's words, "So many people understand the law to be about retribution when someone has done something that doesn't line up."[7] Linda encourages including an Addressing Change and Engaging Disagreement module in every agreement:

The Addressing Change and Engaging Disagreement module takes a restorative response to conflict, restoring connections, mourning the unmet need and looking at the conditions that gave rise to the disruption. The person who is the author of whatever act has been the trigger didn't do the thing they did because they're a bad person. They did it because it made sense in the context they were in. Addressing Change and Engaging Disagreement gives us a way to look at that context, look at those conditions and take responsibility across the board. This allows us to avoid making someone an accused. As soon as there is an accused, there's a danger of retribution or coercion. We're no longer going to have an open, healing conversation.[8]

In Breyting's founder agreement, there is a lengthy conflict-resolution process outlined that begins with Von and Fred getting together for drinks and discussing their differences. If that isn't sufficient, a peer review follows, then mediation. The process continues all the way to valuing the company, should they need to part ways. In their work, the Breyting team engages independent artists. In agreements with these individuals, Breyting's values are shared and artists are asked to share theirs too. Breyting then asks how artists want to be treated if they fall short on delivery, according to their arrangement. From Von's perspective, "We're going so much deeper than lawyers do in each of our agreements."[9]

## The Role of Lawyers

We are each capable of shaping our own agreements, and those agreements need to integrate with a conventional legal system. Lawyers help us check our plans to ensure we're not getting ourselves into trouble with the larger system. It's helpful to remember the conventional system tells us what we can't do, not what we can do.

When conflicts arise and we have a cocreated conflict-resolution module in place, a conversation facilitator is often who's needed most. Some lawyers have the appropriate training and right mind-set to fill this role. Others do not. Von decided he needed to part ways with his attorney. When he wanted to resolve a potential dispute by getting everyone together for tea, his lawyer suggested suing instead. In Von's words, "I needed a peace maker, not a conflict creator."

Before engaging a lawyer, ask yourself what help you specifically want from your lawyer. Does the lawyer understand and support your values and intentions? What power and authority are you passing to the lawyer and what self-determination are you keeping? Choose a partner who will invest the time to translate your values into written agreements that define the relationships you desire to foster.

# 27

# Handbooks, Playbooks and Blogs

Document and
Share How You Work

"If it's not documented, it's not open source."

**ALANNA IRVING**[1]

I N THE LAST twenty-six chapters, we've shared a plethora of ideas, practices and rituals. Every organization we've encountered has a unique story to tell. Many of those organizations have chosen to publicly share how they work through handbooks, playbooks and blogs. Disclosing core operating principles openly is yet another example of the transparency that differentiates self-managing businesses from the traditionally secretive ways in which many choose to function. Rather than believing that we compete to win so others will lose, progressive entities instead focus on achieving a meaningful purpose. In doing so, they share their learning for everyone's benefit, helping others to fulfill their purpose faster.

The team agreements we introduced in chapter 10 are often collected together into a single living artifact, usually called a handbook or playbook. Team agreements only work when they are transparent to everyone involved. How can someone be accountable to an agreement they haven't seen, don't remember, didn't commit to or can't reference? The documents are published in various styles and formats and are made easily accessible and editable.

When the team at ET Group first began shifting to self-organizing after decades in a traditional hierarchy, forty people needed to align. To help, members of ET Group's teamwork and relationships circle led the cocreation of a playbook. It's a small printed booklet that contains the company's purpose along with an overview of the team's structure and high-level operating practices. This small playbook provided sufficient guidance to get the team started, and they now update and reprint it as needed.

Once the first playbook was complete, questions started to arise. The team was looking for more guidance, more clarity. The HR handbook that the company had been using for years no longer fit the team's needs or ways of working. A new online handbook was born as a detailed reference guide to how things work at ET Group. It's an evolving document. Now every member of the team has two places to go for guidance: the playbook provides high-level guidance while the handbook gets into the fine details.

## How Self-Organizing Handbooks Are Different

Traditional companies use employment contracts, job descriptions and policies as tools to articulate expectations and control activities. Often the content of these documents does little to inspire proactive team engagement and goes unreferenced until troubles arise. Cocreated handbooks offer a better alternative.

As first introduced in chapter 4, shifting our use of language is core to successful self-organizing. The documentation we outline in this chapter differs significantly from traditional human resource policy handbooks. HR policies tend to be legalistic and focus on compliance, with command-and-control language. The substance of the content gets pushed down into the organization. Effective team agreements and handbooks differ in six core ways, as shown in the table below.

| Traditional Employee Documentation | Cocreated Team Agreements |
|---|---|
| Cover the maximum number of possibilities that can be contemplated | Cover the events you are currently experiencing or foresee coming up soon |
| Are written by employers and define formal agreements between employees and the company | Are written by the team, for the team, to clarify relationships and collective agreements |
| Use third-person policy- and rule-based language (you should, must, never, are required to) | Use first-person casual language (we agree, find, have come to appreciate, have a shared expectation) |
| Are based on carrots and sticks and a belief that people need to be kept in line | Are based on mutual trust and a belief that everyone has a positive intention |
| Use future-state language (will, when required, should) | Use current-state language (agree, do, share, understand) |
| Are rigid and unchanging | Are adjusted and customized frequently to evolve with the group |

As you may notice, cocreated team agreements have a different feel. Consider this introduction from a traditional handbook:

The purpose of this handbook is to provide employees with an overview and understanding of the core policies that underlie the employment relationship with the company. While it is not possible to cover every situation that employees will face, there are certain basic principles to which every employee must adhere during their course of employment with us. These provisions apply in all jurisdictions where we may conduct business now and in the future.

The policies, practices and benefits, including those described in the handbook, may change from time to time. Management reserves the right to amend, modify, rescind, delete, supplement or add to the provisions of this handbook as appropriate.

Now compare that with an introduction from a self-managing handbook:

> This set of agreements is written by our team, for our team. While this handbook is written primarily for those of us who are employees and ongoing contractors, many sections may prove useful to others in our ecosystem.
>
> In creating this handbook, we avoided as much legal jargon as possible and focused instead on the kinds of relationships we'd like to have with each other. In some cases, we've had to keep the legal jargon to interface with the outside world.
>
> In signing on to our handbook, you are giving an enthusiastic thumbs-up to our culture, values and agreements. Welcome! We think you're going to like it here.

Can you feel the difference? The first is written to protect and the second to clarify, align and unite. As we learned in the previous chapter, much of the legalistic framing of agreements is left over from a different era and is now unnecessary.

## Write Your Handbook

Every handbook we've read is unique. To help you get started, we've created a list of the kinds of agreements and points to consider including. Remember that self-organizing handbooks aim to cover current events rather than contemplate all future scenarios.

### Big picture
Purpose: your story/your why
Values: your shared values
Organization: how you organize yourself and make changes to your governance
Clients: who you prefer to work with (and not work with)
Rituals: the rituals and routines you follow

**Building and strengthening the team**
Hiring: how you go about expanding your team
Diversity: your beliefs about diversity and how you build a diverse team
Professional development: how you support each other to grow your skills and experiences
Exiting: your shared understanding of how and when members leave your team

**Coworking**
Updating agreements: how you update your shared agreements
Location: shared expectations for time spent in office and how you work remotely
Time away: Managing vacation, leaves and absences
Performance: your shared performance expectations
Feedback: how you give and receive feedback
Conflict: managing interpersonal tensions
Health and safety: how you keep your team safe
Quality control: your shared quality expectations for customer deliverables
Technology: the technology you agree to use to make working together easier

**Financial elements**
Compensation: how you think about compensation
Benefits: the perks and benefits you enjoy
Expenses: how the spending of organizational funds is decided

**Information and communication**
Communication: how you communicate with each other, your customers and your partners
Branding: how you use your branding and market your offerings
Transparency: what you share and how you share it
Confidentiality: your shared understanding about how you manage confidential information

Intellectual property: your shared understanding of what belongs to and remains with the organization

**Social responsibility**
Sustainability: how you support a sustainable world
Giving: how you get involved in your local community and give back

It's time to get inspired! To see and experience transparency in action, visit open.buffer.com where Buffer shares its learnings in an ongoing series of blog posts we love. A list of our favorite handbooks can be found in the resources section.

THIS BRINGS us to the end of the book and, we hope, to the beginning of your personal journey of leading in a self-managing context.

We believe the world is ready for, in need of and embarking on a radical transformation of unprecedented scale. At the core of this transformation is a move to more self-organizing, self-managing ways of working and being. Championing this transformation is the number one leadership challenge of our time.

How might you be the best leader you can be for current times? Are you ready to step up and step in with grit, initiative and a willingness to do the essential work of internal transformation? We hope you've discovered new and inspiring ideas that have expanded your thinking.

There is a growing cohort of leaders who are championing this transformation. Are you one of them? Has your thinking shifted? Have you become aware of the potential of ecosystem collaborations that consider and benefit from the whole?

We truly hope the stories, experiments and invitations throughout this book will provide you with support, guidance and the knowledge that you are not alone. We have not given you a standard framework for your upcoming journey nor have we provided a step-by-step guide. Instead, the resources here are offered as encouragement to iterate, experiment and evolve to uncover and amplify your and your organization's purpose.

If you need help, reach out to us. We're continuing the conversation at leadtogether.co and would love to hear your story.

# Acknowledgments

W E OWE A sincere debt of gratitude to all who have contributed to this book:

Alanna Irving, Anthony Cabraal, Björn Lundén, Bogdan Haiducu, Brad Dunkley, Brian Robertson, Bruce Peters, Bryan Peters, Bryan Ungard, Cara Conceller, Carolyn Swora, Chris Ashworth, Christian Kroll, Damien Douté, Dave Hewett, Davi Gabriel da Silva, David Tomás, Dirk Propfe, Doug Kirkpatrick, Ed Frauenheim, Edwin Jansen, Eric Windeler, Erika Bailey, Francesca Pick, George Pór, Greg Judelman, Harm Jans, Heather Fields, Helen Sanderson, Jan Perkins, Jane Watson, Jason Cottrell, Jason Tham, John Breininger, Joost Minnaar, Joshua Vial, Jurriaan Kamer, Karin Tenelius, Kate Beecroft, Keith McCandless, Kent Gregory, Kim Davidson, Kim Wright, Kurtis McBride, Laura Zizzo, Lee Manning, Linda Alvarez, Lotta Croiset van Uchelen, Luz Iglesias, Maria Cristina C. Dela Cruz, Marin Petrov, Mark Kuznicki, Matt McKenna, Paul Mandeltort, Paweł Jędrzejewski, Peter Aprile, Peter Zijlstra, Philip Baumann, Pim de Morree, Ria Baeck, Richard Sheridan, Rob Reed, Robbie Ruuskanen, Rodrigo Bastos, Ryan Zizzo, Samantha Slade, Sara Dunkley, Sean O'Connor, Sheella Meirson, Simon Mhanna, Simon Wakeman, Stuart Voaden, Suchitra Davies-Webb, Tim Jones, Tim Magwood, Todd Valentine, Tom Nixon, Tony Florio, Ved Krishna, Von Coven.

Throughout our writing, we relied heavily on the great work and support of the Brave Works community of leaders, the Corporate

Rebels, Frederic Laloux, Enspiral and Lisa Gill. Thank you for collecting and sharing the stories that help us all Lead Together. Having self-published our previous two books, our appreciation for the team at Page Two is immense. Thank you for sharing your wealth of expertise, providing us with phenomenal guidance and being all-around awesome human beings.

**FROM BRENT:** A long list of individuals have been instrumental in helping me develop to the point where writing this book became possible. Dirk Propfe, Edwin Jansen, Jim Diotte, Peter Shallard, Roberta Beecroft and Susan Basterfield—a special thanks to you for opening doors and windows that have proven to be transformational. To my family and friends—love and gratitude for allowing me an abundance of space and time, and for the encouragement to bring this book to life. And lastly, to you, the reader—thank you for seeking out bold, brave and intentional ways of leading together. The world needs more leaders like you.

**FROM SUSAN:** As someone who always felt a little bit like the nerd sitting in the corner, both in school and in the workplace, I'm thankful to the people who illuminated a different path and changed everything for me—especially the brilliant humans I practice alongside. To my beloved Colin, for everything. And to my families, both traditional and chosen, for your love and support and showing me that it's possible to fulfill one's livelihood by doing work you love with people you love. And most of all to you reading this now: be emboldened to step in and manifest a life-giving workplace.

**FROM TRAVIS:** I'm deeply grateful, inspired and humbled by the hard work so many leaders are willing to put in. They are building a better and different world in the products and services that they create, and they are willing to do the incredible heavy lifting of imagining a new world of work. It's a world where work is immensely more connecting, energizing and just more human. I'm also inspired and energized by all of the amazing communities that have self-organized to help spread this knowledge, including the Teal Team, Institute for Evolutionary Leadership, Responsive Org and last but not least Teal for Startups, which is where our work together as coauthors began. Finally, to my wonderful wife, Nicole, who challenged me to take some of these crazy ideas I loved and put them into a book the second week we were dating. That stone is still casting ripples in my life, and hopefully some of this can be a positive ripple for you as well.

# Resources

WE OFFER you the following list of resources to support you on this path to a new way of working.

## To Learn More about the Emerging Teal/Self-Managing Paradigm

*Better Work Together: How the Power of Community Can Transform Your Business* (Wellington, New Zealand: Enspiral Foundation, 2019) by producing authors Anthony Cabraal and Susan Basterfield. A compendium of stories, practices, tools and lessons from one of the world's preeminent globally distributed self-organized collectives. betterworktogether.co

*Brave New Work*: *Are You Ready to Reinvent Your Organization?* (New York: Portfolio/Penguin, 2019) by Aaron Dignan. An excellent, easy read about the future of work. The book includes a helpful operating system canvas. bravenewwork.com

*Corporate Rebels: Make Work More Fun* (Eindhoven, Netherlands: Corporate Rebels, 2020) by Joost Minnaar and Pim de Morree. A fantastic source of stories and inspiration drawn from the authors' travels to some of the world's most progressive organizations. You can learn more about their book and read their extensive blog at corporate-rebels.com.

*Enlivening Edge*. A free, searchable online magazine with over 1,000 articles, stories and perspectives about the evolution of organizations and social systems. enliveningedge.org

*Holacracy: The New Management System for a Rapidly Changing World* (New York: Henry Holt and Company, 2015) by Brian Robertson. An introduction to Holacracy, which has influenced how many self-managing organizations are shaped. holacracybook.com

*Leadermorphosis* hosted by Lisa Gill. A podcast exploring the emerging world of self-management and progressive organizations through the firsthand experiences of thought leaders and practitioners. leadermorphosis.co

*Reinventing Organizations: A Guide to Creating Organizations Inspired by the Next Stage of Human Consciousness* (Millis, MA: Nelson Parker, 2014) or *Reinventing Organizations: An Illustrated Invitation to Join the Conversation on Next-Stage Organizations* (Millis, MA: Nelson Parker, 2016) both by Frederic Laloux. Arguably the most comprehensive piece of writing about the Teal paradigm currently available. Additional valuable resources, including a video series by the author, can be found at reinventingorganizations.com.

## To Deepen Your Skills of Leading Together

The work of Dr. Brené Brown. Taking an honest look at our personal and professional areas of development requires vulnerability, which is Brené's specialty. Her body of work includes a variety of books, recorded workshops and one of the top five TED Talks of all time. brenebrown.com

*Going Horizontal: Creating a Non-Hierarchical Organization, One Practice at a Time* (Oakland, CA: Berrett-Koehler Publishers, 2018) by Samantha Slade. Becoming our best leadership self requires breaking old habits and experimenting with new practices. *Going*

*Horizontal* introduces readers to seven practices core to self-management. goinghorizontal.co

The Integrative Enneagram. An assessment tool based on an archetypal framework that offers in-depth insight to individuals, groups and collectives. There is an endless number of assessment tools available to help us learn more about ourselves. This tool is preferred by many on the Teal journey because it speaks to levels of consciousness. integrative9.com

*Joy, Inc.: How We Built a Workplace People Love* (New York: Portfolio/Penguin, 2015) by Richard Sheridan. CEO and "chief storyteller" Richard Sheridan details how the Menlo Innovations team removed the fear and ambiguity that typically make a workplace miserable and turned the company into an atmosphere full of energy, playfulness, enthusiasm and maybe even...joy.

*Leadership and Self-Deception: Getting Out of the Box* (Oakland, CA: Berrett-Koehler Publishers, 2018) by the Arbinger Institute. Through the story of a man facing challenges at work and at home, this book shows how we blind ourselves to our true motivations and, in the process, sabotage our effectiveness and happiness. arbingerinstitute.com

## To Improve Your Team's Decision-Making Capacity

"The Advice Process." A guide to how the team at Equal Experts uses the advice process can be found at advice-process.playbook.ee.

*The Decision Maker: Unlock the Potential of Everyone in Your Organization, One Decision at a Time* (Seattle, WA: Pear Press, 2013) by Dennis Bakke. The book provides a simple framework called the advice process that enables everyone to make good decisions. decisionmakerbook.com

"Generative Decision-Making." An introduction to the generative decision-making process can be found at percolab.com/en/generative-decision-making-process.

## To Build a Deliberately Developmental Organization

*An Everyone Culture: Becoming a Deliberately Developmental Organization* (Boston, MA: Harvard Business School Publishing, 2016) by Robert Kegan and Lisa Laskow Lahey. A book about creating cultures where everyone can overcome their own internal barriers to change and learn to use errors and vulnerabilities as prime opportunities for personal and company growth.

## To Create Legal Agreements Aligned with the Philosophy of *Lead Together*

*The Book of Agreement: 10 Essential Elements for Getting the Results You Want* (Oakland, CA: Berrett-Koehler Publishers, 2002) by Stewart Levine. A demonstration of how agreements for results are far superior to agreements for protection, the book outlines ten principles for creating agreements and provides over thirty specific templates.

*Discovering Agreement: Contracts That Turn Conflict into Creativity* (Candescence Media, 2016) by Linda Alvarez. An approach to generating legally enforceable documents that embed responsive, resilient operating systems into contractual relationships in support of sustainable, agile, adaptable value-based business relationships. discoveringagreement.com

## To Facilitate Authentic Conversations

*Crucial Conversations: Tools for Talking When Stakes Are High* (New York: McGraw-Hill, 2002) by Al Switzler, Joseph Grenny, Kerry Patterson and Ron McMillan. The subtitle of this book says it all. vitalsmarts.com/online-store

Liberating Structures. A series of thirty-three practical, open-source, how-to methods for meeting, planning, deciding and relating to one another. liberatingstructures.com

Open Space Technology. A method for organizing and running a meeting or multiday conference, where participants create the agenda on the fly to address important issues. openspaceworld.org

The World Café. A structured conversational process in which groups of people discuss a topic, often with predefined questions to help participants get curious and encourage collective action. theworldcafe.com

## To Explore Diversity

*The Person You Mean to Be: How Good People Fight Bias* (New York: Harper Business, 2018) by Dolly Chugh. How to confront difficult issues including sexism, racism and inequality, with practical tools to avoid being a well-intentioned barrier to equality. dollychugh .com/book

## Our Favorite Handbooks

Crisp operating model: theagilitycollective.github.io/dna/docs
Enspiral: handbook.enspiral.com
ET Group: handbook.etgroup.ca
Greaterthan: handbook.greaterthan.works
Ian Martin Group: teal.ianmartin.com
Loomio: loomio.coop
Valve: valvesoftware.com/hu/publications

## Our Favorite Blogs and Newsletters

Buffer: open.buffer.com
Corporate Rebels: corporate-rebels.com

The Moment: themoment.is/ideas
Nearsoft: nearsoft.com/blog
The Ready: theready.com/newsletter

## Other Companies That Inspire Us

Avivo Live Life: avivo.org.au
The Barefoot Lawyer: barefootlawyer.uk
Careershifters: careershifters.org
Fairground Accounting: fairground.co.nz
Optimi: optimi.co.nz
Tautoko Services: tautoko.org.nz
Tergar Asia: tergarasia.org
Yash Pakka: yashpakka.com

# Company Profiles

ALL THE companies we have featured offer inspiring examples of helpful practices. Those that we know to be Teal and/or practicing self-management—the most progressive "lead together" companies—are marked with an asterisk.

I-DEGREE/Shift A Toronto-based consulting firm partnering with organizations to define and align their values. 1-degreeshift.ca

**Bazaarvoice** A digital marketing company headquartered in Austin, Texas. bazaarvoice.com

**Bee Talents** A Poland-based IT recruitment and HR support agency. beetalents.com

**Björn Lundén AB**\* A Swedish knowledge and software company supporting small- and medium-sized companies. bjornlunden.se

**Bol.com**\* The Netherlands' leading web shop for books, toys and electronics. bol.com

**Breyting Community Roaster**\* A cause-oriented coffee roasting company in Florida. communityroaster.com

**Buffer**\* A fully distributed team working in fifteen countries, providing a social media management software platform. buffer.com

**Bullfrog Power** Canada's leading green energy provider, based in Toronto. bullfrogpower.com

**Buurtzorg\*** A Dutch home-care organization making use of innovative independent nurse teams. buurtzorg.com

**Carpenter Oak\*** A designer and maker of oak-framed buildings in the UK. carpenteroak.com

**ConsenSys** A blockchain technology company building Ethereum blockchain infrastructure and applications. consensys.net

**Corporate Rebels\*** A future of work research firm and blog publisher. corporate-rebels.com

**Counter Tax Lawyers\*** A Toronto-based firm specializing in tax disputes and litigation. countertax.ca

**Crisp\*** A consulting company based in Stockholm with a unique DNA. crisp.se and dna.crisp.se

**Culture Amp** A people and culture platform helping organizations collect, understand and act on employee feedback. cultureamp.com

**Cyberclick\*** A leading online advertising and digital marketing agency in Spain. cyberclick.es

**Decurion Corporation** A Los Angeles–based operator of businesses ranging from entertainment centers to seniors' living facilities and commercial real estate. decurion.com

**Deeson\*** A leading UK-based digital agency creating transformational digital platforms using open source technology. deeson.co.uk

**Ecosia\*** A Berlin-based social business and internet search engine provider. ecosia.org

**EMPAUA** A European Salesforce consultancy working with companies on their digital transformation. empaua.com

**Enspiral\*** A primarily New Zealand–based collective of entrepreneurs, changemakers and activists collaborating on initiatives, projects and world-changing ventures. enspiral.com

**Equal Experts** A multinational consultancy providing tailored, end-to-end services in software development and delivery. equal experts.com

**ET Group\*** A Toronto-based self-managing technology integration company. etgroup.ca

**Exact Media (renamed Connections)** A Toronto-based ecommerce company offering targeted sampling and coupon placements inside parcel shipments. connectionsbytsw.com

**FAVI\*** A subcontractor and automotive supplier that develops and optimizes die-cast components, located in France. favi.com

**Figure 53** A Maryland-based maker of software that controls media playback in live performances. figure53.com

**Fitzii\*** A division of the recruiting firm Ian Martin Group based in Oakville, Canada. fitzii.com

**FreshBooks** A Toronto-based provider of cloud-based accounting software for small businesses and self-employed professionals. freshbooks.com

**FX Agency** A corporate communications firm based in the Netherlands. fxagency.nl

**Gravity Payments** A Seattle-based credit card processing and financial services company. gravitypayments.com

**Greaterthan\*** A consulting firm providing training and consulting for organizations wanting to rethink and retool power, governance and value. greaterthan.works

**Hack and Paint\*** Hack and Paint was an award-winning game studio focused on creating the next generation of games and experiences for virtual reality.

**Haier** A Chinese multinational manufacturer of home appliances and consumer electronics. haier.net

**HolacracyOne\*** The team stewarding the Holacracy movement and evolution of the practice. holacracy.org

**Ian Martin Group\*** A progressive recruitment and project-staffing firm with offices in Canada, the US and India. ianmartin.com

**Jack.org** A Canadian charity that trains and empowers young leaders to dismantle barriers to positive mental health. jack.org

**Johnsonville Foods** A Wisconsin-based company that is one of the largest sausage producers in the United States. johnsonville.com

**LifeLearn** A provider of online solutions helping veterinary practices optimize client communications, maximize efficiency and improve profitability. lifelearn.com

**Mantle314\*** A Toronto-based consultancy focused on climate-related risk and strategies to thrive. mantle314.com

**Maptio\*** An online software tool helping organizations map who is responsible for what and who is helping whom. maptio.com

**Marco Specialties** A California-based provider of parts and supplies to pinball machine owners. marcospecialties.com

**Menlo Innovations\*** A software design and development firm based in Ann Arbor, Michigan. menloinnovations.com

**Miovision** Creators of intelligent solutions for traffic data collection and advanced traffic signal operations. miovision.com

**Morning Star\*** A California-based worldwide market leader in tomato processing. morningstarco.com

**Myplanet** A Toronto-based software studio. myplanet.com

**Nulogy** A Toronto-based supply chain enterprise software provider. nulogy.com

**Once Again Nut Butter\*** An employee-owned producer of nut butters based in New York State. onceagainnutbutter.com

**Percolab\*** A Canadian- and European-based international systems cocreation and codesign firm. percolab.com

**Precision Nutrition\*** A global provider of nutrition coaching, nutrition software and professional certification based in Toronto. precisionnutrition.com

**Rackspace** Managed cloud computing service provider based in Texas with operations around the world. rackspace.com

**Rebel Group** International advisory firm specializing in the development of public-private partnerships. rebelgroup.com

**Retrium** A fully distributed team providing software for team retrospectives. retrium.com

**Schuberg Philis\*** An IT outsourcing company in the Netherlands. schubergphilis.com

**SideFX** A developer of 3D animation and visual effects software for use in film, commercials and video games based in Toronto. sidefx.com

**Sobol.io\*** A software platform for distributed and self-organizing teams. sobol.io

**Spotify** A Swedish music streaming and media services provider headquartered in Stockholm. spotify.com

**Sylius\*** A Poland-based open source ecommerce platform. sylius.com

**Target Teal\*** A Brazilian consulting agency helping organizations reinvent their practices, structures and working relationships. targetteal.com

**Terramera** A Vancouver-based sustainable agriculture cleantech company. terramera.com

**TGB Architects** An architectural and social design firm based in Seattle. tgbarchitects.com

**The Moment\*** An innovation design studio in Toronto, helping organizations and teams to prepare for the future. themoment.is

**The Ready\*** A US design and transformation firm dedicated to helping organizations discover a better way of working. theready.com

**TOMS** A shoe company based in California known for its commitment to give a new pair of shoes to an impoverished child each time it sells a pair of shoes. toms.com

**Tuff Leadership Training\*** A Stockholm-based training company teaching a style of leadership that produces motivated, responsible employees and self-reliant teams. tuffleadershiptraining.com

**WD-40 Company** The manufacturer of the oil, lubricant, cleaner and rust remover. wd40.com

**Wellbeing Teams\*** An organization of small, self-managed, values-led and neighborhood-based teams delivering care and support within communities. wellbeingteams.org

**Zappos\*** Online retailer of shoes, clothing, handbags and accessories, known for providing an exceptional customer experience. zappos.com

# Notes

## Preface

1  Frederic Laloux, *Reinventing Organizations: A Guide to Creating Organizations Inspired by the Next Stage of Human Consciousness* (Millis, MA: Nelson Parker, 2014), 239.

## Introduction to an Emerging Paradigm

1  Stephen Covey quoted in "The Seven Habits of Highly Effective People," FranklinCovey, accessed June 8, 2020, franklincovey.com/the-7-habits.html.

2  Aaron Dignan, *Brave New Work: Are You Ready to Reinvent Your Organization?* (New York: Portfolio/Penguin, 2019), 8.

3  Aaron Dignan, *Brave New Work: Are You Ready to Reinvent Your Organization?* (New York: Portfolio/Penguin, 2019), 8.

4  Tom Nixon, "Resolving the Awkward Paradox in Frederic Laloux's *Reinventing Organizations*," Medium, April 14, 2015, medium.com/maptio/resolving-the-awkward-paradox-in-frederic-laloux-s-reinventing-organisations-f2031080ea02.

5  John F. Kennedy, "John F. Kennedy Moon Speech—Rice Stadium," NASA, accessed June 8, 2020, er.jsc.nasa.gov/seh/ricetalk.htm.

6  Tom Nixon, "Resolving the Awkward Paradox in Frederic Laloux's *Reinventing Organizations*," Medium, April 14, 2015, medium.com/maptio/resolving-the-awkward-paradox-in-frederic-laloux-s-reinventing-organisations-f2031080ea02.

## Chapter 1: Leadership Redefined

1   Albert Einstein quoted in "Einstein's Big Ideas," *Nova* (PBS), accessed June 10 2020, pbs.org/wgbh/nova/einstein/wisd-nf.html.

2   Lisa Gill and Lotta Croiset van Uchelen, "Lotta Croiset van Uchelen from Schuberg Philis on Self-Steering Teams and Wholeness," *Leadermorphosis* (podcast), episode 11, November 23, 2017, 36:39, leadermorphosis.co/episode-11-lotta-croiset-van-uchelen-from-schuberg-philis-on-self-steering-teams-and-wholeness. With edits by permission of Lotta Croiset van Uchelen.

3   Simon Wakeman, interview with Brent Lowe, September 6, 2019.

4   Lee Manning, interview with Brent Lowe, August 30, 2019.

5   Lisa Gill and Karin Tenelius, "Karen Tenelius from Tuft Leadership Training on Giving Away the Authority," *Leadermorphosis* (podcast), episode 12, December 8, 2017, 34:42, leadermorphosis.co/episode-12-karin-tenelius-from-tuff-leadership-training-on-giving-away-the-authority. With edits by permission of Karin Tenelius.

6   Lisa Gill and Tom Nixon, "Tom Nixon from Maptio on Creative Authority in Self-Managing Companies," *Leadermorphosis* (podcast), episode 5, June 13, 2017, 41:23, leadermorphosis.co/episode-5-tom-nixon-from-maptio-on-creative-authority-in-self-managing-companies#. With edits by permission of Tom Nixon.

7   Mark Kuznicki, email to Brent Lowe, November 15, 2019.

## Chapter 2: Power

1   Francesca Pick, "Cut the Bullshit: Organizations with No Hierarchy Don't Exist," Medium, March 3, 2017, medium.com/ouishare-connecting-the-collaborative-economy/cut-the-bullshit-organizations-with-no-hierarchy-dont-exist-f0a845e73a80.

2   Dacher Keltner, "Don't Let Power Corrupt You," *Harvard Business Review*, October 2016, hbr.org/2016/10/dont-let-power-corrupt-you.

3   Balázs Szatmári, "We Are (All) the Champions: The Effect of Status in the Implementation of Innovations" (PhD diss., Rotterdam School of Management, Erasmus University, 2016). hdl.handle.net/1765/94633.

4   Jane Watson, "On Power & Transparency," Talent Vanguard, May 12, 2019, talentvanguard.com/2019/05/12/on-power-transparency/. With edits by permission of Jane Watson.

5   These power framework definitions are derived from the work of Tuesday Ryan-Hart (see vimeo.com/273147036) and Elizabeth Hunt (see medium. com/@elizabeth_1480/le-pouvoir-%C3%A0-linfini-repenser-nos-relations-de-pouvoir-32655a3d5b5d).

6   Peter Aprile, conversation with Brent Lowe, October 17, 2019.

## Chapter 3: Transition Stages

1   Tim Jones, conversation with Brent Lowe, January 25, 2019.

2   Peter Aprile, conversation with Brent Lowe, October 17, 2019.

3   Bryan Peters, conversation with Brent Lowe, October 10, 2019.

4   Edwin Jansen, "How People Actually Adopt Self-Management," Medium, January 27, 2019. medium.com/@EdwinJansen/how-people-actually-adopt-self-management-934b13477ce4.

5   Simon Wakeman, interview with Brent Lowe, September 6, 2019.

6   Kathryn Maloney, "Dear Beloved Clients, Please Start by Doing," Medium, July 16, 2018, medium.com/the-ready/dear-beloved-clients-please-start-by-doing-not-thinking-8dff9dd0ac98.

7   Harm Jans, email to Brent Lowe, June 3, 2020.

8   Peter Aprile, conversation with Brent Lowe, October 17, 2019.

9   Lisa Gill and Samantha Slade, "Samantha Slade from Percolab on Practicing Self-Management," *Leadermorphosis* (podcast), episode 10, October 30, 2017, 32:37, leadermorphosis.co/episode-10-samantha-slade-from-percolab-on-practicing-self-management. With edits by permission of Samantha Slade.

10  Leo Widrich interviewed in Jeff Haden, "The $7 Million Company with No Managers," LinkedIn, August 4, 2015, linkedin.com/pulse/7-million-company-managers-one-jeff-haden/.

11  Lisa Gill and Helen Sanderson, "Helen Sanderson from HAS on Reinventing Home Care," *Leadermorphosis* (podcast), episode 9, October 11, 2017, 45:30, leadermorphosis.co/episode-9-helen-sanderson-from-hsa-on-reinventing-home-care. With edits by permission of Helen Sanderson.

### Chapter 4: Conscious Language

1   Peter Block, *Community: The Structure of Belonging* (Oakland, CA: Berrett-Koehler Publishers, 2009), 115–16.

2   Jason Cottrell, conversation with Brent Lowe, May 9, 2020.

3   Anthony Cabraal and Susan Basterfield (producing authors), *Better Work Together: How the Power of Community Can Transform Your Business* (Wellington, NZ: Enspiral Foundation, 2019), 279–81.

4   Courtney Seiter, "Peek inside a Startup's Slack Room: The Top Words We Use at Buffer," Buffer, January 5, 2016, open.buffer.com/top-words-of-buffer/.

### Chapter 5: Resistance

1   Seth Godin, "Introduction," *Linchpin: Are You Indispensable?* (New York: Portfolio, 2010).

2   Steven Pressfield, "Resistance Wakes Up with Me," Steven Pressfield, October 2, 2019, stevenpressfield.com/2019/10/resistance-wakes-up-with-me/.

3   Edwin Jansen, conversation with Brent Lowe, February 6, 2020.

4   Frederic Laloux quoted in Simon Confino, "How to Best Influence Your Team's Culture," *HuffPost*, January 12, 2018, huffpost.com/entry/how-to-best-influence-your-teams-culture_b_5a58b891e4b00b4ea8d083c7.

5   Lisa Gill and Jurriaan Kamer, "Jurriaan Kamer from Agile CIO on Agile Organisations and Beyond," *Leadermorphosis* (podcast), episode 3, May 30, 2017, 32:23, leadermorphosis.co/episode-3-jurriaan-kamer-from-agile-ceo-on-what-it-means-to-be-a-truly-agile-organisation.

### Chapter 6: Purpose

1   Patrick E. McKnight and Todd B. Kashdan, "Purpose in Life as a System That Creates and Sustains Health and Well-Being: An Integrative, Testable Theory," *Review of General Psychology* 13, no. 3 (2009): 242–51, doi.org/10.1037/a0017152.

2   Caterina Bulgarella, "Purpose-Driven Companies Evolve Faster Than Others," *Forbes*, September 21, 2018, forbes.com/sites/caterinabulgarella/2018/09/21/purpose-driven-companies-evolve-faster-than-others/#1bfa4c9955bc.

3    Frederic Laloux, *Reinventing Organizations: A Guide to Creating Organizations Inspired by the Next Stage of Human Consciousness* (Millis, MA: Nelson Parker, 2014), 194.

4    "We're More Than Just a Company That Sells Products," WD-40 Company, accessed June 8, 2020, wd40company.com/our-company/.

5    Isaac Davison, "Whanganui River Given Legal Status of a Person Under Treaty of Waitangi Settlement," *New Zealand Herald*, March 15, 2017, nzherald.co.nz/nz/news/article.cfm?c_id=1&objectid=11818858.

6    Chris Finlayson quoted in Colin Dwyer, "A New Zealand River Now Has the Legal Rights of a Human," NPR's *The Two-Way*, March 16, 2017, npr.org/sections/thetwo-way/2017/03/16/520414763/a-new-zealand-river-now-has-the-legal-rights-of-a-human.

7    *Reinventing Organizations Wiki*, s.v., "Teal Organizations," accessed June 8, 2020, reinventingorganizationswiki.com/Teal_Organizations.

8    Alison Alexander, "The Power of Purpose: How Organizations Are Making Work More Meaningful," Northwestern School of Education and Social Policy, accessed June 8, 2020, sesp.northwestern.edu/masters-learning-and-organizational-change/knowledge-lens/stories/2016/the-power-of-purpose-how-organizations-are-making-work-more-meaningful.html.

9    Cheryl Heller, "Mission? Vision? Values? Forget It," Unreasonable Group, June 8, 2016, unreasonablegroup.com/articles/mission-vision-values-forget-it/.

10    "About TOMS," TOMS, accessed June 8, 2020, toms.co.uk/about-toms.

11    "What Is This?" Crisp DNA, accessed June 8, 2020, dna.crisp.se/docs/index.html.

12    Adam Leipzig, "How to Know Your Life Purpose in 5 Minutes," TEDxMalibu, video, 10:33, February 1, 2013, youtu.be/vVsXO9brK7M.

## Chapter 7: Values, Principles and Aspirations

1    Elvis Presley quoted in Rich Smith, "Values Are Like Fingerprints," Atlas Medstaff, *Adventures in Nursing* (blog), May 1, 2019, atlasmedstaff.com/adventures-in-nursing/values-are-like-fingerprints/.

2  Jackie Le Fevre quoted in Helen Sanderson, "Values and Beliefs—What They Mean for Wellbeing Teams," LinkedIn, January 10, 2017, linkedin .com/pulse/values-beliefs-what-mean-wellbeing-teams-helen-sander son-frsa/.

3  Natalia Lombardo, "When Values Collide," Medium, March 31, 2018, medium.com/the-tuning-fork/when-values-collide-48991f119902.

4  Helen Sanderson and Jackie Le Fevre, "Values in Practice—from Intention to Action," Helen Sanderson, September 12, 2018, helensand erson.net/2018/09/values-in-practice-from-intention-to-action/.

5  Doug Kirkpatrick, "Creating the Twenty-First-Century Organization through Organizational Self-Management in the New World of Work," Doug Kirkpatrick, accessed June 8, 2020, dougkirkpatrick.com/speaking/.

## Chapter 8: Psychological Safety

1  Amy Edmondson quoted in Michael Boykin, "An Introduction to Psychological Safety," *Range*, accessed June 10, 2020, range.co/blog/ introduction-to-psychological-safety.

2  Charles Duhigg, "What Google Learned from Its Quest to Build the Perfect Team," *New York Times Magazine*, February 25, 2016, nytimes. com/2016/02/28/magazine/what-google-learned-from-its-quest-to-build-the-perfect-team.html.

3  "Tool: Foster Psychological Safety," re:Work, accessed June 8, 2020, rework.withgoogle.com/guides/understanding-team-effectiveness/steps/ foster-psychological-safety/.

4  Amy Edmondson, "Building a Psychologically Safe Workplace," TEDxHGSE, video, 11:26, May 4, 2014, youtu.be/LhoLuui9gX8.

5  Lisa Gill and Mari Petrov, "People from Hack and Paint on Self-Management in a Remote Team," *Leadermorphosis* (podcast), episode 15, March 27, 2018, 37:57, leadermorphosis.co/episode-15-people-from-hack-and-paint-on-self-management-in-a-remote-team. With edits by permission of Marin Petrov.

6  Simon Wakeman, interview with Brent Lowe, September 6, 2019.

7  Joost Minnaar, "Ruthless Experimentation: 5 Best Practices," Corporate Rebels, accessed June 8, 2020, corporate-rebels.com/ ruthless-experimentation/.

## Chapter 9: Radical Responsibility

1  Fleet Maull, "Radical Responsibility," LinkedIn, July 20, 2016, linkedin. com/pulse/radical-responsibility-fleet-maull/.

2  Lisa Gill and Björn Lundén, "Björn Lundén from BL Information on Scrapping Stupid Rules in Companies, " *Leadermorphosis* (podcast), episode 17, May 2, 2018, 37:17, leadermorphosis.co/episode-17-bjorn-lunden-from-bl-information-on-scrapping-stupid-rules-in-companies. With edits by permission of Björn Lundén.

3  Sir Edmund Hillary, 1977, quoted in Robert D. McFadden, "Edmund Hillary, First on Everest, Dies at 88," *New York Times*, January 10, 2008, nytimes.com/2008/01/10/world/asia/11cnd-hillary.html.

4  Lisa Gill and Tom Nixon, "Tom Nixon from Maptio on Creative Authority in Self-Managing Companies," *Leadermorphosis* (podcast), episode 5, June 13, 2017, 41:23, leadermorphosis.co/episode-5-tom-nixon-from-maptio-on-creative-authority-in-self-managing-companies#. With edits by permission of Tom Nixon.

## Chapter 10: Agreements

1  Thomas Paine, "Practice Accountability," *Illuminated Living*, May 20, 2019, illuminatedlvg.com/2019/05/practice-accountability.html.

2  Paweł Jędrzejewski, conversation with Brent Lowe, June 28, 2019.

3  Bruce Peters, "Promises Made, Promises Kept," TEDxRochester, video, 12:45, April 16, 2014, youtu.be/WNSJvOqTfQE.

4  Bruce Peters, conversation with Brent Lowe, June 6, 2019.

5  Rodrigo Bastos, conversation with Brent Lowe, June 6, 2019.

6  Alanna Irving, "Breathe in Leadership, Breathe out Leadership: Enspiral's Organisational Refactor," Medium, May 19, 2019, medium.com/enspiral-tales/breathe-in-leadership-breathe-out-leadership-enspirals-organisational-refactor-884d0babf6b7.

7  Kurtis McBride, conversation with Brent Lowe, June 9, 2017.

8  Brené Brown, "Brené Brown: 3 Ways to Set Boundaries," *HuffPost*, updated December 6, 2017, huffpost.com/entry/how-to-set-boundaries-brene-brown_n_4372968.

## Chapter 11: Clear Roles

1   Casey Stengel quoted in Toni Mollett, "Casey Stengel: America and
the World Need a Major Motion Picture about Casey Stengel. Now!"
[brochure], accessed June 10, 2020, caseystengel.org/wp-content/
uploads/2010/11/stengel_brochure.pdf.

2   Neel Doshi and Lindsay McGregor, *Primed to Perform: How to Build the
Highest Performing Cultures through the Science of Total Motivation* (New
York: HarperCollins, 2015), 169.

3   Edwin Jansen, conversation with Brent Lowe, February 6, 2020.

## Chapter 12: Decision-Making

1   Samantha Slade, *Going Horizontal: Creating a Non-Hierarchical
Organization, One Practice at a Time* (Oakland, CA: Berrett-Koehler
Publishers, 2018), 118.

2   Damien Douté, "The 6 Types of Decision-Making Processes Explained
with Ice-Cream," Medium, October 3, 2018, medium.com/@doute.d/
the-6-types-of-decision-making-processes-explained-with-ice-cream-
541991529f3d.

3   Dave Hewett, interview with Travis Marsh, November 14, 2019.

4   Dennis Bakke, *The Decision Maker: Unlock the Potential of Everyone in Your
Organization, One Decision at a Time* (Seattle, WA: Pear Press, 2013).

5   Sheella Mierson, "Case History: Distributed Leadership Changes
Everything in a Manufacturing Company," Sociocracy Consulting,
accessed June 8, 2020, sociocracyconsulting.com/wp-content/uploads/
Case-Study-of-OANB.pdf.

6   Mary Poppendieck and Tom Poppendieck, *Lean Software Development:
An Agile Toolkit* (Upper Saddle River, NJ: Pearson Education, 2003), 57.
Access a few sample chapters at ptgmedia.pearsoncmg.com/images/
9780321150783/samplepages/0321150783.pdf.

7   Jeff Atwood, "The Last Responsible Moment," Blossom, accessed June 8,
2020, blossom.co/index.html%3Fp=98.html.

8   Cloverpop, "7 Breakthrough Decision Practices," Cloverpop white
paper (undated), 5, cloverpop.com/hubfs/Whitepapers/Cloverpop_7_
Breakthrough_Decision_Practices.pdf.

## Chapter 13: Feedback

1    George Pór, email to Brent Lowe, June 8, 2020.

## Chapter 14: Interpersonal Tensions

1    Mary Parker Follett, *Freedom and Co-ordination: Lectures in Business Organisation* (London: Management Publications Trust, 1949).

2    Chris Ashworth, email to Brent Lowe, July 8, 2019.

3    Simon Wakeman, interview with Brent Lowe, September 6, 2019.

4    Pim de Morree, "Morning Star's Success Story: No Bosses, No Titles, No Structural Hierarchy," Corporate Rebels, accessed June 8, 2020, corporate-rebels.com/morning-star/.

5    Marshall B. Rosenberg, *Nonviolent Communication: A Language of Life*, 3rd ed. (Encinitas, CA: PuddleDancer Press, 2015).

## Chapter 15: Meaningful Meetings

1    Jason Fried, "The Two Biggest Drags on Productivity: Meetings and Managers (Or, as We Call Them, M&Ms)," *Inc.*, October 31, 2013, inc.com/jason-fried/excerpt-easy-on-the-mms.html.

2    Kate Beecroft, "Strategies to Guide Virtual Community Conversations," Virtual Communities for Impact, accessed June 10, 2020, communities forimpact.org/case_study/strategies-to-guide-conversations/.

## Chapter 16: Personal Growth

1    Bryan Ungard quoted in Susan Basterfield and Kate Fulton, *Rethinking Organisations*, Western Australia Individualised Services (WAiS), June 2019, waindividualisedservices.org.au/wp-content/uploads/2019/06/WAIS_RethinkingOrganisation_Paper_FINAL_screenview.pdf.

2    Bryan Ungard quoted in Susan Basterfield and Kate Fulton, *Rethinking Organisations*, Western Australia Individualised Services (WAiS), June 2019, waindividualisedservices.org.au/wp-content/uploads/2019/06/WAIS_RethinkingOrganisation_Paper_FINAL_screenview.pdf.

3    John Stepper, "New! Working Out Loud Circle Guides v3.0," Working Out Loud, August 5, 2015, workingoutloud.com/blog/new-working-out-loud-circle-guides-v3-0. See also John Stepper, *Working Out Loud:*

*A 12-Week Method to Build New Connections, a Better Career, and a More Fulfilling Life* (Vancouver, BC: Page Two, 2020).

## Chapter 17: Transparency

1   Keith Rabois quoted in Mathilde Collin, "More Than a Buzzword: How We Practice Transparency at Front," Medium, February 12, 2019, medium.com/@collinmathilde/more-than-a-buzzword-how-we-practice-transparency-at-front-d415b94fd8a4.

2   Sheella Mierson, "5 Pitfalls of a Top-Down Hierarchy and What to Do about Them," The Sociocracy Consulting Group, sociocracyconsulting.com/whitepaper/.

3    "Transparency," Buffer, accessed June 8, 2020, buffer.com/about#transparency.

4   Ryan Buell, "Operational Transparency," *Harvard Business Review*, March–April 2019, hbr.org/2019/03/operational-transparency.

5   Duncan Oyevaar quoted in "Rebellious Practices: The Power of Open-Book Management," Corporate Rebels, accessed June 8, 2020, corporate-rebels.com/rebellious-practices-open-book-management/.

## Chapter 18: Compensation

1   Peter Koenig, Money and Source Masterclass, Riverslea, New Zealand, January 2020.

2   Doug Kirkpatrick, conversation with Susan Basterfield, June 3, 2020.

3   Erika Bailey, conversation with Brent Lowe, May 26, 2020.

4   Greg Judelman, conversation with Brent Lowe, October 25, 2017.

5   *Reinventing Organizations Wiki*, s.v., "Compensation and Incentives," accessed June 8, 2020, reinventingorganizationswiki.com/Compensation_and_incentives.

6   *Reinventing Organizations Wiki*, s.v., "Compensation and Incentives," accessed June 8, 2020, reinventingorganizationswiki.com/Compensation_and_incentives.

7   Charles Davies, "Don't Argue about Money in Restaurants," LinkedIn, October 9, 2019, linkedin.com/pulse/dont-argue-money-restaurants-charles-davies/.

8   Francesca Pick, conversation with Susan Basterfield, June 1, 2020.

9   Cara Conceller, interview with Travis Marsh, November 18, 2019.

10  Mike Moyer, *Slicing Pie Handbook: Perfect Equity Splits for Bootstrapped Startups* (Lake Forest, IL: Lake Shark Ventures LLC, 2016), 2.

## Chapter 19: Diversity and Inclusion

1   Mahatma Gandhi quoted in "Mahatma Gandhi,"
    Goodreads, accessed June 10, 2020, goodreads.com/
    quotes/7352037-our-ability-to-reach-unity-in-diversity-will-be-the.

2   Nicholas Kristof, "Our Biased Brains," *New York Times*, May 7, 2015,
    nytimes.com/2015/05/07/opinion/nicholas-kristof-our-biased-brains.
    html.

3   Emilio J. Castilla and Stephen Benard, "The Paradox of Meritocracy in
    Organizations," *Administrative Science Quarterly* 55, no. 4 (December 1,
    2010): 543–676, doi.org/10.2189/asqu.2010.55.4.543.

4   Naomi Eisenberger, "The Neural Bases of Social Pain: Evidence
    for Shared Representations with Physical Pain," *Psychosomatic
    Medicine* 74, no. 2 (February/March 2012): 126–35, doi.org/10.1097/
    PSY.0b013e3182464dd1.

5   Liz Guthridge, "Why Social Pain Hurts Your Workplace Performance
    (and How to Avoid It)," *Forbes*, November 13, 2017, forbes.com/sites/
    forbescoachescouncil/2017/11/13/why-social-pain-hurts-your-workplace-
    performance-and-how-to-avoid-it/#6c3b60be7fc7.

## Chapter 20: Future Colleagues

1   Jim Collins, *Good to Great: Why Some Companies Make the Leap... and
    Others Don't* (New York: Harper Business, 2001), 42.

2   Claudio Fernández-Aráoz, "21st-Century Talent Spotting," *Harvard
    Business Review*, June 2014, hbr.org/2014/06/21st-century-talent-spotting.

3   Doug Kirkpatrick, "12 Keys to the Workplace of the
    Future," *HuffPost*, August 13, 2016, huffpost.com/entry/
    twelve-keys-to-the-workpl_b_7986378.

4   Matt McKenna, conversation with Brent Lowe, May 28, 2020.

5   Courtney Seiter, "How We Hire: A Look inside Our Hiring Process,"
    Buffer, accessed June 8, 2020, open.buffer.com/hiring-process/.

### Chapter 21: The New Joiner Experience

1   E.E. Cummings quoted in "E.E. Cummings,"
    Goodreads, accessed June 10, 2020, goodreads.com/
    quotes/806-it-takes-courage-to-grow-up-and-become-who-you.

2   John Sullivan, "Extreme Onboarding: How to WOW Your New Hires
    Rather Than Numb Them," LinkedIn, July 15, 2015, business.linkedin
    .com/talent-solutions/blog/2015/07/extreme-onboarding-how-to-wow-
    your-new-hires-rather-than-numb-them.

3   John Sullivan, "Extreme Onboarding: How to WOW Your New Hires
    Rather Than Numb Them," LinkedIn, July 15, 2015, business.linkedin
    .com/talent-solutions/blog/2015/07/extreme-onboarding-how-to-wow-
    your-new-hires-rather-than-numb-them.

4   Joost Minnaar, "4 Powerful Lessons to Successfully Run a Self-Managed
    Company," Corporate Rebels, accessed June 8, 2020, corporate-rebels.
    com/rebel-group/.

5   Sophie Rödl, "Culture First: My Onboarding Experience at EMPAUA,"
    EMPAUA, August 9, 2019, blog.empaua.com/culture/first-weeks-empaua/.

6   Barbara Malewska, "Not Looking Back—Key Takeaways from My
    Onboarding Process," Bee Talents, April 15, 2019, beetalents.com/blog/
    onboarding-process-my-story/.

### Chapter 22: Exiting Colleagues

1   Jeffrey McDaniel quoted in "The Honesty of Trees in Winter," *A Day
    in the Life*, January 30, 2014, sites.psu.edu/rclshannon/2014/01/30/
    the-honesty-of-trees-in-the-winter.

2   John Sowell, "Company Led by Idaho Native Who Set $70k Minimum
    Pay Avoids Layoffs as Revenue Halved," *Idaho Statesman*, March 31, 2020,
    idahostatesman.com/news/business/article241642826.html.

### Chapter 23: Bold Strategy

1   Jim Whitehurst, "How to Plan in a World Full of Unknowns," LinkedIn,
    April 11, 2019, linkedin.com/pulse/how-plan-world-full-unknowns-
    jim-whitehurst.

2   Michael Sheetz, "Technology Killing Off Corporate America: Average
    Life Span of Companies under 20 Years," CNBC, August 24, 2017, cnbc.
    com/2017/08/24/technology-killing-off-corporations-average-lifespan-
    of-company-under-20-years.html.
3   Karn Manhas, "What If You Posed Your Company's Mission Statement
    as a Question?" *Quartz*, July 2, 2019, qz.com/work/1654371/mission-
    statements-are-over/.

## Chapter 24: Rituals

1   Tim Leberecht and Gianpiero Petriglieri, "Andrés Iniesta's Farewell,
    and How to Make Endings Count at Work," *Harvard Business Review*,
    May 30, 2018, timleberecht.com/article/andres-iniestas-farewell-and-
    how-to-make-endings-count-at-work/.
2   Nicholas Hobson, Juliana Schroeder, Jane Risen, Dimitris Xygalatas and
    Michael Inzlicht, "The Psychology of Rituals: An Integrative Review and
    Process-Based Framework," *Personality and Social Psychology Review* 22,
    no. 3 (August 2018): 260–84, doi.org/10.1177/1088868317734944.
3   Steven Handel, "The Difference between Routines vs. Rituals," The
    Emotion Machine, January 29, 2010, theemotionmachine.com/routines-
    vs-rituals/.
4   Ornish Living, "The Science Behind Why Naming Our Feelings
    Makes Us Happier," *HuffPost*, May 15, 2015, huffpost.com/entry/
    the-science-behind-why-na_b_7174164.
5   Courtney Seiter, "27 Questions to Ask Instead of 'What Do You Do?'"
    Buffer, accessed June 8, 2020, open.buffer.com/27-question-to-ask-
    instead-of-what-do-you-do/.
6   Amanda Fenton, "Check-In Question Ideas," Amanda Fenton Consulting,
    April 12, 2014, amandafenton.com/2014/04/check-in-question-ideas/.
7   Pim de Morree, "Team Work: The Bare Essentials," Corporate Rebels,
    accessed June 8, 2020, corporate-rebels.com/the-bare-essentials/. With
    edits by permission of Pim de Morree.
8   Szabolcs Emich, conversation with Susan Basterfield, July 2017.
9   Lisa Gill and Francesca Pick, "Francesca Pick from OuiShare on a
    Lab for New Ways of Working," *Leadermorphosis* (podcast), episode 4,

June 6, 2017, 9:10, leadermorphosis.co/episode-4-francesca-pick-from-ouishare-on-a-lab-for-new-ways-of-working. With edits by permission of Francesca Pick.

10  Tim Casasola, "How Your Organization Can Make Great Decisions by Default," Medium, December 21, 2018, medium.com/the-ready/how-your-organization-can-make-great-decisions-by-default-950fa976e991.

## Chapter 25: Operating Systems

1   Constance Fenimore Woolson quoted in "Theories Are Like Scaffolding," Quotefancy, accessed June 10, 2020, quotefancy.com/quote/1751080/Constance-Fenimore-Woolson-Theories-are-like-scaffolding-they-are-not-the-house-but-you.

2   *Reinventing Organizations Wiki*, s.v., "Organizational Structure," reinventingorganizationswiki.com/Organizational_Structure, accessed July 10, 2020.

3   Bernhard Bockelbrink, James Priest and Liliana David, "The Seven Principles," Sociocracy 3.0 (2017), sociocracy30.org/the-details/principles.

## Chapter 26: Legal Agreements

1   Brené Brown, *Dare to Lead: Brave Work. Tough Conversations. Whole Hearts.* (New York: Random House, 2018), 190.

2   Stewart Levine, *The Book of Agreement: 10 Essential Elements for Getting the Results You Want* (Oakland, CA: Berrett-Koehler Publishers, 2002), bkconnection.com/static/The_Book_of_Agreement_EXCERPT.pdf.

3   Kim Wright, conversation with Brent Lowe, January 21, 2020.

4   Von Coven, conversation with Brent Lowe, January 2020.

5   Peter Zijlstra, email to Brent Lowe, January 22, 2020.

6   Stewart Levine, *The Book of Agreement: 10 Essential Elements for Getting the Results You Want* (Oakland, CA: Berrett-Koehler Publishers, 2002), 28, bkconnection.com/static/The_Book_of_Agreement_EXCERPT.pdf.

7   Linda Alvarez, conversation with Brent Lowe, August 22, 2019.

8   Linda Alvarez, conversation with Brent Lowe, August 22, 2019.

9   Von Coven, conversation with Brent Lowe, January 2020.

## Chapter 27: Handbooks, Playbooks and Blogs

1    Alanna Irving, "Sharing Power, Money, and Information," in *Better Work Together: How the Power of Community Can Transform Your Business*, producing authors Anthony Cabraal and Susan Basterfield (Wellington, NZ: Enspiral Foundation, 2019).

# About
# the Authors

## Brent Lowe

Brent is a performance coach who helps leaders show us their best selves within thriving,
purpose-driven teams. His firsthand experience comes from founding and growing four
companies, as well as serving on the leadership teams of three successful founder-led
businesses. He helped those organizations
scale their teams, grow revenues, launch
new ventures, integrate acquisitions and
expand globally. Now, as the scale coach for founder CEOs, Brent
works with entrepreneurs and leaders who are growing the size
and impact of their businesses to tackle local and global challenges. Many of his clients are motivated by the UN's Sustainable
Development Goals and a desire to lead in ways that feel authentic,
inspiring and personally fulfilling. He and his clients share a belief
that leadership goes far beyond delivering financial returns, with
ecosystem stewardship being a core responsibility. Brent lives in
Toronto, Canada, with his wife, Sharon, and their kids, Abby and
Evan. Learn more about Brent's work at brentlowe.com.

## Susan Basterfield

Susan is a catalyst and convener who believes that awareness and discernment can unblock drains and move mountains. From thirty-five-plus years in business—spanning global multinationals, start-ups and schools—arose experiences that, at first unconsciously and now quite consciously, drive her work as a systems transformation partner. Plainly speaking, she believes in getting real about  what's happening and naming it—because when we name it, we create the choice to change it. Her work includes standing shoulder to shoulder with leaders and organizations on their transformational journeys, often over many years, and convening virtual development programs, including the Practical Self-Management Intensive. She is an educator, coach, facilitator, writer and collective entrepreneur. Obsessed with building the capacity to build capacity, Susan seeks out that which is life-giving, dances with complexity and weeds out constraints to potential. She practices with Greaterthan, Better Work Together and Enspiral. Susan and her husband, Colin, chose Aotearoa, New Zealand, as home in 2003. Learn more about Susan's work at greaterthan.works and enspiral.com.

## Travis Marsh

Travis is a facilitator, coach and trainer who
works with companies and nonprofits by introducing mindsets and tools that help dynamic
leadership grow and expand in organizations.
He started his career in engineering and has
worked in sales, marketing, operations, software development and people operations,
and has supported and led teams in several of
those areas. He has worked in multinational
organizations as well as start-ups growing ten-fold per year. This
perspective allows him to see the interconnection and big impact
that small changes in leadership and followership can have. In his
work with clients, he specializes in team and interpersonal dynamics. He also works at the Stanford Graduate School of Business
facilitating a class on interpersonal communication. He coaches
purpose-driven companies, both VC-funded and bootstrapped.
Travis has a deep desire to unleash people's potential by helping
organizations grow and develop. Travis lives in San Francisco, California, with his partner, Nicole. Learn more about Travis's work
at themastersmark.com.

CPSIA information can be obtained
at www.ICGtesting.com
Printed in the USA
LVHW041506111120
671410LV00027B/199